WINNING BASKETBALL FUNDAMENTALS

Lee Rose

Human Kinetics

Library of Congress Cataloging-in-Publication Data

Rose, Lee H.
 Winning basketball fundamentals / Lee Rose.
   p. cm.
 Rev. ed. of: The basketball handbook, c2004.
 Includes index.
 1. Basketball--Coaching--Handbooks, manuals, etc. 2. Basketball--Training.
I. Rose, Lee H. Basketball handbook. II. Title.
 GV885.3.R68 2012
 796.323077--dc23
                                    2012018519
ISBN-10: 1-4504-3162-3 (print)
ISBN-13: 978-1-4504-3162-0 (print)

This book is a revised edition of *The Basketball Handbook,* published in 2004 by Human Kinetics.

The web addresses cited in this text were current as of July 2012 unless otherwise noted.

Acquisitions Editor: Justin Klug; **Developmental Editor:** Laura Podeschi; **Assistant Editor:** Tyler Wolpert; **Copyeditor:** Bob Replinger; **Indexer:** Alisha Jeddeloh; **Graphic Designer:** Joe Buck; **Graphic Artist:** Julie L. Denzer; **Cover Designer:** Keith Blomberg; **Photograph (cover):** Tom Dahlin/Getty Images; **Photographs (interior):** Neil Bernstein, unless otherwise noted; **Photo Asset Manager:** Laura Fitch; **Visual Production Assistant:** Joyce Brumfield; **Photo Production Manager:** Jason Allen, **Art Manager:** Kelly Hendren; **Associate Art Manager:** Alan L. Wilborn; **Illustrations:** © Human Kinetics; **Printer:** United Graphics

We thank Urbana High School in Urbana, Illinois, for assistance in providing the location for the photo shoot for this book.

Human Kinetics books are available at special discounts for bulk purchase. Special editions or book excerpts can also be created to specification. For details, contact the Special Sales Manager at Human Kinetics.

Printed in the United States of America   10 9 8 7 6 5 4 3 2 1

The paper in this book is certified under a sustainable forestry program.

Human Kinetics
Website: www.HumanKinetics.com

United States: Human Kinetics
P.O. Box 5076
Champaign, IL 61825-5076
800-747-4457
e-mail: humank@hkusa.com

Canada: Human Kinetics
475 Devonshire Road Unit 100
Windsor, ON N8Y 2L5
800-465-7301 (in Canada only)
e-mail: info@hkcanada.com

Europe: Human Kinetics
107 Bradford Road
Stanningley
Leeds LS28 6AT, United Kingdom
+44 (0) 113 255 5665
e-mail: hk@hkeurope.com

Australia: Human Kinetics
57A Price Avenue
Lower Mitcham, South Australia 5062
08 8372 0999
e-mail: info@hkaustralia.com

New Zealand: Human Kinetics
P.O. Box 80
Torrens Park, South Australia 5062
0800 222 062
e-mail: info@hknewzealand.com

E5727

To my family:
As always, thanks for your support and for hanging in with me.

Contents

Foreword   vi

Preface   vii

Acknowledgments   ix

Key to Diagrams   xi

1 Six Guiding Principles 1

2 Playing and Coaching 29

3 Performance Rating System 47

4 Individual Offensive Skills 65

5 Offensive Priorities 105

6 Team Offense 127

7 Defensive Skills and Tactics 167

8 Team Defense 199

9 Tactics for Special Situations 225

Index   258

About the Author   265

Foreword

I have to hand it to whoever titled this book. It not only fits the subject matter, and what will result (winning!) if you apply the information effectively, but it also captures what comes to mind regarding Lee Rose's coaching forte.

Well over 30 years ago as an assistant coach at Virginia Commonwealth University, I faced the University of South Florida and its highly celebrated new coach. I almost expected an air of arrogance from the opposing bench, occupied by the coach famous for earning a National Coach of the Year Award and leading his two previous schools, UNC-Charlotte and Purdue University, to Final Fours. After all, those were big-time credentials for a coach in the Sun Belt Conference.

But what I observed in that first game and saw in all subsequent contests against USF was a coach who was about his players and team, not about himself. And when you played a Lee Rose–coached squad, you knew you had to play well; the opponent was never going to beat itself.

Lee's teams were so fundamentally sound that they always seemed to play better than the individual talents would suggest. Lee was a master of matchups, frustratingly so for the opposing coach. Every time you thought you had an edge, he'd counter it with the right defense and personnel. You watch it happen time and again and ask, "How does he do that?"

Winning Basketball Fundamentals is the answer. From the first page to the last it's as solid a book as you'll find on the proper execution of techniques and tactics. But what really makes it so valuable are Coach Rose's keen insights and beneficial tools. Whether using the three-point shot, free throws, or screen and roll, you'll pick up new ideas on maximizing production and consistency. And the coach's player performance rating system is an outstanding evaluation tool for games and practice. From the big-picture guiding principles to the situation-specific inbound plays, the content is loaded with wisdom and ready-to-use applications.

The book is easy to navigate, too. The precision with which Lee Rose communicates his knowledge reflects the same type of discipline his teams demonstrated on the court. That composure and control manifest itself into a succinct and straightforward style of presentation that I especially appreciate.

But in addition to all the great things the book has to offer, even more impressive is what Coach Rose does with it. As was the case with *The Basketball Handbook*, Coach Rose will buy a large supply of the books and distribute at no cost to schools in some of the poorest areas of Appalachia. Along with the book comes a positive message about education as the key to a better future. And that's a winning point for all of us in the basketball community to remember.

Tubby Smith
Head coach, University of Minnesota

Preface

Winning Basketball Fundamentals is for coaches at all levels who are seeking ways to improve instructional skills and for players who are interested in developing an all-around game. In all my years of coaching, I've never met a player who didn't need to improve in some area. I've been around good players, excellent players, and great players, but never a perfect player. Whether it's free-throw shooting, dribbling, passing, rebounding, setting screens, using proper shooting technique, or some intuitive trait such as selflessness or good decision making, even a great player can improve parts of his game. This book addresses those areas and more.

If you're a middle school or high school player who wants to know what's expected of you when trying out for a team, you can go to the offensive skills section or learn about defense by checking the defensive tactics segment. If you want to know how to improve your vertical jump or increase your speed, it's here. If you're college bound, you will find drills covering the fundamentals as well as vital information on what to look for and what you can expect when selecting a school.

The further you advance in organized ball, the more you are expected to contribute. If you have good habits, you understand that the more effort you give, the greater the benefits. This axiom is true in sports, but more important, it's true in life. Players and coaches alike need to understand that the disappointment in losing relates directly to the amount of energy expended in trying to win. Ask yourself why young players excel in high school but fall behind as they progress to college. Too often it's because they focus only on the skills that are easy for them and disregard the importance of being well rounded. Whether as a coach or a player, you need to bring to the game a firm understanding of what it takes to be successful and then devise a plan that helps you accomplish your goals.

The first three chapters of Winning Basketball Fundamentals discuss the importance of establishing principles that help both coach and player stay focused; identify roles for players, coaches, and teams; and present a fair and consistent evaluation process. The book moves from the philosophical to the technical in chapters 4 to 9 by defining the offensive and defensive fundamentals and concluding with tactics for special situations. The corresponding drills and diagrams promote development at all levels. If you're a coach, the drills and diagrams serve as excellent teaching aids for practice.

When applicable, I have included personal coaching stories to illustrate a point, but this book is not about my coaching career or the college institutions or pro teams where I have worked. This book is about helping you understand the fundamentals of the game and how to apply that knowledge to your situation. I was the coaching supervisor for the NBA's Development League (NBA D-League) for six years. In that role, I critiqued professional coaches, offering concrete suggestions that helped them develop expertise in their trade. At the present time, I actively mentor basketball coaches at the high school, college, and professional levels. This book addresses many of the issues that I cover with the coaches. I hope that by reading this book, you will come across new ideas that will enhance and improve your game.

Talent alone does not guarantee winning, but talent sharpened by fundamentals certainly offers a better opportunity. Players and coaches who excel in basketball understand that energy unleashed randomly is rarely constructive, so they come to the game seeking ways to improve—ways to get that edge that provides success. Successful coaches have a plan for the team and for each team member. Players need the same kind of road map for their game as they seek improvement. Each drill worked on in practice and every offensive and defensive strategy employed should have a specific purpose. *Winning Basketball Fundamentals* presents proven drills that enhance development for both player and coach.

The information presented in *Winning Basketball Fundamentals* is the culmination of almost a half century of active involvement in basketball. The drills, taken from college and the NBA, are the ones that endured the test of time and proved most effective. I hope they will for you, too.

Acknowledgments

First, I would like to thank the players I have coached. To win, coaches must have talented players, and I was indeed blessed with talented players. But more than that, I coached men of strong character. To each of you, I say thank you for being part of my journey and this book.

My deepest appreciation goes to the unheralded assistant coaches who contributed so much to our success. Following, in chronological order, are the four institutions where I coached and the assistants, in alphabetical order.

Transylvania	Don Lane, Bob Pace, Ron Whitson, Roland Wierwille
UNC Charlotte	Everett Bass, Mike Pratt
Purdue	Everett Bass, Roger Blalock, George Faerber, Billy Kelly, Jeff Meyer
South Florida	Everett Bass, Jan Bennett, Lewis Card, Gordon Gibbons, Mike Lederman, Mike Lewis, Jeff Meyer, Mike Shirley, Mark Wise

I owe a great deal of gratitude and appreciation to two special people who kept me on track with their continuous encouragement and support throughout the writing process. The original manuscript took just over three years to complete, and this revision has taken two years. Yet the experience, knowledge, and theories were collected over a lifetime of coaching. The concept and stories are mine, but without many people giving freely of their time and energy, the original book, let alone this new and improved revision, would never have made it to print. I want to recognize and thank the following:

John Kilgo: John and I forged a lasting friendship when he was the announcer for the UNC Charlotte 49ers during our run to the Final Four in 1976–77. I am indebted to him for the invaluable suggestions, perceptive insights, and basketball knowledge that he shared as an author and radio and TV commentator. He read and reread most of this revision; his support has been invaluable. He has my thanks and deep respect.

Jordan Cohn: Jordan has always encouraged the writing process and has been a source for facts and stats. I am grateful.

I am profoundly grateful to Human Kinetics, principally Ted Miller, for his patience, direction, enthusiasm, and belief in the original publication, as well as this extensive revision. Special thanks to Laura Podeschi, the developmental editor for this revision. Her attention to detail, constant positive input, and encouragement were invaluable in this process. Thanks also to others at HK who contributed to the project, including Justin Klug, Tyler Wolpert, Neil Bernstein, Joyce Brumfield, Joe Buck, Jason Allen, Laura Fitch, Al Wilborn, and Julie Denzer. And finally, thanks to Urbana High School in Urbana, Illinois, for providing the location for the book's photo shoot.

During my formative years I received wonderful training and encouragement from my coaches: Briscoe Evans at Morton Junior High; Elmer "Baldy" Gilb, John Heber, Walter Hill, and Dr. C.T. Sharpton, the principal, at Henry Clay High School; and Harry Stephenson, C.M. Newton, and Jack Wise at Transylvania College.

Shared values and mutual respect were the basis for the relationships I had with those for whom I worked. It is my pleasure to recognize Dr. Irvin Lunger, Dr. James Broadus, Dr. Dean Colvard, Dr. Frank Dickey, Dr. Doug Orr, Wayne Duke, Bill Wall, Vic Bubas, Tay Baker, Fred Schaus, and Dr. Dick Bowers. NBA colleagues Bob Weiss, Willis Reed, Del Harris, Frank Hamblen, Mike Dunleavey, Sam Vincent, Lenny Wilkins, Marty Blake, Mat Winick, Larry Riley, Michael Goldberg, and Senator Herb Kohl, owner of the Milwaukee Bucks, were always encouraging and supportive.

Eleanor Rose: I want to thank Elo for her steadfast confidence and her unselfish commitment of time, energy, and wise counsel. She read and reread every word and every drill, and she is one tough critic. As partners for these past 53 years, we found that few things in our lives equaled the emotional roller coaster we rode while writing and revising this book.

Key to Diagrams

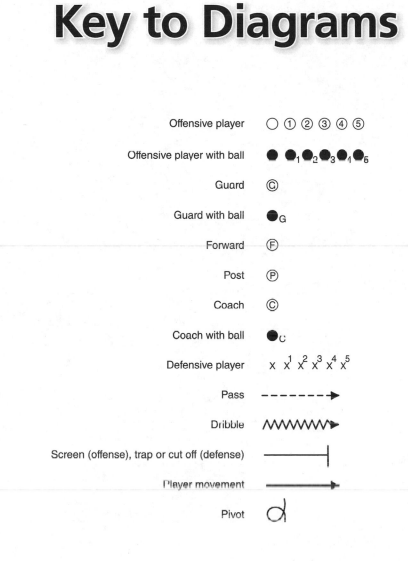

Offensive player	◯ ① ② ③ ④ ⑤
Offensive player with ball	● ●₁ ●₂ ●₃ ●₄ ●₅
Guard	Ⓖ
Guard with ball	●G
Forward	Ⓕ
Post	Ⓟ
Coach	Ⓒ
Coach with ball	●c
Defensive player	X X¹ X² X³ X⁴ X⁵
Pass	- - - - - - ▶
Dribble	∿∿∿∿∿▶
Screen (offense), trap or cut off (defense)	├─────
Player movement	─────▶
Pivot	♂

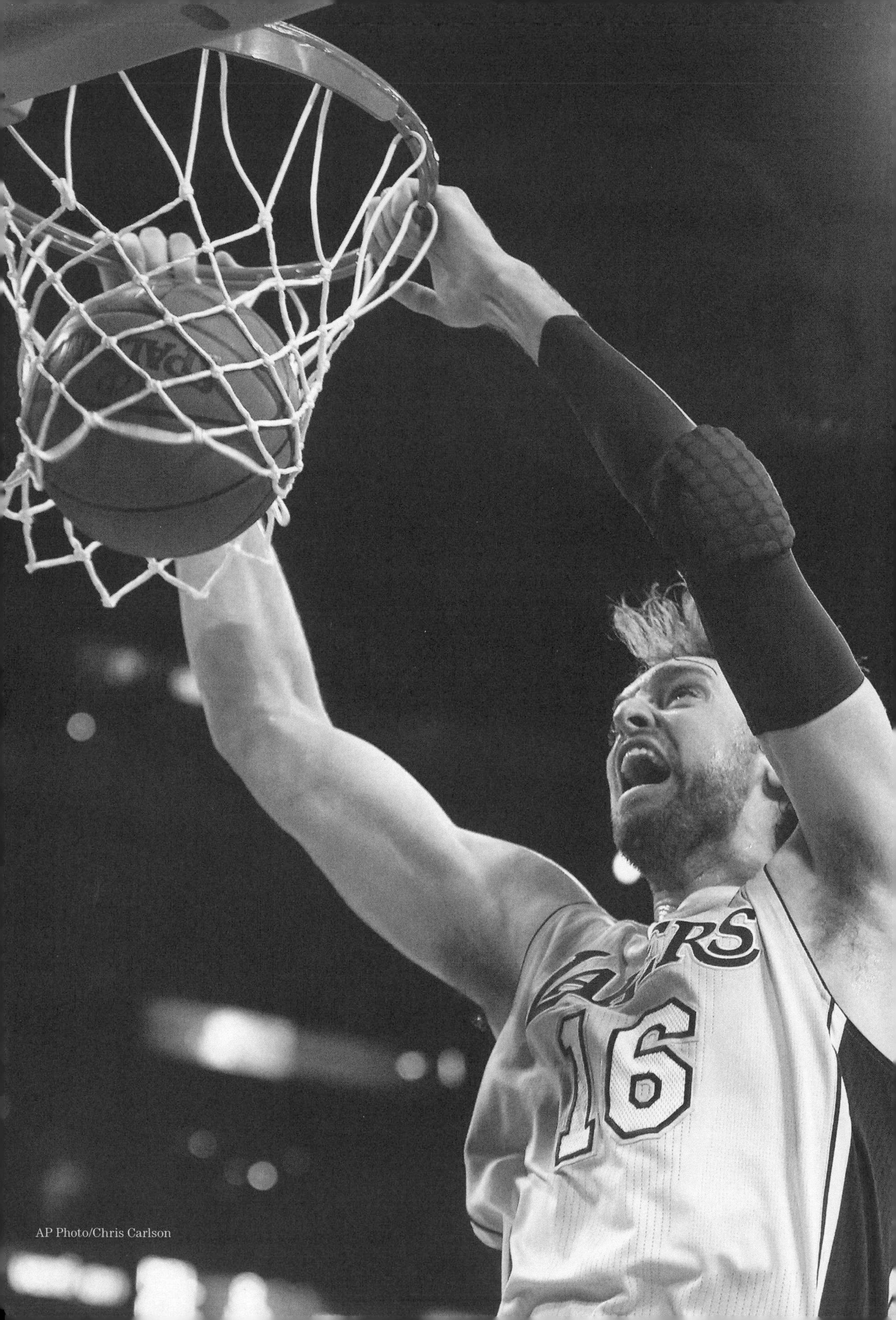

AP Photo/Chris Carlson

Six Guiding Principles

Growing up watching the University of Kentucky's glorious championship basketball teams, from the Fabulous Five of 1948 to Rupp's Runts of the mid-1960s, I learned lessons about the game that would last a lifetime. Foremost among them was that each player and coach had to commit to playing within a set of fundamental beliefs to succeed as a team.

As those Kentucky squads demonstrated, not every club has to subscribe to the same formula to be successful, and players don't have to be similar. Coaches and athletes must take into account many factors, such as experience and individual skills. Historically, NBA and NCAA champions have differed markedly, even from one year to the next.

Still, over the course of a half century as a player and coach, I've found that these six principles characterize consistent, winning teams:

1. Be in good physical condition
2. Play hard
3. Play smart
4. Execute the plan
5. Be unselfish
6. Maximize strengths and minimize weaknesses

Think of your own experience. Did not each of these factors come into play on your best teams? Conversely, weren't the poorer teams lacking in one or more of these dimensions?

Ultimately, winning comes down to talent, but players' abilities are compromised when the squad is deficient in any of these six principles. So, as a player and as a coach, commit to achieving and maintaining them, starting with physical conditioning as the bedrock that must be addressed first.

PRINCIPLE 1:
BE IN GOOD PHYSICAL CONDITION

Elite basketball players are fascinating to watch. They not only adeptly execute skills and tactics but also give maximum effort throughout each game. Even more amazing is that they make it all look so effortless.

Obviously, not every player will perform with the apparent ease of the game's superstars, but with proper physical conditioning, players can improve their output dramatically. Optimal basketball-specific fitness will allow athletes to increase both their minutes played and the quality of those minutes.

The preseason program I recommend is composed of three distinct elements: base building, agility and power training, and performance training. The regimen is demanding, yet realistic and effective. Competitive players love the daily challenges, and they benefit greatly by completing the sport-specific activities featured in this approach.

Players must have an adequate supply of drinking water on hand during all workouts, practices, and games. Proper hydration is essential for good health, efficient body functions, and high-level athletic performance.

The following points explain the three distinct elements of this program.

Build a Base

Previously, conditioning for basketball involved slow and long-duration strenuous activity. Aerobic exercises perhaps included long-distance running, cycling, swimming, or other activities that demanded endurance. Such activities, when well planned and performed at the proper intensity over time, will improve respiration efficiency and heart rate, and such workouts are fine in the off-season for maintaining overall fitness.

But to improve cardiovascular fitness for basketball, the distances that players run should be reduced and the speed of their activity should be increased. For years, the emphasis in training basketball players was on elongated muscles—muscles that are slender, stretched out, and used for running long distances. But the fast-twitch muscle fibers, those that contract more quickly during the shorter periods of high-intensity physical activity, are more important here.

It all starts with athletes developing an adequate anaerobic base to withstand the performance demands that will tax the functioning of this system of the body. Think of it as building the foundation for a house. Although we will add stylistic features specific to the structure as construction progresses, those elements are unlikely to hold up without a solid base from which to build and sustain them. The foundational movements will be anaerobic conditioning, and we will tailor the stylistic features to the sport-specific movements essential for basketball.

According to the American Sports Medicine Institute (ASMI) in Birmingham, Alabama, anaerobic training is "activity that lasts from 30 seconds to 2 minutes." This definition includes interval training, which emphasizes fast-twitch muscle response. Interval training involves working out in intense, limited segments, performed in an exercise-to-rest ratio of 1:2 (for example, 1 minute of exercise for every 2 minutes of rest). Interval training is the preferred method for training basketball players and should make up the major part of anaerobic conditioning.

Interval training activities create an oxygen debt without making athletes feel exhausted or making them more susceptible to injury because of fatigue. Oxygen debt is more commonly called "being winded," and recovery from it requires a period of rest. The more fit a player is, the quicker the recovery occurs. Interval training increases lung capacity and oxygen intake, which enhance recovery and endurance. Players must have endurance to maintain performance throughout games and finish strong.

An interval training program should be conducted in an indoor facility such as a gym or indoor track where administrative props—a clock and a stopwatch—are constant. The clock serves two major functions—it's visible, reflecting the running time for each interval, and it spurs the players to work harder. The incentive for players is to beat the clock, not teammates, although friendly competition occurs. This motivational aspect of the clock is powerful. With players directing their focus to an inanimate object, the coach does not have to play the role of the bad guy. When using a track, a 94-foot (28.7 m) distance must be marked off on one side of the straightaway to replicate a gym floor.

Here's how to structure the interval training. Every team member runs 1 mile (1,600 m), which is divided into intervals of eighths of a mile (200 m). This means that each player runs one-eighth of a mile (220 yards, or 200 m) eight times. Required, predetermined times are assigned to the three positions—guards, forwards, and centers. Five years of personal statistical data on individual players by time and position compiled during preseason conditioning provides predetermined times for each position. (Note that all these times were compiled with college athletes; obviously, times may vary with either less mature high school players or more highly skilled professional players.)

Each player is responsible for running the sprints within that specific period. The goal of all players is to reduce their time daily, thereby increasing their speed. For example, guards begin the first day by running the eighths (200 m) in an allowable time of 44 seconds. On the second day the time drops to 43 seconds, on the third day to 42 seconds, and so on. The time for forwards begins at 44 seconds and then drops to 43. Centers begin the first day at 45 seconds and reduce their time to 44 seconds.

This intense interval training lasts 10 days. It should be supervised, and results need to be recorded. The training is divided into two distinct segments—eighths (1/8) are run on Monday, Wednesday, and Friday, and quarters (1/4) are run on Tuesday and Thursday. The sample workout schedule (table 1.1) reflects both days of the week and required times.

At the beginning of the interval drill, the clock should be set to 24 minutes to avoid having to reset a stopwatch constantly. The clock runs continually until all three groups (guards, forwards, and centers) finish the mile (1,600 m). Typically,

Table 1.1 Sample Workout Schedule

WEEK 1					
	Monday	Tuesday	Wednesday	Thursday	Friday
Distance	1/8 mi (200 m)	1/4 mi (400 m)	1/8 mi (200 m)	1/4 mi (400 m)	1/8 mi (200 m)
Guards (point and shooting)	:44	1:38	:43	1:35	:42
Forwards (small and power)	:44	1:38	:43	1:35	:43
Centers	:45	1:42	:44	1:41	:44

- Times and makeups for the big men should be established in consultation with the players. They are often modified depending on age, weight, and speed.
- Guards and forwards should have no problem making the times for the first week.
- Everyone struggles with breathing in the quarters.

WEEK 2					
	Monday	Tuesday	Wednesday	Thursday	Friday
Distance	1/8 mi (200 m)	1/4 mi (400 m)	1/8 mi (200 m)	1/4 mi (400 m)	1/8 mi (200 m)
Guards (point and shooting)	:41	1:33	:40	1:33	:39
Forwards (small and power)	:42	1:33	:41	1:33	:40
Centers	:44	1:40	:43	1:40	:42

- Goal is to get the big men down to 1:40.
- Excellent runners make all their times.
- Good runners improve their speed considerably.
- Fair runners noticeably increase their speed.

the guards go first. Assistant coaches call and record their times as they cross the finish line. On an eighth-mile (200 m) day, the forwards follow the guards, beginning at the 23:00 mark. Then the centers move to the starting line and begin their run at 22:00. When the centers finish, the guards start again. The players repeat the process for seven more cycles until everyone completes the mile.

The timing process is the same for the quarters except that two-minute intervals separate the running of the groups. The guards begin at 24:00, the forwards at 22:00, and the centers at 20:00. Each group continues in turn until time expires, and each group runs four quarters.

If a player misses a time (that is, does not meet the goal), he runs an additional eighth. When making up eighths, 5 seconds is added to the time requirement: A player running the regular eighths in 42 seconds would be allowed 47 seconds for makeups. A player who fails the makeup is allowed an extra 10 seconds for the third attempt. For a missed turn when using a court, the penalty is two additional eighths. For the quarters, penalty makeups are 15 seconds on the first miss and individually set thereafter. Following a short rest period, players complete all makeups before beginning the exercises in phase II. Players must touch the end lines with both hands on all turns; failure to do so costs an extra interval. The interval begins at the whistle or on the command of "Go." The penalty for a false start is an extra eighth.

The objective of this conditioning is to get players in sufficient condition so that they can complete a two-hour practice without pulling a muscle or injuring themselves; it is not a boot-camp mentality. To prevent injury or illness, the coach should use discretion about when players have pushed themselves as hard as they can.

Train for Agility and Power

After the base is established, the preseason conditioning program must focus on muscular endurance, mobility, flexibility, balance, strength, and power. This work begins directly after the running phase ends.

On Monday, Wednesday, and Friday following the interval work, six basketball-related exercise stations are used. Three exercises—defensive slides, sit-ups, and burpees—emphasize agility, flexibility, and strength. Three exercises focus on plyometrics jump training, emphasizing speed jumping, rope jumping, and rebound jumping. On Tuesday and Thursday following the running, the entire workout consists of plyometrics depth jumping.

Plyometrics is a technique that originated in Russia and Eastern Europe in the mid 1060s. The Soviets achieved great success with plyometrics in their training regimen, especially in track and field. Yuri Verhoshansky, a Russian coach whose success with jumpers is legendary, could be called the father of plyometrics. He succeeded in increasing his athletes' reactive abilities by adding exercise that involved jumping and leaping and that took advantage of the natural elasticity of the muscle tissues.

The six Monday, Wednesday, and Friday drill stations suggested here are supervised by coaches, trainers, and statisticians, who record each player's results. Each exercise lasts 45 seconds, and a 2-minute rest occurs after each activity. The team splits into groups according to position. All groups are supervised, and all begin on the same whistle. Each group is assigned a starting drill. Players rotate in an organized manner until they have completed all six drills. With five groups, one station will be free (open) during each rotation. The goal each day is determined by the average repetitions set the previous day.

SIT-UP

Sit-ups strengthen the abdominal muscles. Establishing a strong core of abdominal muscles helps prevent strains, tears, and injuries that often take a season to heal.

1. The exercise begins with the player lying on his back with knees bent, feet flat on the floor, and hands on each side of the head (figure 1.1*a*).

2. A teammate holds the feet in place, and the player curls himself up. A repetition is complete when the elbows touch the knees (figure 1.1*b*).

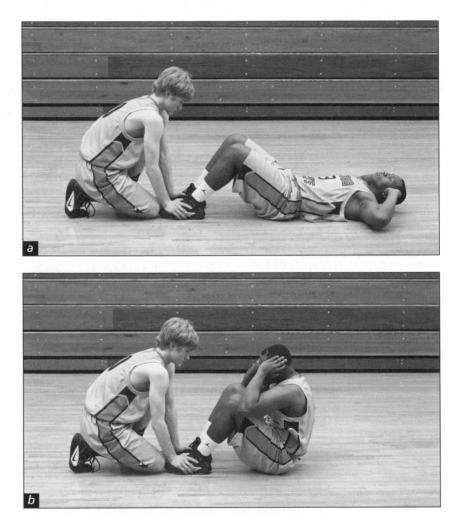

Figure 1.1 Sit-up: *(a)* lie on back; *(b)* elbows to knees.

BURPEE

A burpee, also called a squat thrust, combines multiple exercises and increases strength, mobility, and flexibility. This drill is especially difficult for large players.

1. The player begins standing with his feet close together (figure 1.2*a*).

2. He squats down and places his palms on the floor (figure 1.2*b*). The hands should be shoulder-width apart and outside the knees.

3. The player thrusts his legs backward into a push-up position (figure 1.2*c*) and touches his chest to the floor (figure 1.2*d*).

4. He returns to the push-up position followed by the squat position, stands erect with the shoulders high, and then repeats the drill.

Figure 1.2 Burpee: *(a)* stand; *(b)* squat; *(c)* push-up start; *(d)* push-up finish.

The squat, backward thrust, push-up, and stand-up-straight position make this a physically demanding exercise. From a basketball standpoint, the drill teaches players that they are capable of going on the floor after loose balls and are expected to do so.

DEFENSIVE SLIDE

Defensive slides initiate the learning process for proper defensive position with correct footwork. Slides are great for strengthening the groin, abdominal, and back muscles. Useful props for this exercise are four chairs or orange cones to designate the space needed for sliding.

1. The player begins with his feet spaced apart and arms out (figure 1.3a).

2. He pushes off the right foot, bringing the feet closer together (figure 1.3b), and steps with the left foot (figure 1.3c). He uses short steps without crossing his feet.

3. After four or five slides, the player changes directions to return to his starting position. Repeat.

After performing the drill side to side, players can also perform it moving up and back. The emphasis is on technique—maintaining low body position and proper balance with the knees bent, the back straight, and the head up during the slides. This defensive slide technique helps prevent groin injury. The drill involves constant movement.

Figure 1.3 Defensive slide: *(a)* feet apart; *(b)* push off right foot, bringing feet closer together; *(c)* step with left foot.

SPEED JUMPING

A prop 6 inches (15 cm) in height is needed for this exercise. The exercise improves speed, quickness, endurance, and strength.

1. Speed jumping starts from a standing position with knees bent (figure 1.4*a*).
2. The player jumps over a 6-inch (15 cm) prop (figure 1.4*b*), lands on both feet (figure 1.4*c*), and immediately jumps back to his starting position. Repeat.

Players jump over and back in a continuous motion. The emphasis is on speed and quickness, but safety is also a concern because players often tire at the end of the drill. Because of fatigue, players may have to stop momentarily to gather themselves before finishing the drill.

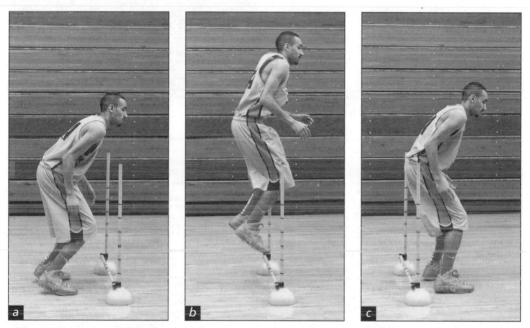

Figure 1.4 Speed jumping: *(a)* load with knees bent; *(b)* jump; *(c)* land on both feet.

REBOUND JUMPING

Rebound jumping develops strength, rhythm, and explosion off a two-footed jump.

1. The drill starts at the free-throw line (figure 1.5*a*) with a running two-step approach.

2. The player gathers at the backboard and explodes off both feet (figure 1.5*b*), slapping the backboard as high as he can with both hands (figure 1.5*c*).

3. After returning to the floor, the jumper quickly returns to the free-throw line and repeats the process while the coach counts the jumps.

The object is to increase speed, height, and number of touches each day.

Figure 1.5 Rebound jumping: *(a)* Start at free-throw line with two-step approach; *(b)* explode off both feet; *(c)* slap backboard.

ROPE JUMPING

Rope jumping is vital for timing, rhythm, and strengthening the legs and ankles.

1. The exercise begins by jumping off both feet for 15 seconds (figure 1.6*a*).

2. The player then switches to the right leg for 15 seconds (figure 1.6*b*).

3. Finally, the player finishes with the left leg for 15 seconds (figure 1.6*c*).

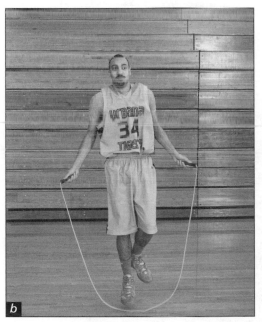

Figure 1.6 Rope jumping: *(a)* both feet; *(b)* right leg; *(c)* left leg.

On Tuesday and Thursday, the players focus on plyometrics depth jump training. The instant uplift off one leg provides increased tolerance, development, and efficiency in the stretch-shortening cycle of muscle action. During the stretching, a greater amount of elastic energy is stored in the muscle. The muscle then reuses this elastic energy in the following concentric action to become stronger. Make sure that players work with a qualified instructor and become familiar with correct jumping technique.

DEPTH JUMPING

Begin with boxes measuring 12, 18, 24, 30, and 36 inches (30, 45, 60, 75, and 90 cm) high with a flat base 36 inches (90 cm) in length and 36 inches in width. Begin by placing boxes in a row, 24 inches (60 cm) apart, beginning with the smallest and ending with the tallest.

1. A player begins by jumping onto the 12-inch (30 cm) box (figure 1.7, *a-c*).

Figure 1.7   Depth jumping: *(a-c)* jump to 12-inch box.

2. The player immediately jumps down and springs onto the 18-inch (45 cm) box (figure 1.7, *d-f*), quickly jumps down and elevates onto the 24-inch (60 cm) box, and so on.

3. Completing as many boxes as is comfortably safe, the player reverses and returns down the boxes one at a time using the same springing action.

After touching the floor, the player immediately begins a new repetition. A player completes three to six repetitions—both legs, right leg, and left leg—for one set. The second set begins after a two-minute rest.

Figure 1.7 *(continued)*   Depth jumping: *(d-f)* jump to 18-inch box.

Train for Performance

The final component of preseason conditioning is full-court work in which players choose the teams and officiate their own games. Veteran leadership on a team can be helpful in ensuring that less mature and inexperienced teammates play hard every second they're on the court, which in turn gives them the greatest conditioning benefits.

The first team to make 10 baskets wins; winners stay and losers sit. With 15 players, there are three teams. Each team plays at least two games. Full-court play helps players develop stamina and endurance. Players are tired, sometimes exhausted, after extending themselves to make their running times in the eighths and performing their agility and power exercises. Therefore, scrimmages are often sloppy and poorly played.

To make the necessary progress, individual squad members must push themselves and work their way through the fatigue. After three or four days of adding scrimmages to the workouts, players should improve their cardiorespiratory recovery rate and be more capable of demonstrating high-level skills through the end of the session.

PRINCIPLE 2: PLAY HARD

In 1958 I graduated from Transylvania University—a small, academically sound school in Lexington, Kentucky, that had its own rich basketball history and tradition. We learned quickly to be comfortable and secure in our own shoes, because being located in the same city as the University of Kentucky, we knew that we would always be in its long shadow. After serving as captain of the basketball team and earning my degree in physical education, I sought a job in coaching.

For me, money wasn't the issue; an opportunity was what I was searching for. I jumped at the offer to coach high school in the small town of Versailles, Kentucky, located about 12 miles (20 km) from Lexington. For teaching five classes, coaching three sports—basketball, football, and baseball—and driving the school bus to athletic events, my salary was $3,200 annually, which was fine with me. This was my chance to coach basketball, and it was a golden opportunity.

Many people have a story like mine that involves working hard. But if basketball is a person's dream, to play it or coach it or both, hard work and dedication have to be part of the equation. I'm not much impressed with young people who say they want to coach but then turn down an opportunity because they don't want to live in a small town off the beaten path. To get your break in coaching or in playing basketball, you have to be willing to start small and work hard. Period. Anything less than total effort on the part of high school and college players and coaches will not produce consistent winning. Players and coaches at those levels must do several things to ensure maximum effort on a consistent basis because, when everything else is equal, effort usually determines the winner.

David Hunziker, our student clock supervisor at Transylvania College, showed us by example that slacking off was unacceptable. Although stricken with cerebral palsy, he took great pride in handling his duties without a slip, was a key member of our staff, and set a great example for our team. He was such an inspiration to everyone in the program that none of us could imagine complaining or letting up.

The following points summarize ways in which to work hard.

Maintain Focus

Like most things in life, winning in basketball requires a keen, sustained effort. Forget the shortcuts and distractions; there aren't any. Winners realize that they must stay focused, work their way to the top, and understand, going in, that discouraging setbacks will occur along the way.

Whether working on individual skills alone on an outdoor court or taking part in a team practice in the middle of the season, total concentration is essential to learning, retention, and execution. Injuries such as turned ankles and pulled muscles are commonplace in practice when players lose concentration and don't maintain intensity.

Be Efficient

One way that a coach can prevent players from being distracted is by keeping practices interesting, productive, and upbeat. Individual sessions should move briskly, preferably with a clock regulating the amount of time spent on each drill. Drills should not exceed 5 minutes, except for scrimmages. Blocks of time ranging as high as 20 minutes can be devoted to a specific aspect of the game (shooting, defensive footwork, boxing out) as long as drills vary throughout the period. Variety keeps players from becoming bored and helps them maintain concentration. More is accomplished in less time, and practice is more productive for everyone involved.

Players can be efficient by making it to practice on time, dressing properly, being attentive, focusing on and executing drills correctly, competing intently, and supporting teammates and coaches with a positive attitude.

Compete Every Day

Whether you're a high school freshman trying out for the junior varsity team or a professional player battling for a roster spot or a place in the starting lineup, a practice environment that promotes healthy competition can help you flourish. High school players can find opportunities to compete as close as the local church league, YMCA, or even the neighborhood hoops. College players and beyond can take even the simplest offensive drill to the next level of competition. For example, individual shooting drills should end with a winner. Keep tabs on who is first to make a certain number of shots and declare a winner. After a winner emerges, change the drill. For team shooting drills based on curls, fades, and pop-outs off pin-downs, say that the first team to make five baskets wins. Having worked with great NBA shooters such as Dell Curry, Glen Rice, Dale Ellis, and Ricky Pierce, I can tell you that such competition drives them.

Seek Extra Work

The time before and after practice is player improvement time, or PIT. Whether working on ballhandling, rebounding, defense, or shooting, players who put in an extra 15 to 30 minutes a day will improve faster than those who show up right at the start of practice and leave as soon as it ends. PIT also provides an excellent opportunity to improve coach–player relationships. Players who master skills and feel better about their coaches will be more motivated from one practice to the next. Many coaches are making PIT an integral part of practices rather than optional. PIT is essential for young players as well as seasoned veterans at any level who aren't getting significant playing time.

PRINCIPLE 3: PLAY SMART

Energy unleashed randomly is rarely constructive. Dr. Jim Broadus, the dean of education at Transylvania College, was a frequent visitor to our basketball practices. An analytical man, he was always questioning why we did certain things. For instance, he wanted to know why, in our press offense, we worked against seven defenders. (We did this to make the offense work harder.) The players' intense concentration fascinated Dr. Broadus, and he wondered whether they could duplicate it in the classroom. We discussed the difficulties in teaching competition and cooperation. He was always interested in the teaching process and enjoyed the give-and-take between player and coach. His questions underscored the importance of why one particular drill and plan was better than another. Further, his questions emphasized that you should do everything with a purpose—that you should plan your work and work your plan. Staff meetings and the practice court are where you develop the plan and where players learn to succeed through smart play.

The following points summarize ways in which to play smart.

Focus on Intelligence

In deciding how to run a program, a coach can drive the team, push it, or lead it. Although a coach usually favors one style over another, all three methods will probably surface during the long season. The most effective coaches understand that the cornerstone of a winning program includes not only basketball success but also academic success for each player. To maintain a flourishing, well-rounded program, the coach should become involved in the total educational process.

On the court, players can demonstrate basketball intelligence by adhering to school and team policies, supporting teammates, being early and staying late for individual improvement sessions before and after practice when possible, and being cooperative whenever called on to do so. Off the court, players need to assume responsibility for their academics and meet classroom requirements, eat responsibly and maintain healthy habits, chose friends wisely, and stay out of harm's way.

TRASH TALKING

Alex English, a member of the Basketball Hall of Fame and the 1983 NBA scoring champion, coached the Charleston Lowgators of the NBA Developmental League in 2001–2002. I was supervisor of coaches for the league at that time, and during a practice session, I observed that Coach English's players were trash-talking each other. During our critique session, I asked Coach English why he permitted trash talking during practice. He just shrugged his shoulders, as if he didn't know or hadn't thought about it. My reply to him was "You don't have a player good enough to trash-talk in the NBA." He agreed and stopped the trash talking with a few comments at the team meeting that night.

Practice With a Purpose

Players cannot play smart without understanding the fundamentals, and they learn those fundamentals in practice. Teams that are not fundamentally sound and dedicated to the same purpose and goals will have a hard time playing, especially when they face adversity. Some players who make the game look easy, such as Chris Paul of the Los Angeles Clippers, might leave the impression that they are playing by instinct and guts, but statistics reveal another story. In the 2011-12 season Paul averaged 19.8 points per game, shot 47.8 percent from the field, 86.1 percent from the free-throw line, and 9.1 assists per game. Practice sessions offer players the opportunity to experiment and come to know their strengths as well as develop a shared purpose with teammates.

Develop a Solid Foundation

The coach must seek to develop the foundational offensive and defensive skills of players, from the high school to the professional level. As young players rise through the ranks, much attention—usually too much attention—is given to points scored. The leading scorer is not necessarily the team's best player, although that wouldn't always be apparent to those who read newspaper accounts of games.

Players who score a lot of points are not necessarily good shooters. Shooters might be scorers, but it doesn't always work the other way around. In many instances, big, young players score many points simply because they are bigger than their defenders. With stars twinkling in their eyes because of the media coverage that they receive for scoring points, they might not understand that they need to improve their passing and dribbling or increase the range on their jumper. The coach must remind them of what they need to work on, because as players move up the basketball ladder their lack of overall skills will catch up with them.

The game requires much more than just scoring points. Good defensive habits are essential. Players need to learn early to stay in front of their opponent, stay down on jump shooters, avoid reaching and grabbing on dribble penetration, and use good rebounding techniques. The players who go on to good college and professional careers have developed both offensive and defensive skills to become complete players.

Keep Fouls Under Control

After players have learned the foundational skills, they should begin to realize that fouling and putting the opponent on the line is costly. Intelligent play is impossible if players foul because they lack fundamentals or play out of position because of lackadaisical effort. Coaches need to drive home the point that excessive fouling is often a path to defeat. After all, a 15-foot (4.5 m) shot from directly in front of the basket with no defensive opponent shouldn't be too hard for a top player.

I had a system at UNC Charlotte, Purdue and South Florida where I substituted a player as soon as he picked up his first foul. That rule serves a couple of purposes. First, substitutes recognize that they are important to the team because they know that they are going in as soon as the starter at their position fouls for the first time. Knowing that they are going to get into the game, substitutes concentrate more in practice. They don't have the mind-set that they are just substitutes and don't need to work hard in practice. Second, as the starter leaves the game after one foul, he receives a strong message that random fouling hurts the team. By sitting awhile, the player has time to focus on not picking up a careless second foul. This policy also includes sitting starters after their second and third fouls to avoid early foul problems.

Get the Ball to the Right Player

Coaches and players should work hard in practice to ensure that the right person receives the inbounds pass in late-game situations. A team protecting a lead late in the game should make every effort to get the ball to the best foul shooter because they know that the opponent is going to foul as soon as the inbounds pass is completed.

The old NBA Charlotte Hornets used a play called the line to inbound the ball against pressure. Players would line up single file and then break randomly to open areas on the floor. Opponents would foul the player receiving the inbounds pass. We realized that Glen Rice, our best free-throw shooter, should be our first option in those situations. If we succeeded in getting the ball to Rice, opponents were reluctant to foul him because he shot 85 percent from the foul line. Not fouling immediately took time off the clock, which played into our hands.

Know your best options and use them.

PRINCIPLE 4: EXECUTE THE PLAN

A game often boils down to two or three possessions in the endgame. Close games usually go to the team that executes with poise late in the contest. Knowing this, coaches spend hours working on late-game situations. They emphasize getting the proper passing angles, setting good screens, balancing the floor in a manner that makes it difficult for the opponent to guard the offensive players or get a double team, and having all players on the court work hard in their roles so that one of them can get an open shot. Coaches and players learn that mental mistakes breed physical errors; thus, good teams focus on the task, play with intensity, and keep a positive mind-set.

Just getting a shot in late-game situations isn't enough; the goal is to get a high-percentage shot. Doing so takes discipline and poise, which come in part from proper preparation. All players on the court—passer, screener, decoy, and shooter—must perform their roles correctly for the team to reach its goal. One of the truths of basketball is that the failure of one player to do his job can negate the work of four teammates who did theirs perfectly. Basketball is the true team game, with five players working as one to accomplish a single purpose. And if we're paying attention, all of us—coaches and players—will learn something new in every game, which will help us down the road.

The following points summarize ways in which to execute the plan.

Don't Experiment in Games

After trailing Jacksonville for most of the game, South Florida (my team at the time) used a full-court, 1-3-1 press to pull within 2 points with five seconds to go. Jacksonville fouled our center, who went to the free-throw line for two shots and a chance to tie the game. The press had worked well, so we decided to stay in it. But we needed to adjust our alignment because our center was shooting the free throws. If he made the free throws, his new role would be to take the up position in the press to guard the inbounds passer, while the small forward needed to rotate back and guard the basket against any long pass or layup attempt.

Our center made the two free throws to tie the score and then took his proper defensive position, guarding the Jacksonville player who was throwing the ball inbounds. The entry pass went to Jacksonville's guard, who immediately attacked the sideline off the dribble. Instead of attacking the wing defenders, he threw a long pass to Jacksonville's center, who hit an uncontested layup at the buzzer. Our small forward had lined up correctly before the foul shots were taken, but when Jacksonville threw the ball in, he left his assignment under the basket and ran to midcourt, his usual position, forgetting that he had exchanged spots with the center.

As South Florida's head coach, I learned two important lessons from this experience: First, don't try things in a game that the players have never practiced; second, remember that although some players are capable of making adjustments on the fly during the heat of a close game, others are not as adaptable and need to stay within their comfort zones. Failure to execute in the endgame cost us a possible victory.

Players should also avoid experimenting in games; as with coaches, practice is the time to make major adjustments.

Play Your Trump Card at the Right Time

Most good teams know the value of proper execution. Baseball teams practice the suicide squeeze, even though they seldom use the play. Football teams practice the quarterback sneak, although they use it sparingly. Basketball teams work on full-court, short-clock situations almost daily. Teams should spend time practicing minute details because such situations might arise in any game. When I was head coach at Transylvania, we were in the finals of the Kentucky Intercollegiate Athletic Conference tournament against Union College of Barbourville, Kentucky. Union had home-court advantage by virtue of being the higher seed. Much was at stake, because the winner would advance to the National Association of Intercollegiate Athletics (NAIA) playoffs, and the loser's season would end.

Transylvania had the ball out of bounds in a tie game 94 feet (28.7 m) from the basket with four seconds left in regulation. We had practiced a play all season for precisely that situation, and when the players came to the time-out huddle they already knew what our strategy would be. Still, for the play to work, each player had to carry out his assignment. Our guards were positioned opposite each other on the sidelines at midcourt. Our tallest player, Bob Ecroyd, lined up at our free-throw line, and our center was at midcourt. On the call of "Hike," Ecroyd set a back screen for our center as our two guards took three hard steps into the backcourt and then pivoted and ran toward the frontcourt as the ball was thrown to Ecroyd at midcourt. Ecroyd's first option was to pass to one of the guards, but that option wasn't available. His second option, which he executed, was to drive to the basket and shoot. The ball banked in at the buzzer, and we were on our way to Kansas City and the NAIA national tournament. The back screen, the sprinting by the guards, their reverse pivots, the long pass to Ecroyd at midcourt, and his catch, dribble, and shot all culminated in perfect execution. The true essence of coaching and playing is execution.

PRINCIPLE 5: BE UNSELFISH

I've never met a coach who enjoys coaching a selfish player, and I've never met a player who enjoys playing with a selfish teammate. Basketball players learn early that shooting and ballhandling are the skills that coaches look for when selecting teams. Unfortunately, as coaches select the better players for Amateur Athletic Union (AAU), middle school, and high school teams, selfish play is already built into the system.

Unselfishness isn't achieved by trying to prove to teammates, coaches, and fans that you aren't selfish, but rather by maintaining a mind-set and approach to playing in which all decisions and actions reflect one desire—to help the team be as successful as it possibly can be. In some situations this might mean pulling up on a drive and dishing it to a teammate breaking open to the basket; in others it might mean taking the open jumper. The point is that when a player thinks first and foremost about functioning in the most effective manner to accomplish team goals, selfishness is not an issue.

The 2011 men's NCAA tournament had excellent examples of unselfish teams who beat higher seeds throughout the competition. Starting with Butler's second run to the Final Four in two years, the number 8 seed Bulldogs upset number 1 seed Pittsburg in the second round; number 13 seed Morehead flattened powerful

Louisville, the number 4 seed; and the University of Richmond from the Atlantic 10 Conference, a number 12 seed, beat SEC power and number 5 seed Vanderbilt. Perhaps the ultimate example of unselfish team play in the 2011 NCAA tournament was Virginia Commonwealth University, a play-in team seeded number 11, who crushed number 1 seed Kansas on their way to the Final Four.

The following points summarize ways in which to be unselfish.

Share the Ball

High scorers make the teams, are voted to all-star teams, and receive media attention from those who don't understand the game on any level other than point scoring. Given this situation, it's not surprising that many young players become selfish. They look at taking shots and scoring as the principal way to succeed.

Coaches spend hours teaching players about shot selection. Bad shots can destroy a team in many ways. Effective coaches teach players that poor shot selection can cause several problems:

- The team is in poor offensive rebounding position; no one knows when to go to the boards.
- Bad shots make the team vulnerable to fast breaks and easy baskets for opponents. Who rotates back?
- Poor shot selection destroys team morale; the shooter puts selfish interest above team success.
- When players take bad shots, teammates have no incentive to make screens and cuts.
- The fire-at-will, one-and-done offensive approach leads to chaos and confusion.

The coach should clarify at the beginning of the season the difference between a good shot and a bad shot. Players need to know the parameters

Ball handlers are taught to move the ball, hit the open teammate, and pass ahead on fast breaks. Selfish players might choose to hold the ball rather than pass ahead to a teammate in transition, thus destroying the advantage of having numbers on their side in a fast break. Think of some of the outstanding players in today's game. Derrick Rose, Chris Paul, Kobe Bryant, Steve Nash, and Rajon Rondo come quickly to mind. These players do not have to dominate the ball to be effective. In fact, they go out of their way to involve their teammates and spread the scoring load, making it harder for opponents to guard them. Chris Paul averages 9.8 assists per game, Rajon Rondo 8.1 assists, and Derrick Rose 6.8 assists. Kobe Bryant has 5,418 assists over his career thus far. Their approach is not only unselfish basketball but also the smart way to play. Good coaches design half-court sets that highlight player and ball movement. When this movement stops, the offense breaks down. For their own good as well as for the success of the team, players should share the basketball. They'll find that making a good pass that leads to a teammate's basket is just as rewarding as scoring themselves.

Help Teammates on Defense

Defense is the cornerstone of good basketball. Good defensive teams can often hang in there with teams that have better talent. And even teams with exceptional talent know that there are going to be nights, especially on the road, when their shots aren't falling. The way to win on such nights is through good defense. By keeping the other team from shooting a high percentage, a team's chances of victory skyrocket. Good athletes who are willing can learn to play effective defense, and good defensive teams are almost always in the game.

What does a player need to play good defense? Defenders bring high energy, toughness, unselfishness, enthusiasm, the ability to move their feet quickly, and good anticipation. The best defensive players always stand ready to lend a helping hand to a teammate who gets beat. Great camaraderie can be built on defense. The beauty here is that the unselfishness seeps over to the offense and helps foster unselfish behavior there. Defense can be fun, and the best defensive teams take pride in their defensive effort. Coaches can learn many things about players from watching them play defense.

Here are nine defensive hustle indicators that players should use when trying out for a team:

1. Get down in an athletic position and assume a defensive stance.
2. Slide the feet without crossing them.
3. Sprint to catch up and get level to the ball when you fall behind.
4. Contain by staying in front of the dribbler.
5. Contest every shot that your opponent takes.
6. Deny ball-side cuts.
7. Box out on rebounds.
8. Dive on the floor for loose balls. Such conduct is contagious.
9. Take no plays off. If you need rest, ask the coach to remove you from the game. Don't try to catch your breath on defense.

Eliminate the Virus

Sooner or later, selfish players will poison the team. Coaches must move quickly and decisively to eradicate the selfish virus. If a coach lets one team member get by with selfish play, then other players eventually are going to say, "He lets Joe do it. Why shouldn't I?" Then your team is doomed.

Bill Russell, the great center of the Boston Celtics, dominated with unselfishness. One evening I was seated next to Tom "Satch" Sanders, a Boston teammate of Russell's. I asked him what made Boston so effective. He said it was because of Russell. "He controlled the ball 90 percent of the time for us but scored only 10 percent of our points," Sanders said. Russell understood that players succeed by winning, not by individual scoring statistics. Although the NBA has produced many star players, only the truly unselfish ones such as Russell, Michael Jordan, Larry Bird, Magic Johnson, Isiah Thomas, and more recently, Shaquille O'Neal, Kobe Bryant, David Robinson, and Tim Duncan have provided the necessary leadership to win the NBA title.

PRINCIPLE 6: MAXIMIZE STRENGTHS AND MINIMIZE WEAKNESSES

Players bring various skills to the game. Some are scorers and shooters, others are good ball handlers, some are best at rebounding, others excel on defense, and still others provide overall leadership and enhance team chemistry. Good coaches know what each player on their team does well and not so well, and serious players want to know the truth about their skills, whether they're playing on an AAU team, at summer camp, or on a school team.

One NBA team charts 67 different parameters of defense and grades players daily on those measures. The following points summarize ways in which to maximize strengths and minimize weaknesses.

Record Workout Results

Table 1.2, a first-look evaluation form used for tryouts and practices, provides the coach with specific information for accurate comments when discussing a player's strengths and weaknesses.

A coach analyzes and determines his team's assets and liabilities through record keeping and workouts, eventually refining the players' roles to build a cohesive unit. Roles define the shooters, the rebounders, and the defenders. Most of the time these roles are self-evident. When players understand and accept their roles, the potential for conflict diminishes. Perceptive coaches understand that players can disagree about style of play. Guards, naturally, prefer an offense that features the perimeter shot as the first option, whereas the big players want their touches in an offense that emphasizes going inside first. Highly talented teams enjoy the luxury of being able to attack inside and outside, but the coach of less-talented teams must make clear what style will dominate. The head coach seeks input from assistants on style of play but makes the final decision.

To make sure that there is no confusion, the coach, not the player, has the final word on what role the player will play to help the team succeed. In the team's first meeting of the season, the coach must cover several issues, such as policies, regulations, and discipline. At this time, all players should fill out a form indicating their strengths, weaknesses, and individual goals for the year (table 1.3). Compiling and reviewing their responses should help reduce the potential for conflicts and get everyone pulling in the same direction.

Table 1.2 Observation Chart

Name: _____ Scale: 1–5 (5 is best)

EVALUATION			
Offensive skill	**Rating**	**Defensive skill**	**Rating**
Shooting		Proper stance	
Perimeter shots		Contains	
Dribbling		Contests	
Passing		Gives help or support	
Moves ball ahead		Stops dribble drive	
Offensive rebounding		Defensive rebounding	
Attitude		Hustle	
DISCUSSION POINTS			
Strengths	**Rating**	**Weaknesses**	**Rating**
Shooting		Proper stance	
Dribbling		Contests	
Attitude		Gives help or support	
Contains		Stops dribble drive	
Defensive rebounding		Perimeter shots	
Hustle		Passing	
		Moves ball ahead	
		Offensive rebounding	

From L. Rose, 2013, *Winning basketball fundamentals* (Champaign, IL: Human Kinetics).

Table 1.3 Player Goals

Name: _____

1. Team goals	Please explain answer

2. Individual goals	Please explain answer	

3. Statistical improvement	Projected	Last year's statistics
Field goals		
Free throws		
Rebound average		
Assist average		
Turnover average		
Personal fouls		
Points per game		
Shots per game		
Attitude (scale: 1–5; 5 is best)		

4. Academics	Projected	Last year
Grade classification		
Grade point average		
Major		
Academic counselor		
Graduation date		
First semester courses		

(continued)

Table 1.3 Player Goals *(continued)*

5. Playing strengths and weaknesses (please list and elaborate)	Strengths	Weaknesses
	1.	1.
	2.	2.
	3.	3.
	4.	4.
	5.	5.

From L. Rose, 2013, *Winning basketball fundamentals* (Champaign, IL: Human Kinetics).

Use Statistics

Used properly, statistics can help define strengths and weaknesses. Statistics and charts (see chapter 3) compiled during practice are valuable resources in establishing roles for players. Tracking players' progress is an important way of showing them where they need to improve and where they stack up against other players at their position. Statistical systems can measure individual players and teams over a season or a specific number of games. Gathering this information is part of the process, but more important is knowing how to apply it. Valid statistics are one tool that helps coaches identify their team's strengths and weaknesses. They are not an end all, but used properly they provide valuable guidance. Statistics track a player's progress in certain areas and, along with other things that happen in practice, can determine playing time.

Statistics are like a report card for the player. They show strengths and weaknesses without any bias. After statistics are compiled following each game, the coaches should discuss them with the players. In these individual meetings, the statistics are reviewed and discussed, and input is given as to how players can improve their deficiencies.

Finish the Game With Your Best Players

One of the biggest challenges for coaches and players is to make sure that the best players are on the floor at the end of close ball games. Players should be quick to recognize when a teammate is in foul trouble and make adjustments to help on defense, crash the boards, or sprint back to cover the basket to give help. Joe Barry Carroll, a seven-footer (213 cm) and a number one NBA draft pick in 1980 from Purdue, was so valuable to our team that when he picked up his fourth foul, we had to find ways to keep him in the game. We might change the defense or adjust matchups. The coach must be aware of personal fouls, fatigue, and injuries and know who the best pressure free-throw shooters are so that the strongest possible team is on the floor at the end of the game. UConn did exactly that in its 2004 NCAA semifinal win over Duke by holding out Emeka Okafor for almost 16 minutes in the first half of the game so that he would be available for the second-half finish.

Plan the work and work the plan is good advice for anyone attempting to be successful in any enterprise. During the early planning stage, the coach should establish trustworthy principles that serve as the foundation on which to build a successful basketball program. These six guiding principles—be in good physical condition, play hard, play smart, execute properly, be unselfish, and maximize strengths and minimize weaknesses—enable the coach and players to begin on a solid foundation with a clean, unambiguous road map. With the principles firmly in place, we move to the important roles that players and coaches undertake as leadership qualities unfold.

Playing and Coaching

From its creation in 1891 by James Naismith, basketball has been an evolving American sport. The National Federation of State High School Associations conducted a participation survey in 2010–11. According to this survey, 984,777 athletes were participating in basketball. This figure included both male (545,844) and female (438,933) players. These sums place high school basketball third by numbers in student participation (after football, 1,109,836, and outdoor track and field, 1,054,587). The popularity of basketball continues to grow; age-specific programs are offered in elementary schools, church leagues, intramurals, and AAU programs. Junior high programs that have become feeder systems for high schools have never been more competitive; large-city schools have as many as 100 kids trying out for 15 spots. AAU programs that play throughout the summer provide a great opportunity for growth and skill development. The enthusiasm, interest, and participation in the sport of basketball have never been higher.

As the game continues to grow, rules, equipment, court dimensions, game strategy, and the size of the players and their skill sets continue to change and improve. Concurrently, coaches develop new tactics to maximize their collective and individual players' talents within the stipulated rules.

RULES AND ROLE CHANGES

Players' increased size, superb athleticism, and advanced skills have made rules changes necessary. Big men, such as Bob Kurland, George Mikan, Wilt Chamberlain, and Lew Alcindor (Kareem Abdul-Jabbar) had tremendous influence on changing and rewriting the rules concerning goaltending, dunking, free throws, and others.

Coaches, too, have prompted rules changes. North Carolina's Dean Smith and peers that adopted his four-corner offense took advantage of great ballhandlers and the absence of a shot clock at the college level. As more teams tried to shorten the game by keeping the ball away from bigger, more athletic opponents, college decision makers and television advertisers became concerned that the public would lose interest and that television ratings would slide. So in the mid-1980s, to increase scoring and eliminate stalling tactics, three rules changes were instituted:

1. 45-second shot clock
2. Three-point field goal
3. Elimination of defensive hand checking

Each of these changes had a dramatic effect on how the modern game of basketball is played. The shot clock and three-point shot forced coaches to revise their strategies. Zone defenses were at first thought to be more effective because teams had to shoot the ball within a prescribed time and defenders had to move out on the court and guard the three-point line. But soon, good ball movement against the zone produced more open perimeter shots, which called for more man-to-man defenses.

In addition, the elimination of hand checking encouraged the dribble-drive attack. For years, defensive players were allowed to put one hand on an offensive player's hip and thus control the direction and speed of the offensive opponent. In the mid-1980s, however, this rule changed. If the offensive player was facing the defender, the defender was not allowed to touch him. The advantage quickly shifted from defense to offense, and the dribble-drive offense (see chapter 6) became a popular offensive attack.

The shot clock and the three-point shot, along with the enforcement of the no-hand-checking rule, produced the results that rules makers desired. The shot clock in college basketball was reduced to 35 seconds in 1993, and the three-point arc was moved back to 20 feet, 9 inches (6.32 m) in 2008.

Coupled with the rules changes, players were getting bigger, stronger, faster, and more skilled, which rendered traditional role labels antiquated. For years, the roles of basketball players fell into three basic categories: guards, forwards, and centers. As players improved, however, position designations became more specific:

Point Guard (1)   It's been said that coaches who really appreciate point guards are the ones who've had to play without one. The point guard becomes the coach on the floor. In most cases the point guard is the vocal leader on the floor and always knows the time on the clock, the score, the number of time-outs remaining, how many fouls each team has committed, and who to foul when it is necessary. The point guard must have great peripheral awareness and make good decisions with the ball. Point guards are unselfish and think *pass first, shoot second*. Great point guards generate a lot of assists because they look to distribute the ball. They need to be fast and quick and have the ability to separate and create space when dribbling. Four outstanding NBA point guards are Derrick Rose, Chris Paul, Russell Westbrook, and Steve Nash.

Shooting Guard (2)   The shooting guard has a scoring touch. The two-guard position requires great perimeter shooting skills. The primary role for the two guard is to produce points. Typically, the two guard is big, from 6 feet, 3 inches (190 cm) to 6 feet, 7 inches (201 cm), and athletic, like Kobe Bryant (6 feet, 6 inches, or 198 cm), LeBron James (6 feet, 8 inches, or 203 cm), Joe Johnson (6 feet, 7 inches, or 201 cm), and Ray Allen (6 feet, 5 inches, or 196 cm). But size is not a requirement; Monta Ellis of the Milwaukee Bucks and Steph Curry of Golden State, both just a little over 6 feet (183 cm), play both point guard and shooting guard.

Shooting guards should be able to handle the ball, beat opponents off the dribble, and penetrate. They should also have good catch-and-shoot skills coming off curls and pin-down baseline screens. A major asset is their ability to hit open-court shots off the fast break, and two guards must be good free-throw shooters because in late-game situations they are involved in handling the ball and taking the last shots.

Small Forward (3)   Three words describe the small forward: diversity, size, and scoring. The small forward is a highly skilled player who has many of the two-guard skills. They are usually a bigger version of the two-guard and have the ability to play inside on the low post and outside on the perimeter. Small forwards can rebound and attack off the dribble immediately, filling one of the fast-break lanes. They are good open-court players and have ballhandling, passing, and decision-making capabilities. There is no standard size for small forwards; they can range from 6 feet, 5 inches (196 cm) to 7 feet (213 cm). The term *small forward* is somewhat misleading, especially with players like Kevin Durant at 6 feet, 9 inches, Kevin Garnett at 6 feet, 11 inches, and Dirk Nowitzki at 6 feet, 11 inches.

In reality, the more skills the small forward brings to the team, the more difficult it is for the opponent to match up. Successful teams need at least three players who can score in the upper teens to 20s, and the small forward should be one of them.

Power Forward (4)   Power forwards are usually big and powerful, emphasizing strength more than finesse. This position requires a player to be physically strong. Power forwards must rebound aggressively, protect the basket, block shots, and defend competitively. They need to have a midrange jump shot out to 17 feet (5 m) and a low-post game. They are not required to score big numbers but should consistently score 8 to 10 points per game with a good field-goal percentage. NBA crossover players like Tim Duncan and Blake Griffin, both dominant scorers, are the exception, not the rule, for the power forward position. In most situations, the power forward is willing to sacrifice scoring for defense and rebounding. P.J. Brown, who played for both the Charlotte Hornets and the New Orleans Hornets, was an excellent example of what it takes to play this position.

Center (5)   As the saying goes, "Offense separates the great ones." Centers are ideally big, strong, mobile, and able to handle the ball well. They should have a scoring touch around the basket. The better centers are excellent passers and have peripheral awareness, like Pau Gasol, and they are good rebounders and shot blockers who have quick jumping ability, like Dwight Howard. Low-post players need to have soft hands, sound footwork, and good body balance. The best centers are good free-throw shooters, permitting their teams to go through them late in games. Glaring exceptions to this are Shaquille O'Neal and Wilt Chamberlain, who had lifetime free-throw averages of 53 percent and 51 percent respectively.

Essential for good low-post players is a go-to move that is practically unstoppable. This move could be a skyhook, a step-back jumper, an explosive power move, or a face-up jumper with drive options. An old Kentucky saying, "Great centers don't come down the pike very often," has been the case since basketball began.

Versatility, power, and quickness are priorities at all positions. The days of the one-dimensional player are history. The multiskilled, multipositional player has become not the exception, but rather the desired norm.

Of course, the appreciation for multitalented players that can affect a game in many positive ways for a team is nothing new. In the early 1960s, Oscar Robertson, a 6-foot-5-inch (196 cm) point guard and scoring guard, dominated college

DUKE'S ZOUBEK AND PLUMLEE

College basketball coaches today face considerable uncertainty because many of their bigger and more talented players apply for the NBA draft long before their college eligibility is up. Therefore, coaches find themselves in a position where they must be able to find young talent and then, through teaching, growth, and physical development, help them become better players.

Duke University won the 2010 NCAA championship without a dominant, can't-miss future NBA All-Star. They had a core of solid players returning in Kyle Singler, Jon Scheyer, and Nolan Smith, but to compete for the title they needed their big men to come through. Their team effort is an excellent example of putting all the pieces together.

Duke had not been in the NCAA finals since 2004, and one reason appeared to be the lack of a stronger inside presence. Two major improvements occurred. First, Brian Zoubek, at 7 feet, 1 inch (216 cm), had the size and strength but needed experience and confidence, which he improved on as a junior. Second, Miles Plumlee, at 6 feet, 10 inches (208 cm), provided excellent backup support on the inside. Zoubek and Plumlee combined to provide a double-double (10 points, 11 rebounds) while establishing a physical defensive presence. Offensively, the big men came through by providing the inside power necessary to win the championship. They had talent but not necessarily early-round NBA talent. Development and patience paid off as Zoubek and Plumlee proved invaluable in Duke's title run.

basketball at the University of Cincinnati before spending 14 glorious years in the NBA. He was All-NBA 11 times and was chosen for the NBA All-Star Game 12 times. He is the only player in NBA history to average a triple-double for an entire season. Arguably the greatest all-around player ever, he became the prototype of the big guard who could play on the perimeter as well as post up inside.

By the mid-1970s, big men who could play multiple positions were beginning to dominate basketball. Larry Bird and Magic Johnson, both 6 feet, 9 inches (206 cm), burst on the scene, followed in 1985 by 6-foot-6-inch (198 cm) Michael Jordan. Jordan's Chicago Bulls won six NBA championships. As Jordan was reaching the twilight of his playing career, Kobe Bryant, also 6 feet, 6 inches, came to the NBA straight out of high school in 1996 to pick up the mantle of the big guard and dictate how the game would be played.

Today the all-around, multiple-position, go-to players are becoming the rule rather than the exception. Numerous star players with multiple talents are ready to accept the torch when Bryant decides to call it a career. Among them are LeBron James, 6 feet, 8 inches (203 cm); Kevin Durant, 6 feet, 9 inches (206 cm); Blake Griffin, 6 feet, 10 inches (208 cm); and Dwayne Wade, 6 feet, 4 inches (193 cm).

What makes these players special? They're virtually impossible to guard one on one because of their strength and explosiveness as well as their superb ability to handle the ball and see the court. Getting players such as Bryant, James, or Durant open or isolated in space isn't hard. It just takes execution and the ability to read defenses.

PLAYING

Basketball players come in all shapes and sizes. The only requirement a player has for making any team, regardless of the level, is to bring some kind of skill that the squad needs. No rule stipulates that you be large or small, short or tall, heavy or thin, fast or slow, because all types of physical skills and character traits are needed to assemble a team.

Furthermore, it's what you do with what you've got that matters. For example, although small by conventional standards, point guards Earl Boykins at 5 feet, 5 inches (165 cm), Tyrone Bogues at 5 feet, 3 inches (160 cm), Spud Webb at 5 feet, 6 inches (168 cm), current Detroit Piston Will Bynum at 6 feet (183 cm), and Chicago Bulls player John Lucas III at 5 feet, 11 inches (180 cm) have all parlayed ballhandling skills and uncommon quickness into excellent NBA careers.

As the game has grown, one of the biggest changes for both players and coaches has been the emphasis on position-specific skills. Increased competition, the advent of AAU travel teams, and larger school enrollments have made it necessary for coaches to explain to younger players the importance of developing their physical attributes as early as possible. For example, if a young player is tall and can rebound and defend, the coach will emphasize the skills specific to the power forward because the chance is good that he will grow into a power post player.

When trying out for team, players must bring two things with them—a good work ethic and a confident, positive attitude. As young players try out for a team, they may soon realize that they do not have all the skills, but they should never give up. For instance, a player who is big but not fast can find a place if he has good instincts and passing skills and knows how to set solid screens. An athletic rebounder with good speed who doesn't shoot well can complement the team's defense. A small guard who has limited rebounding or low-post defensive ability but who is able to make good playmaking decisions is ideal on a team that uses pressing defenses.

Upon first making a team, players must realize that many roles are viable within the team concept. A team has 5 starters, 5 backups to the starters, and, on a 15-member team, 5 backups to the backups! As starters graduate and move on, all the backups move up and assume responsibility for a new role. For that reason young athletes must practice hard every day and improve on their fundamental skills. Players must stay focused and help the coaching staff by executing their roles and contributing to the team effort.

Players should never give up and must continue playing and developing their skills. A young player who played for me at the University of North Carolina at Charlotte was cut as a sophomore in high school. He asked his coach what he could do to improve his game, and the coach told him to play in the school's intramural program. He did. Next year as a junior, he tried out again and was cut. Again he played in the intramural program and worked on his game. As a senior he made the team. They had a good season, and he was offered a scholarship to college. Following a successful collegiate career, he was drafted by the Boston Celtics. In his fourth season with Boston, they played Houston for the NBA title. Boston won, and Cedric "Cornbread" Maxwell, who was cut twice in high school but never quit, was voted MVP of the NBA playoffs. Remember that confidence, perseverance, and hard work always pay off. That is not to say that every player who works hard and doesn't give up will become the MVP of the NBA playoffs, but without that hard work and determination the chances would be zero.

COACHING

The old-school approach that coaches coach and players play fails on many fronts today. The coach–player relationship is much more reciprocal now. Rather than dictating every decision and action on and off the court, current coaches seek input from players, listen to their suggestions and concerns, and attempt to implement their preferences when it is in the team's best interest to do so.

Yet the roles and responsibilities of coach and player are distinct in many ways. Clearly, as adults with oversight duties and ultimate authority, coaches must have the knowledge and vantage point to serve the best interest of the program and all participants in it. Players, on the other hand, are focused on how they fit into the team and how much playing time they can garner.

If nothing else, the one interest that coaches and players share is the desire to succeed. When the coaching staff's definition of success matches that of the players and becomes everyone's primary aim, the two function together most effectively.

Becoming a Coach

The lure of coaching differs somewhat for everyone. Some are spurred by their experience of playing for an admired role model. Others find the opportunity to teach and develop athletes appealing. Competitive types see it as way to challenge themselves against peers. Still others enjoy the intricacies of planning and drawing up plays to set things into motion. Some are drawn to coaching because it is a natural progression of participation when their talents and physical status do not permit them to continue as players. But perhaps the best and most common of all reasons for getting into basketball coaching is passion for the sport.

As a young kid I participated in sports, and the competition involved provided recognition. I was inspired to work harder and always to try to do better the next time I stepped on the court. I was small in stature in a "big man's game," so the challenge of overcoming that size disadvantage served as a great motivator through grade school, high school, and on through college.

Although I played baseball and basketball as a collegian, the latter sport became my favorite and ultimately my vocational vehicle. I feasted on the game's competitiveness and intensity and was consumed by the quest for knowledge in teaching techniques and devising strategies.

Be assured that there are many ways to get into the coaching profession. A person can plan for it in college by taking required courses or by coaching in intramural programs at school. Countless parents volunteer at the local high school and get involved at the youth level, others get caught up in the AAU team in their area, and numerous others get drawn in to help out local professional teams. At one time a prerequisite to coaching in college was a college degree, but that is not necessarily true anymore.

Networking and personal contacts are a vital component to obtaining a job in every field. From elementary school to the NBA, contacts become important as you go through life, and many people who have children or friends in coaching will get involved by helping out and suddenly decide to pursue a coaching career. Cultivating friends as you go through high school and college can pay great dividends after you graduate and begin looking for a coaching opportunity. People who get involved by volunteering find themselves drawn to coaching and many times get started at the most basic level. Coaches come from all walks of life, and that background influences how they approach the game.

Coaches and Systems

In my time, one of the great truisms for young coaches seeking to learn about the great game of basketball was this: "Always go to clinics, even if you only pick up one new idea. It's worth it." Seldom was one idea all that was learned. We coaches listened intently to the great masters of the game and drank up their knowledge.

Four styles of play, and the great coaches who taught them, had a great influence on my viewpoint on the manner in which the game should be played.

My journey of learning started with my college coach, C.M. Newton, a University of Kentucky product and an Adolph Rupp disciple. Rupp coached at the University of Kentucky from 1932 to 1972 and won four NCAA championships. He was renowned for his outstanding teams. Coach Rupp dominated the Southeastern Conference with a fast-break offensive philosophy highlighted by quick, fast guard play and a strong inside game. He used drills that complemented that style of play. For years that was the focus of my offense.

Following Coach Rupp was a bright new coach on the West Coast by the name of John Wooden. He coached the UCLA Bruins from 1948 to 1975, winning 10 NCAA championships. For me, Coach Wooden embodied the complete coach. Just by watching his team play we learned about dignity, decorum, and discipline. A strict fundamentalist, Coach Wooden was also extremely creative, especially with his unique ability to change his system of play from year to year based on his players' skills and talent. This approach taught me the importance of maximizing skills and minimizing limitations. Regardless of the talent pool, the coach needs to find a system of play that works. Coach Wooden had terrific philosophical sayings that were put on our chalkboards, such as "Be quick, but don't hurry," "Never mistake activity for achievement," "It's not so important who starts the game, but who finishes it," and "It's the little details that are vital. Little things make big things happen."

The third coach whose style I emulated was Coach Dean Smith, who became head coach at the University of North Carolina in the early 1960s, about the same time I got into coaching. Smith was a leader in the Atlantic Coast Conference and won two NCAA championships. Game management was one of his greatest assets, and watching his teams play was a real treat. Coach Smith's innovations—changing defenses frequently, using a unique substitution system, using time-outs, and employing the famous four-corners offense, were instrumental in forming my ideas about controlling tempo and end-game coaching. Specifically regarding Coach Smith's foul policy and substitution pattern, he always protected his players for the final five minutes of the second half. His early foul substitution rule was an essential part of his strategy and was a personal influence on the many aspects of my game management.

The fourth coach who had a great influence on my thinking was Tay Baker at the University of Cincinnati (UC). Coach Baker was an assistant under Ed Jucker when Jucker won back-to-back NCAA titles in 1961 and 1962. Tay was a dedicated, defensive-minded coach, and for the three years that I assisted Coach Baker at UC, we were one of the best defensive teams in the country.

These four coaches, Adolph Rupp, John Wooden, Dean Smith, and Tay Baker, were the men whose basketball philosophies influenced my coaching life. I read their books, used their quotes, watched their teams play, and focused on them as they managed their games from the bench. They were disciplined, organized, and controlled. They did not publicly humiliate their players, executed well out of time-outs, and never beat themselves. Did they have talent? Of course they did. Did they know how to use that talent? Of course they did. Did they win? Yes—they did.

During the course of my coaching career, I've come to appreciate the tactical approaches of several other coaches beyond Rupp, Smith, Wooden, and Baker. Two such coaches are Phil Jackson and Tex Winter.

Jackson was a role player for the New York Knicks during that franchise's glory days in the early 1970s. From the bench he observed the skillful strategic maneuvering of his coach, Red Holzman, and then went on to hone his coaching skills in the Continental Basketball Association, where he won the 1984 championship with the Albany Patroons. When Jackson took over as head coach of the Chicago Bulls in 1989, one of his first moves was to retain Chicago's assistant coach, Tex Winter.

GREAT PLAYERS, NOT SO HOT AS COACHES

I believe that winning is a by-product of hard work, a positive support system, and the good fortune of having talented basketball players. And those three things are required to win at each level. Talent alone does not ensure success.

Former players with outstanding talent often have difficulty grasping this fact as coaches. As a result, their coaching experience is often disappointing and short lived. Here is a short list of truly great players—Hall of Fame players—whose coaching results never matched their great accomplishments as players.

Coach	Record	Winning Percentage
Dave Debusschere	79-190	29 percent
Wes Unseld	202-345	37 percent
Elgin Baylor	86-135	39 percent
Willis Reed	82-124	40 percent
Bob Cousy	141-209	40 percent

In 2001 I was hired as the coaching supervisor of the newly formed NBA Development League. My job was to help former NBA players make the transition from playing to coaching at the professional level. There were eight teams in the NBDL and 2 coaches per team. These 16 aspiring coaches were all looking to advance into the NBA. Each year I conducted clinics for them about all facets of the game of basketball. I covered topics from drafting players, organizing practice sessions, and teaching offensive play sets and defensive shell coverage to preparing for interviews, making professional connections, and negotiating contracts.

Winter had been a long-time, highly successful college coach whose offensive attack originated from his playing days under Sam Barry at the University of Southern California in 1946–47. Interest in his approach escalated to the point that in 1962, Winter published a book titled *The Triple-Post Offense*. He tinkered with and improved this offense in college and professional head coaching jobs through the years and eventually even gave it a new name: the triangle offense (see chapter 6).

The floor balance and spacing of the offense, its ball and player movement, backdoor cuts, pick-and-rolls, post-ups, flash post and step-ins, isolations, and weak-side pin-downs, all flowing out of one basic set, appealed to Jackson, perhaps harkening back to the tremendous movement and teamwork demonstrated by the Knicks teams that he played on. And in Winter, Jackson had both the in-depth knowledge of the finer points of the offense and an experienced master at teaching it. Together, Jackson and Winter created—with considerable help from

GREAT COACHES, NOT SO HOT AS PLAYERS

All pro coaches—and really coaches at every level—need a talented roster to be successful and must have talent continuing to flow into the program to win consistently. A number of coaches have built their teams and systems around star players and have been extremely successful.

Winning percentage reflects a coach's success, and many non-NBA players have been extremely successful as NBA coaches. Greg Popovich's system centered on David Robinson and Tim Duncan, and his Spurs have won four NBA titles (736-362 at San Antonio). Chuck Daly, with Isiah Thomas, Joe Dumars, and Bill Laimbeer, won two NBA titles (638-437 at Detroit). These and other coaches who never played a minute in the NBA developed unique styles and systems around their stars to produce winning programs.

Coach	Record	Winning Percentage
Greg Popovich	736-362	67 percent
Mike Brown	272-138	66 percent
Stan Van Gundy	431-282	60 percent
Chuck Daly	638-437	59 percent
Jeff Van Gundy	430-318	57 percent
Eric Spoelstra	194-118	60 percent

This list shows that top coaches can come from a variety of backgrounds. But all winning coaches share a knack for dealing with administration, staff, players, and media. The five coaches just listed were able to confront the challenge and succeed at the pro level.

the great Michael Jordan—an attack that was a nightmare for opposing defenses and dominated the NBA, winning six NBA titles over the next nine years.

Yes, Jackson was fortunate to have great players throughout his NBA coaching career. Jordan, Scottie Pippen, Shaquille O'Neal, and Kobe Bryant would make most offenses potent. But the triangle offense helped those players and their teammates function as a unit, improved their efficiency and consistency, and made it impossible for opponents to focus their efforts on stopping only one or two players.

I had the pleasure of observing and scouting the triangle offense during the Bulls' magical championship years and found the experience compelling. Their system reminded me of an experience I had when I was an assistant coach at the University of Cincinnati during the mid-1960s. Tay Baker, UC head coach, called the assistants together and asked us to list all the plays that we'd like to put into our half-court offense. An elaborate list of two- and three-man plays was put on the chalkboard. When everyone had their say, Coach Baker had us work together as a staff to put the plays in a continuity pattern. This wonderful learning moment was one that I duplicated throughout my coaching career. Developing and using the ideas of assistant coaches can be extremely productive.

Assistant Coaches and Support Staff

As Phil Jackson's choice of Tex Winter illustrated, one of the most important decisions that a head coach makes is choosing wisely when picking assistant coaches. Warren Buffet says that three attributes are important when hiring people: The first is integrity, the second is intellect, and the third is work ethic. And, he adds, if the candidate doesn't have the first one, forget the second two.

Finding dependable assistants that bring diversity, knowledge, integrity, and loyalty to the staff should be the goal of every head coach. I think it's important to hire assistants who can bring a different perspective than your own to the table. Selecting assistants who come from different backgrounds provides new ways of looking at issues, and it expands the entire coaching staff's understanding with new information and more possibilities.

Regardless of the team—high school, college, or professional—the head coach determines duties and responsibilities for the staff. He needs to prioritize the agenda and make sure that the assistants' major assets are reflected in their assignments. This approach not only assigns responsibility but also defines the coverage area and boundary for each assistant's input. Here are just a few of the important areas that must be assigned and covered in high school and college:

Academics   First, for those coaching in educational institutions, is the ever-important academic supervisor. One assistant is assigned to oversee all academic issues: classes, labs, attendance, nightly study hall, and making sure that the correct courses are taken in the right sequence and in a timely manner to meet the academic standards toward graduation. This position is crucial.

Recruiting   Second, on the college level, comes the chief recruiter. This assistant maintains all the important information relative to recruiting contacts, visits, and game schedule. And this assistant maintains a depth chart on all five positions showing graduating classes year by year.

Scheduling   Having someone on the staff responsible for scheduling is important. Regardless of whether it's high school, college, or the NBA, scheduling games is a year-round process. Although most teams participate in league play and most of their games are assigned, dates still need to be filled. In some cities (Charlotte, for instance), public schools do not compete with private schools; therefore, private schools must scramble to find opponents. The same demand is placed on college teams. Conferences dictate about three-fourths of the schedule, leaving the schools as many as 12 games to locate. The head coaches in high school and college will discuss their priorities about home and away games and then leave it up to the assistant to obtain dates and provide options for the head coach. In some situations, the athletic director assists in making contacts and assigning dates.

Although the league assigns all games in the NBA, many of the arenas have issues because of multiple bookings for such activities as concerts, horse shows, boxing events, and college games. Scheduling becomes a big issue when a team has multiple back-to-back games; someone must be aware of all events to ensure that no double booking occurs.

Equipment   In most situations, an equipment manager is a full-time position on the athletic staff and is responsible for ordering, stocking, and laundering all equipment. Equipment includes home and away uniforms, practice jerseys, and practice equipment such as basketballs, jump ropes, and vests of different colors.

Video   A video technician is responsible for filming all games and having clips or full games available for practice. Having game copies available is also important, because most coaches will want to take the game film home following each game. The film coordinator has the responsibility of setting up and taking down all the video equipment and of maintaining complete files on all the games.

Statistics for Practice and Games   Keeping accurate statistics is the best tool that coaches have when discussing a player's role and explaining his positive and negative attributes. Some coaches like only game stats, whereas others are more specific and require a whole statistical staff for keeping practice stats on a daily basis. Assigning an assistant coach to oversee that daily stats are kept is well worth the time. To cover this procedure, volunteer students are a useful resource. Seeing the correlation between game and practice results is always interesting. Most people like looking at the box score, but it doesn't always tell the full story; a performance rating chart (see chapter 3) is invaluable here.

Travel   Overseeing travel logistics involves a myriad of details, beginning with scheduling the trip. Depending on whether the team travels by bus or plane, these logistics vary, but the attention to detail must not. The assistant must make sure that all information is conveyed to the players, stressing that they must be on time, dressed properly, and have their equipment (even if the equipment manager is taking care of their game equipment, they still must be sure to bring any personal equipment). Again, depending on the level, food arrangements must be planned and made ahead of departure. If overnight arrangements are necessary, room assignments must also be taken care of before departure.

Practice Responsibilities   Many chores must be attended to if practices are to run smoothly. Taping ankles is a major one. Although a trainer typically does this, some high schools and small-college programs do not have trainers and must rely on coaches to handle this job. Other jobs that must be handled to make practices run smoothly are making sure that the floor is clean, rolling out ball racks, making sure that the proper amount of air is in the balls before practice starts, getting out different colored vests to divide players into teams, being sure that jump ropes and other such equipment are available for players, and ensuring that the game clock is on and running. Again, the equipment manager or a student helper may do this, depending on the level or situation.

Assistant coaches are assigned offensive and defensive drills and teams to work with throughout the practice. During scrimmage work they will normally oversee one team and officiate at the same time. Many details must be handled, and they need to be designated before practice starts. Preparation is the key.

Game-Day Duties   On game day, one assistant is designated as the advance scout, and that person puts the opponent's lineup on the greaseboard or chalkboard with specific defensive assignments. The opponent's plays are diagramed and explained, and their go-to play at crucial times is emphasized. Baseline and sideline out-of-bounds plays are drawn up and explained. Coaches always want to show the opponent's press attack and the way in which they intend to combat it. Of major importance is listing the opponent's poorest free-throw shooters so that the team will know whom to foul if it is necessary. There will be a discussion about whether pressing defenses will be used and when they intend to press, after made field goals or made free throws.

Following the scouting report, the team goes on the floor to warm up with the assistant coaches. The assistant coaches may participate in drills by passing, or they may just observe to make sure that the players are not horsing around. Following layups and position-specific shots, the team goes back to the dressing room where the head coach makes a few comments. The team then returns to the floor.

During the game, assistant coaches will be assigned either an offensive or defensive chart, which they will refer to at halftime to see where the opponent is hurting them. All coaches are responsible for bench behavior throughout the game, and when the game ends, all coaches see to it that their team leaves the floor in an orderly manner. An assistant will secure a box score and get it to the head coach, who will either make some comments or dismiss the team.

Team Chemistry and Leadership

Winning teams, almost without exception, are made up of players and coaches who are committed to shared goals and have a single agenda: doing what ensures the team's success.

Then why don't all coaches—high school, college, NBA—demand it? Because building team chemistry is like trying to grab a fistful of Jell-O. It's harder than it looks. Chemistry is not something tangible that can be created by a coach's

PLAYER EVALUATION THE NBA WAY

Thousands of dollars, miles of exhaustive travel, and untold hours are spent tracking and evaluating college basketball prospects. The same holds true for the NBA, except that their scouts are also looking in the European leagues and at current NBA players for trade opportunities. Hundreds of experts at the college and professional levels are constantly evaluating talent and monitoring players' character.

The annual NBA Predraft Combine provides a variety of player evaluations. Some involve physical tests, others are mental, and all the prospects at the combine undergo in-depth interviews. NBA teams can also request a battery of psychological tests or have the prospect take such a test when he visits their franchise. College recruiters, however, must depend primarily on recommendations from high school and AAU coaches, teachers, guidance counselors, and principals. Psychological tests may be requested but are not required.

The last thing that a coach wants is to bring in a player who has character issues that could destroy the chemistry of the team. To borrow a quote from Abraham Lincoln, the 16th president of the United States:

> Reputation is the shadow. Character is the tree. Our character is not just what we try to display for others to see, it is who we are even when no one is watching. Good character is doing the right thing because it is right to do what is right.

Coaches at all levels occasionally make a mistake in measuring a player's talent, but they can overcome it with good coaching. But making a mistake in judging a player's character can be fatal to a team's chances for success.

Character transcends race, religion, education, position, age, gender, and personality. People sometimes think of character as something a person either has or doesn't have. They say, "He has character," meaning that he has good character. We recognize the truth that everyone has character and that coaches must distinguish between good and bad character. Character mistakes bring all kinds of scrutiny to an athletic program, resulting in administrative investigations and team distractions. All these produce the same negative result: destruction of team chemistry. The big issues develop when the most talented player is also the team's most disruptive player, one who requires high maintenance and demands special treatment. Coaches want their best players to be their most dependable leaders in the classroom, on the practice floor, and away from campus. Coaches who sacrifice the many for the few make a colossal mistake. An unspoken but very real question among NBA teams is this: How many disruptive players can one team have on its 12-player roster?

speech or turned on like a light switch. Chemistry is an elusive bond, a feeling of unity that is vital for good teams but difficult to capture.

Good chemistry is more than huddling, stacking hands, and shouting in unison, "Defense!" Building team chemistry involves composition, behavior, structure, and relationships in which teammates all work together toward a specific goal. A few obvious players who exemplify these special chemistry qualities include Steve Nash, David Robinson, Dirk Nowitzki, Tim Duncan, and playmakers Derek Fisher and Jason Kidd.

Although there are no guarantees that a coach can build chemistry with a given team, I found that three basic principles must be established and put in place if it's to be accomplished. The coach must create an environment where good chemistry can flourish. Here we will take a look at five chemistry-building steps that every coach should consider.

1. Be fair and consistent. The most important time a coach will ever spend is when he is defining the concept of fairness. Nothing is more important to an individual player than feeling that he is competing on a level playing field. If the coach's rules and guidelines on fairness are subjective, he is asking for problems and probably a long, unproductive season. The coach must create or design a fairness system that eliminates any hint of bias or deception—one that is completely free of playing favorites. It's not easy, but it is necessary. The system I designed and created to maintain fairness on my teams is called the performance rating system, which is explained in chapter 3.

Every day the coach puts his integrity on the line with the team. Players understand how and when they are evaluated, and if a discrepancy appears, they recognize it immediately. For example, in my system, a player who grades out better on the depth chart should play ahead of those below him. If this does not happen and the player with the lower ranking plays ahead, the higher-ranked player will never forget it and will know that he is playing against a stacked deck. After policies have been established, regardless of the issue, if the coach rules unjustly or inconsistently, the players will know it and the coach will lose the trust factor. Whether the offense is being late for practice, not attending a class, or stealing from a teammate, the coach must enforce the rules voted on by the team. The goal for every coach should be to build a program that promotes mutual respect. Being consistent is a vital part of that concept.

2. Take on your best player. For a disciplined system to work, the coach must have the fortitude to penalize the best player, or the biggest bully on the team, when and if rules are broken. Having been in the NBA for over 20 years, I've had many experiences—some good, some not so good. On one of the NBA teams I coached with, we were running a shooting drill. The squad was divided into two equal teams, and we were shooting three-point shots. It was a competitive drill at the end of practice to see which team could make 15 shots the quickest. Among the rules was that for the shot to count, the player had to shoot from behind the three-point line. As the drill got under way, one player began cheating by not getting behind the three-point line. I cautioned him, saying, "They only count if you are behind the line." The next time around, he again shot the ball in front of the line, so I called him on it. He became irate, and I asked him to leave practice, which he eventually did (getting run out of practice meant that he would be fined). The next day in practice our trainer (who was in charge of collecting fine money) asked me if I had run that particular player out of practice. I said yes, and the trainer said that I should know that the head coach called him and rescinded the fine. No further mention of the situation occurred, but a team is a small unit and information gets around. The team found out, and respect for the head coach was compromised.

3. Build a relationship of trust through policies and input. A coach must build relationships of trust with his players, regardless if he coaches at the high school, college, or professional level. Gaining trust is not a given. It's not automatic, nor can it be built overnight. Trust begins to germinate when the players really believe that the coach wants and encourages their input and participation in making the rules and policies that govern the team. When players serve on team committees that help determine team policies, define acceptable player behavior, and set academic standards, conditioning goals, and expectations, they believe that they have ownership in the system. Why would they want to break a rule that they helped write? Policy participation opens the door for players to take a more active role in what transpires on the game floor. Having a healthy trust system—the coaches trust the players and vice versa—covers what goes on in the locker room, at practice, at individual and team meetings, and with bench decorum. All concerned have absolute understanding that the coach wants and encourages input and will never embarrass the players in public.

One sure way to destroy trust is for the coach to jump all over players during the game. Practices and halftimes are private and out of view of the public. They are the appropriate times for a coach to address the players. A good contract that a coach can have with the players is this: "The practices are ours; the games are yours." Even if a player makes a mistake coming out of a time-out and covers the wrong opponent, resulting in the winning basket for the other team, the player knows that the coach will not throw him under the bus to the media after the game. Neither will criticism occur following the game, not when emotions are running high. Immediately after the game, a wise coach might limit his remarks to "That was a good win" or "I think we're better than that." The mistake can be corrected during video study the next day. Video is known as the truth machine. Players often say, "The eye doesn't lie." They're too smart to argue with what they're looking at on video. I've learned that it takes seasons to build up trust, but it only takes suspicion without proof to destroy it. That's how fragile trust is. My advice to coaches is to maintain composure, withhold critical comments, and never personally attack a player. Let the machine—or the eye—do its work.

4. Explain the difference between a reason and an excuse.   The difference between a reason and an excuse is enormous. This distinction has great ramifications on how we exercise judgment on the activity. Team rules and penalties should be determined and voted on by the players and coaches. Some things are sacred in team building: being on time for all activities, meeting classroom assignments, adhering to dress codes and trip requirements, and respecting others and their opinions. When a violation occurs, the parties involved refer to the players' agreement and resolve the disagreement. An explanation during the rules discussion about reasons and excuses helps clarify the issue. For example, when a player oversleeps and is late for practice, that is an excuse. When a player driving to practice is hit from behind by another car and is detained by the police, that is a reason. Players understand and respect this form of leadership.

5. Eliminate subjectivity in evaluations.   Rules apply equally across the board to players, but their personalities are different. The coach must recognize and respect those differences. If you really want to destroy team morale, let your star player get away with stuff. Show him favorable treatment. That approach is a killer. For example, if the coach overlooks a road trip curfew that is reported, the entire team will know about it within hours. If the coach shows favoritism in handling such a violation, he will more than likely lose the support of the team. Such mistakes have been known to cost a coach a job. There must be no star treatment. None. How can a team have chemistry if the 10th player on the roster believes that one set of rules governs his behavior while a completely different set—a more lenient set—governs the star player? The coach must demonstrate that all team rules apply evenly for every player.

Coaches are famous for doing all that they can to motivate their players and themselves. Some use movies before big games, others have former players come in to speak to the team, but almost all use quotes and sayings from successful people. Coaches hope that these comments will cause the players to think higher and deeper about their goals and how they should move forward.

Here are five positive statements that apply not only to basketball but also to the broader issues in life, such as academics, graduation, and individual personal growth. Whether you are a coach or player, consider these five leadership thoughts to drive your determination:

1. Confidence is empowerment; believe in yourself and take control.
2. The disappointment in losing is equal to the amount of energy expended in trying to win.
3. It is not how many times you get knocked down but how many times you get back up.
4. Put reason over emotion. Basketball is a game of chess, and checkmate is the goal.
5. Practice to improve. If you always do what you've always done, you'll always get what you've always got.

CHAPTER 3

Performance Rating System

Objective evaluation of individual and team performance can be a challenge for both players and coaches. Each of us is predisposed to favor certain styles and facets of play. And athletes have the additional bias of their own ego involvement, which makes it difficult for them to fairly assess how their game measures up. Therefore, most coaches develop or use available performance assessment tools to gauge more accurately how their individual athletes and team are playing.

In my case, this tool is called the performance rating system (or PRS). The PRS provides the most comprehensive and factual analysis in basketball. It includes individual statistics in five performance categories:

1. Shooting
2. Rebounding
3. Ballhandling
4. Defense
5. Violations

REASONS BEHIND THE PERFORMANCE RATING SYSTEM

Simply put, the PRS is an objective evaluation system that removes guesswork when a coach evaluates and selects players. I created it after realizing that basketball players compete for playing time every practice, so accurate and fair statistics should be kept during practices as well as in games to determine a player's production.

The PRS details exactly what a player has accomplished or failed to accomplish during a game or practice. In essence, a number value is assigned for each statistic and then converted and posted on a position-specific depth chart after each game or practice. Following are three key reasons behind my creation of the PRS.

1. It stresses the importance of individual production. On the whole, this procedure helps players understand the importance and significance of their individual production. For instance, a player who depends solely on scoring will soon find that as a one-dimensional player (shooting), he will have a hard time grading well in this system. Therefore, all players must work on their total game every day to improve.

2. It promotes learning. Second, the process of having all players contribute their input and vote on their value preference for each statistic is a learning procedure in itself. To present the PRS to a team, a coach must examine each statistic and come up with unbiased values. For instance, which is more important: a field goal or a pass that leads to the field goal? Which is harder to get: an offensive rebound or a defensive rebound? What is the value of a steal, a blocked shot, or taking a charge? How do you take away points for violations such as over and back, a technical foul, or basket interference?

3. It emphasizes objectivity. Third, and most important, having a fair evaluation system goes a long way in helping build and maintain team chemistry. Nothing destroys a team quicker than team members' sensing that favoritism plays a key part in awarding playing time. Without an objective evaluation system, a coach doesn't stand a chance of measuring a player's realistic value to the team.

Five people who watch the same game will likely give five different responses when you ask them detailed questions about the performance of any player on the court. Most people can identify the high scorers during the game, but when you ask, "What did you think of his defense, his ability to play the passing lanes, his rebounding technique, his use of screens, and his rotation out of double teams?" you'd get varied opinions. Everyone has a unique personal perspective that includes subjective preferences and selective attention. So, your analysis might lead you to favor player A, whereas I might be more impressed by player B.

Clearly, a legitimate method of analyzing basketball players' performance benefits everyone. Whether used to determine who makes the cut, who starts, or who is contributing the most to winning games, the assessment system used should be nonjudgmental, accurate, reliable, and data based.

The PRS is an objective evaluation system that removes guesswork when a coach evaluates and selects players to overcome partiality. This objective evaluation system aids the coach not only in measuring the players' contributions to the team but also in presenting the information to the players.

As players and coaches work through converting box score statistics into a value conversion table, players begin to realize how statistics can take on a different meaning. Players, coaches, parents, friends, and sports writers all know scoring statistics, but understanding the PRS allows players to increase their knowledge of other important statistical measures. There is no single best solution for assigning values, and players and coaches will determine values from entirely different perspectives.

PRACTICAL USES OF THE PERFORMANCE RATING SYSTEM

The benefits of the PRS for coaches and players are numerous. Overall, coaches and players appreciate it for the fact that it creates an environment for individualized success that is fair, competitive, and motivating. For me, the process served as an invaluable evaluation tool on countless occasions. Following are just a couple of examples.

Competitive Success   When coaching in the 1984 World University Games in Kobe, Japan, my staff and I had eight days of practice to get 12 players to play as a team. USA select teams are put together by a USA Basketball committee. Two players were chosen at each position, and two additional skilled specialists were chosen to fill a role as a shooter, defender, big man, or point guard. All players in this instance were starters on major college teams, representing Kansas, Kentucky, Auburn, St. Joseph's, Louisville, Nebraska, Missouri, Virginia Tech, Alabama at Birmingham, South Florida, and Miami of Ohio. All reported to practice expecting to start.

We explained the objective evaluation system to the players at the first practice. The players liked the concept and quickly grasped the weighted values assessed for each statistical category. They appreciated the fact that all five starting positions were open and that no one had been given a starting role. Twelve highly competitive athletes left the locker room satisfied that the evaluation process was fair, equal, and consistent. Each believed that he could win a starting position based on his skill and production. Competitors like to start on an even playing field. All that the good ones ask for is a fair chance with no favored treatment; if that is granted, no one feels victimized by the selection process.

Eliminating subjectivity from the evaluation showed these players the importance that the coach placed on integrity. That was a top priority. The real beauty of using this system, for both the coach and the players, is the clear message that there will be no free passes, handouts, individual agreements, or entitlements. The only way that players get playing time is to earn it by their production. A daily performance rating demonstrates the players' consistency and reflects their position ranking on the team. Players cannot slough off in practice and maintain their position in the lineup.

Motivating Success   The PRS proves to be an effective motivational tool for players and coaches. I saw the real effect of the system in the amazing improvements we made at the University of South Florida. Ranked 248th out of 252 NCAA Division I teams, South Florida was coming off its fourth straight losing season with a 6-21 record when the coaching change occurred in 1980. One of our first moves was to initiate the PRS.

The players loved it, and some would not leave practice until the PR was posted. A team that had previously been riddled with chaos and confusion experienced not one major incident the entire year. That first season at South Florida was one of the most gratifying experiences in a long list of wonderful coaching memories.

We ended the season 18-11, hosted a first-round NIT game against UConn before 10,259 fans, and won the vote as the nation's most improved team. I credit the PRS for the turnaround.

COMPONENTS OF THE PERFORMANCE RATING SYSTEM

The first step to producing accurate statistics is to create a daily performance rating (PR). A daily PR is like a daily test score. Each basketball statistic is assigned a weighted value depending on the importance that the coach and players place on specific categories. For example, a made free throw counts +1 and a missed free throw –2. An offensive rebound rates +2, but a defensive rebound is only +1. By assigning a value to each category—shooting, rebounding, assists, turnovers, violations, and blocked shots—you can produce a numeric score for each practice and game. The coach should explain the conversion formula to players so that they understand it, accept it as an objective measuring stick of performance, and realize that players with the highest PR scores at each position earn playing time.

This objective system records each player's daily contributions by charting his every move during practices and converting individual production results to a corresponding numbering system. The idea is to have clear guidelines, eliminate misunderstandings, and avoid confusion by ensuring that each player has a fair opportunity.

The performance rating system hinges on four factors, some of which have been hinted at earlier:

1. Objectivity as the aim
2. Easy implementation
3. Weighted performance criteria
4. Number-based evaluation

Objectivity as the Aim

Changing from an opinion-based evaluation process to an objective process may not be easy, but it's worth the effort to ensure good decisions and reduce player hostilities. Nothing is more important to team morale than fair treatment by the coach. Players recognize when coaches play favorites and don't treat all team members fairly. The result of such behavior is team disintegration. Whether you call it team morale, harmony, or team chemistry, players get along for valid reasons, and effective leadership is one of them. Players grumble, complain, and create dissension when they think that their trust has been violated. Before long they lose confidence in their coach.

The PRS provides these benefits:

- Provides a useful analytical tool
- Determines a player's weaknesses

- Reflects a player's strengths
- Operates on objective data
- Indicates daily progress
- Eliminates players' concern about fairness
- Provides invaluable data for coach–player discussions
- Offers motivational aid for self-improvement
- Exposes one-dimensional players
- Provides a great system for building team harmony and selecting captains

Easy Implementation

Implementation of PRS begins with the recruitment of at least 12 volunteer staff from the student body, interns, and student managers. In an orientation meeting, coaches explain PRS, identify chart responsibilities, and underscore the need for a specific time commitment. The PRS is implemented for practices, home games, and film analysis of road games. The team supplies the minimal required equipment, including charts, pencils, and a written explanation of the fundamentals to be recorded. Training consists of identifying and defining the fundamental that each volunteer keeps—offensive rebounds or defensive rebounds, assists or turnovers, field goals made or missed, and so forth—and showing how to record the results.

The staff of volunteers works directly with the PRS director to implement the system and record all the statistics. Here are the roles of key staff and their steps for implementation at a glance.

PRS Director Assign a PRS director responsible for coordinating the PRS. The director oversees the volunteers and makes daily assignments, keeps accurate daily statistics, and posts the PR daily in a designated place.

Volunteers The volunteer staff keeps statistics on all five-on-five work that occurs during the practice. The PRS director makes sure that all charts are properly administered, recorded, and collected. At the top of the charts, volunteers must fill in the type of work being done that day. After they finish their work, the volunteers sign their worksheets and pass the forms on to the PRS director, who tabulates and posts the practice results. The same process applies for games and video analysis.

The second step is to train the staff to divide statistics into the following categories:

- All half-court work
- Controlled full-court work
- Scrimmages
- Practice games and intrasquad games
- Regular-season games

In general, volunteers familiar with basketball are preferred; former high school players make excellent volunteers because they know the game and understand the terminology.

Weighted Performance Criteria

A weighted system for basketball statistics directly reflects the importance that the coach places on specific categories within the structure of the game; a weighted evaluation system means that a specific value is assigned to a particular category.

For years coaches and players depended on the NCAA box score to assist them in analyzing the game. A box score can tell you who shoots the most and who the leading scorers are, who gets the most rebounds, and who turns the ball over the most times. But it does not put a value on any of the categories. The PRS is designed to provide a plus or minus value for each category, and therefore each player, in the game. The PRS provides game and practice information that helps players and coaches be aware of who is doing a fundamental job on defense, who is boxing out, who is taking charges, who is setting solid free-up screens, and who is going to the floor for loose balls. The PRS recognizes the little things that make the big things possible.

Here are the steps to creating both offensive and defensive weighted performance criteria:

1. Assign a numerical value to each component of the game.

2. Create necessary forms and separate them by categories—shooting, rebounds, violations, turnovers, assists, and so on. Volunteers record daily statistics on these eight categories.

3. Before each practice, the PRS director passes out folders with forms labeled as follows. Each form has all players listed in alphabetical order.

   a. Shots made and missed (two-point field goals, three-point field goals, free throws)

   b. Rebounds (offensive, defensive)

   c. Assists

   d. Turnovers

   e. Steals

   f. Personal fouls

   g. Blocked shots

   h. Violations

4. Determine a plus (+) and minus (−) value for each category. The point value will vary depending on coach and player perceptions of what is important.

So, how do coaches and players decide what's important? The statistical weighted system for the PRS is designed to be fair for all. Instead of making the leading scorer the most important player on the team, a weighted system rewards players who rebound, block shots, make assists, get steals, and do the blue-collar work necessary for winning. Following each game, my players might have looked at the box score, but they knew that their PR number more accurately reflected what they did that night.

Number-Based Evaluation

The players believe in the PRS process because they approve of the entire weighted system, fundamental by fundamental. See tables 3.1 and 3.2. In looking at the weighted numbers, you'll notice that only a few have modifications. A player gets a +2 for an offensive rebound and a +1 for a defensive rebound because an offensive rebound is much more difficult to get. What player would argue with that? None. A made free throw is a +1 and a missed free throw is a –2. Why? Because a free throw is a free shot, taken totally unguarded. As Larry Bird says, hitting free throws requires only two elements—concentration and practice. Free throws decide nearly all close games. For example, the University of Kentucky lost close games in both the 2010 and 2011 NCAA tournaments because of missed free throws (13 and 8 respectively), while in the 2012 NCAA tournament, they hit 15 of 21 free throws for a respectable 71 percent to defeat Kansas for the national title. Have I ever had a player disagree with the +1 and –2 concept? Never.

Also refer to the basic game violations in tables 3.1 and 3.2. Such violations are the thoughtless acts that get teams beat. No player has ever given a good reason why he should be in the lane for three seconds, or get a technical foul, or goal tend, or commit any other violation. This system of evaluation is applied equally

Table 3.1 Sample Offensive Value Sheet

(+) Value		(–) Value	
SHOOTING			
Made two-point field goal	+2	Missed two-point field goal	(–2)
Made three-point field goal	+3	Missed three-point field goal	(–3)
Made free throw	+1	Missed free throw	(–2)
Screen that frees shooter	+1	Shot that is blocked	(–1)
REBOUNDING			
Offensive rebound	+2		
Tip-out recovery	+2		
BALLHANDLING			
Assist or pass that leads to the score	+3	Bad pass or turnover	(–2)
Steal or interception	+2	Traveling	(–2)
Taking a charge	+3	Committing charging foul	(–3)
BASIC GAME VIOLATIONS			
		Three seconds in the lane	(–5)
		Technical foul	(–5)
		Goal tending	(–3)
		Basket interference	(–3)
		Over and back	(–3)
		Free-throw violation	(–3)
		Jump ball	(–3)
		Out of bounds	(–3)

Table 3.2 Sample Defensive Value Sheet

(+) Value		(–) Value	
SHOOTING			
Blocked shot	+2	Personal foul two-point field goal	(–2)
Protect basket, no layup	+2	Personal foul three-point field goal	(–3)
Front low post	+2	Unnecessary personal foul	(–1)
		Foul jump shooter	(–3)
REBOUNDING			
Tip-out recovery	+2	Permitting offensive rebound	(–2)
Defensive rebound	+1	Failing to box out	(–2)
		Permitting offensive put-back	(–3)
BALLHANDLING			
Taking a charge	+3	Personal foul	(–1)
Steal	+3	Failing to see ball transition	(–2)
Deflection	+2	Permitting middle dribble	(–2)
Diving on floor for ball	+2	Not getting back on defense	(–2)
		No help when one player away	(–2)
		Slow on low-post double team	(–2)
		Failing to close out	(–2)
		Poor execution after time-out	(–3)
		Substitution mistake	(–3)
BASIC GAME VIOLATIONS			
		Three seconds in the lane	(–5)
		Technical foul	(–5)
		Goal tending	(–3)
		Basket interference	(–3)
		Over and back	(–3)
		Free-throw violation	(–3)
		Jump ball	(–3)
		Out of bounds	(–3)

across the board. That is what players want. The coach can modify the numbers based on his philosophy. My philosophy was to eliminate the mental mistakes that get teams beat. I believed that this particular PRS formula did the job.

After players are rated according to the PRS, they are grouped in a depth chart according to position, 1 through 5. The depth chart, shown in table 3.3, reflects the player's daily PR score.

Table 3.3 Sample Depth Chart

Point guard	Shooting guard	Small forward	Power forward	Center
1.	1.	1.	1.	1.
2.	2.	2.	2.	2.
3.	3.	3.	3.	3.

From L. Rose, 2013, *Winning basketball fundamentals* (Champaign, IL: Human Kinetics).

APPLICATION OF
THE PERFORMANCE RATING SYSTEM

After the coach has established the number formula, it is applied for each player based on scrimmage and game results. To understand how a game and players might be graded, let's examine the 2010 NCAA championship game between Duke and Butler. To get the most accurate analysis, statistics should be taken off game video. Box scores do not tell the entire story, especially when it comes to violations called off the ball; blocked shots, lane violations, and bad passes are not always easy to determine accurately during the game. But for the purpose of converting statistics here, the championship game box score statistics will achieve our objective (see tables 3.4 and 3.6).

An abbreviated list of categories—field goals, free throws, rebounds, personal fouls, turnovers, assists, blocked shots, and steals—illustrates how to convert a player's game statistics into a player's PR number (see tables 3.5 and 3.7). The coach must make the final determination regarding a few specific violations (for example, when it is difficult to tell who tipped in an offensive rebound, knocked a ball out of bounds, or committed a foul, or when it is unclear whether a pass that went awry was the fault of the passer or the receiver). The PRS represents the total of each player's statistical contribution for that day.

Table 3.4 Duke Team Statistics Box Score

Player	Min	FGM-A	3PM-A	FTM-A	REB (O/D)	AST	STL	BLK	TO	PF	PTS
Thomas	35	3-5	0-0	0-0	(1/3)	0	2	0	3	4	6
Singler	40	7-13	3-6	2-2	(1/8)	2	1	2	2	1	19
Smith	40	5-15	1-5	2-5	(1/2)	4	0	0	3	0	13
Scheyer	37	5-12	1-5	4-5	(1/5)	5	1	2	2	3	15
Zoubek	31	3-4	0-0	2-4	(6/4)	1	0	2	1	4	8
Mi. Plumlee	9	0-2	0-0	0-0	(1/2)	0	1	1	1	2	0
Dawkins	5	0-1	0-1	0-0	(0/0)	0	0	0	0	0	0
Ma. Plumlee	3	0-0	0-0	0-0	(0/1)	0	0	0	0	0	0
Totals		**23-52**	**5-17**	**10-16**	**(11/25)**	**12**	**5**	**7**	**12**	**14**	**61**

Table 3.5 Duke Individual Performance Ratings

Player	Plus (+)	Minus (–)	PR score	Positives	Negatives
Thomas	+16	–14	+2	REB, STL	PF
Singler	+41	–20	+21	REB, AST, BLK	
Smith	+28	–36	–8	AST	FG, 3P, TO, FT
Scheyer	+43	–27	+16	REB, AST, BLK	3P
Zoubek	+31	–12	+19	REB, FG, BLK	PF, FT
Mi. Plumlee	+8	–8	0	N/A	N/A
Dawkins	0	–3	–3	N/A	N/A
Ma. Plumlee	+1	0	+1	N/A	N/A
Totals	**+168**	**–120**	**+48**		

Table 3.6 Butler Team Statistics Box Score

Player	Min	FGM-A	3PM-A	FTM-A	REB (O/D)	AST	STL	BLK	TO	PF	PTS
Hayward	40	2-11	0-3	8-8	(3/5)	1	1	0	1	1	12
Veasley	38	1-9	0-5	0-0	(3/0)	3	0	0	2	2	2
Mack	31	5-14	2-4	0-0	(1/4)	2	2	0	2	1	12
Nored	27	3-8	1-2	0-0	(1/5)	1	1	0	2	3	7
Howard	19	3-8	0-0	5-8	(2/2)	0	0	0	1	4	11
Jukes	18	4-6	2-3	0-2	(2/2)	0	0	0	0	4	10
Hahn	11	1-1	1-1	0-0	(0/1)	0	0	0	0	1	3
Vanzant	15	1-1	0-0	0-0	(0/1)	0	0	0	0	2	2
Smith	1	0-0	0-0	0-0	(0/0)	0	0	0	0	0	0
Totals		**20-58**	**6-18**	**13-18**	**(12/20)**	**7**	**4**	**0**	**8**	**18**	**59**

Table 3.7 Butler Individual Performance Ratings

Player	Plus (+)	Minus (–)	PR score	Positives	Negatives
Hayward	+28	–28	0	REB, FT	FG, 3P
Veasley	+17	–29	–12	O-REB	FG, 3P
Mack	+28	–25	+3	REB, AST, 3P	FG
Nored	+19	–21	–2	REB	FG
Howard	+17	–22	–5	REB	FG, FT, PF
Jukes	+16	–13	+3	REB, FG, 3P	PF, FT
Vanzant	+3	–2	+1	FG	
Hahn	+4	–1	+3	3P	
Smith	0	0	0	N/A	N/A
Totals	**+132**	**–141**	**–9**		

When analyzed by comparative statistics, tables 3.8 and 3.9 give a look into those important fundamental categories that made the difference in this 61-59 championship game between Duke and Butler. The shooting categories favored Duke (+71 and –106 for –35 total) over Butler (+71 and –122 for –51 total). Rebounding went to Duke in a close battle; Duke was +36 and Butler was +32. Butler had fewer turnovers (8 to 12), but Duke excelled in assists (12 to 7), fewer personal fouls (14 to 18), and more steals (5 to 4). The one category that really sticks out and may have had a great influence on the outcome was Duke's ability to dominate blocked shots, by a 7 to 0 margin. Game video would show how many layups and put-backs were eliminated.

Table 3.8 Comparison of Team Totals

	DUKE PERFORMANCE RATING			BUTLER PERFORMANCE RATING		
	Stats	Plus (+)	Minus (–)	Stats	Plus (+)	Minus (–)
FGM-A	23-52	+46	–58	20-58	+40	–76
3PM-A	5-17	+15	–36	6-18	+18	–36
FTM-A	10-16	+10	–12	13-18	+13	–10
REB (O/D)	36 (11/25)	+47		32 (12/20)	+44	
AST	12	+36		7	+21	
PF	14		–14	18		–18
TO	12		–24	8		–16
STL	5	+10		4	+8	
BLK	7	+7		0	0	
Totals		+171	–144		+144	–156
Overall score		+27				–12

Table 3.9 Comparison of Individual Totals

	DUKE			BUTLER		
	Stats	Plus (+)	Minus (–)	Stats	Plus (+)	Minus (–)
FGM-A	23-52		–12	20-58		–36
3PM-A	5-17		–21	6-18		–18
FTM-A	10-16		–2	13-18	+3	
REB (O/D)	36 (11/25)	+47		32 (12/20)	+44	
AST	12	+36		7	+21	
PF	14		–14	18		–18
TO	12		–24	8		–16
STL	5	+10		4	+8	
BLK	7	+7		0		
Totals		+100	–73		+76	–88
Overall score		+27				–12

Table 3.10 reflects the PRS value conversion for each of the nine statistical categories, broken into similar components: shooting, positive factors, and negative factors. Following in table 3.11 are the PR scores of Duke and Butler within each of these components and the difference between them.

The PRS can also provide a quick snapshot of player production. Compare Butler's top three producers to Duke's top three producers in table 3.12. Singler had a +41 and a –20 for a +21, Zoubek a +31 and a –12 for a +19, and Scheyer a +43 and a –27 for a +16. Compare this production to Butler's top three producers, Hayward with a +28 and a –28 for 0, Mack a +28 and a –25 for a +3, and Jukes a +16 and a –13 for a +3. Butler's top three produced a +72 and a –66 for an overall +6. Meanwhile, Duke's top three produced a +115 and a –59 for an overall +56.

After analyzing all the PR data in its various forms, we can observe that Duke won because of several reasons:

1. Zoubek had an excellent game. He had the second-highest PR at +19 and led in rebounding (10).
2. Duke had 7 blocked shots; Butler had 0.
3. Duke's three most reliable point producers scored 47 points, whereas Butler's top three scored just 35.
4. Duke's top three players (+56) had higher PRs than Butler's top three players (+6).
5. Duke's combined PRs (+27 to Butler's –12) and all-around play prevailed.
6. Duke had three players with very good individual PRs (Singler, +21; Zoubek, +19; and Scheyer, +16); Butler's best were Mack, +3, and Jukes, +3.

Table 3.10 Related PRS Components

Shooting	Positive factors	Negative factors
FG	AST	PF
3P	REB	RO
FT	STL	
	BLK	

Table 3.11 PRS Scores Broken Into Related PRS Components

	Duke	Butler	Difference
Shooting	–35	–51	+16 (Duke)
Positive	+61	+59	+2 (Duke)
Negative	–82	–98	+16 (Duke)
Totals	**–56**	**–90**	**+34 (Duke)**

Table 3.12 Top Three Team Producers

DUKE TOP THREE				BUTLER TOP THREE			
Player	**Min**	**FGM-A**	**3PM-A**	**PR**	**Player**	**Min**	**FGM-A**	**3PM-A**	**PR**
Singler	40	7-13	3-6	+21	Mack	31	5-14	2-4	+3
Zoubek	31	3-4	0-0	+19	Jukes	18	4-6	2-3	+3
Scheyer	37	5-12	1-5	+16	Hayward	40	2-11	0-3	0
Totals		**15-29**	**4-11**	**+56**	**Totals**		**11-31**	**4-10**	**+6**

SCRIMMAGE EVALUATION USING THE PERFORMANCE RATING SYSTEM

Although most of the focus of PRS has been on games so far, this grading program begins on the first day of practice. Following the normal offensive and defensive fundamental drills and the necessary teaching segments, a 30-minute slot is allotted for scrimmaging in each practice. Statistics are tracked during all scrimmages using the PRS. If the team consists of 15 players, each player has 20 minutes of scrimmage each day. John Wooden, widely recognized as the greatest collegiate coach ever, was a proponent of daily scrimmaging. A schedule that would accommodate 15 players might look like this (three teams—A, B, and C—each scrimmaging 20 minutes per day):

10 minutes	A vs. B
10 minutes	A vs. C
10 minutes	B vs. C

Total scrimmage time is 30 minutes. Players inevitably evaluate their progress against teammates, so it's important to incorporate an all-purpose offense (see chapter 6) that gives each player an equal chance to succeed. Chances are that the offense used for evaluation will not be the primary offense used by the team, but players' positions, ballhandling, and rebounding responsibilities are automatically built in. Therefore, the offense used and the administration of the workouts must have certain basic attributes. The evaluation process eliminates as much ambiguity as possible by incorporating these five requirements:

1. The offense is fair and allows all players to show their ability.
2. Playing time is the same for everyone. Devise a plan to ensure this.
3. Players rotate daily to eliminate any assertion that the teams could be stacked.
4. Hire outside officials to ensure impartial refereeing.
5. Grade everyone using the same PRS.

RESULTS OF THE PERFORMANCE RATING SYSTEM

The PRS is based on the hypothesis that as players minimize their weaknesses and improve their strengths, the team automatically improves. This is how it should work:

1. The PRS encourages players to strive for positive results because by doing so they get more playing time. When players reduce their individual mistakes, shoot better percentages, and play more effectively, the team has better results. As the positive replaces the negative, team execution improves.

2. The PRS eliminates guessing about who the most effective players are.

3. Practice results are tabulated and posted for all players to see.

4. No one can take advantage of the system because everyone must practice to have a PR number. If players don't practice, they have no PR number. Without a PR number, they see no game time. Rather than lose a full day of production, players learn to play through sore muscles, nagging irritations, and bad days.

5. Players quickly learn the importance of collecting statistics across the board; the more rounded their game, the better their chance for collecting numbers. Team production goes up as individual execution improves.

6. The system rewards positive play and penalizes poor play. Players pick up on the concept that production precedes playing time. They soon realize that a positive score demands work and complete concentration. The PRS (shooting only) scale in table 3.13 provides an example of how to tabulate one player's shooting performance and shows how difficult it is to depend on scoring alone for a PRS plus rating.

Table 3.13   Individual PRS Shooting Scale

PRS SHOOTING SCALE				
FG made	+2	FG missed		−2
3P made	+3	3P missed		−3
FT made	+1	FT missed		−2
SAMPLE (SINGLER'S SHOOTING STATISTICS FOR DUKE VS. BUTLER)				
FGM-A		3PM-A	FTM-A	
4-7		3-6	2-2	
PRS SCORING (SINGLER'S SHOOTING STATISTICS CONVERTED INTO PRS)				
	Made	Positive	Missed	Negative
FG	4	+8	3	−6
3P	3	+9	3	−9
FT	2	+2	0	0
Totals	9	+19	6	−15
PR (for shooting only)		+4		

In the table 3.13 example, Singler of Duke hit 57 percent of his two-point field goals, 50 percent of his three-point field goals, and 100 percent of his free throws. He scored 19 points and was positive (+4) on the PRS. This example illustrates the fact that just scoring seldom leads the PRS rankings. Singler also had 9 rebounds for 10 points, 2 assists for 6 points, 2 blocked shots for 4 points, and 1 steal for 2 points, bringing his positive PR total to +41. His negative total came to a –20, which gave him an overall total of +21 for the game.

The PRS should help players improve their shooting skills because to score a plus in field-goal shooting, they must shoot better than 50 percent, and to be positive in free-throw shooting, they must hit above 70 percent. A minus in the PRS indicates a problem. In most shooting situations, the concern is shot selection—taking forced shots, launching out-of-range shots, or failing to finish on drives. Of course, shooting is only one category, and players have many opportunities to collect additional positive numbers with rebounds, assists, steals, and all-around good play.

The PRS works as planned. The PRS allows players to concentrate on their game and not worry about whether the coaches notice their rebounds or assists, whether scoring is the only important statistic, or whether the coaches intend to play favorites. When these issues are eliminated, the selection experience becomes a healthy environment in which players and coaches can have friendly conversations in full view of everyone without other players suspecting favoritism. Anyone—player, coach, or parent—who has ever competed on a team understands the value of eliminating favoritism, and the PRS does that.

HUSTLE BOARD

The PRS is a comprehensive analysis of a player's production. The PRS promotes fairness, team play, and accuracy. Yet coaches can use additional methods to motivate and inspire players to enhance their contributions. One of the best I've found is recognizing extra effort through hustle board statistics. Many teams at all levels use the hustle board as an indicator of special accomplishment and recognition.

At the beginning of the year, coaches and players put together a list of important fundamental statistics that are easily recognized and basic but reflect extra effort and in most cases a willingness to sacrifice by going on the floor, by absorbing some physical contact, or, when boxing out, by forgetting all else and maintaining contact until a teammate retrieves the ball. Note that any player can perform these actions, but not all are geared toward this type of physical play. For that reason the word *hustle* is used to define these plays. Players understand that performing these actions is difficult, and they respect those who make such plays. Special recognition is always given to these players through a mention in practice and a symbolic star or emblem placed on the front of their lockers. This approach is similar to putting an emblem on a football helmet to indicate special accomplishments.

Following are some examples of hustle boards that coaches can use. The person who keeps these hustle board statistics must understand basketball. In most situations, an assistant coach or volunteer coach should be assigned this job.

Hustle Board #1 The six categories listed on hustle board #1 (table 3.14) present a difficult overall slate, but each action is basic and easily recorded. Some coaches like the categories on this hustle board because they are all objective.

Table 3.14 Hustle Board #1

Description	Goals to qualify
Take	2 offensive charges
Retrieve	2 offensive rebounds
Deflect	2 passes
Dig out	2 steals
Block shot	1 shot
Tip out	1 missed shot or free throw

Hustle Board #2 Hustle board #2 (table 3.15) represents a different slate with some different fundamental coverages. Each of these plays is important and demands extra effort. All of these plays benefit the team, and emphasizing them on the hustle board will definitely improve each player's all-round performance.

Table 3.15 Hustle Board #2

Description	Goals to qualify
On the floor	2 charges or dives for loose balls
Forced turnover	2 in which team retrieves ball
Screen	2 that free up a player
Front post	1 denied entry pass
Hustle play	1 sprint back on defense
Give foul	1 on layup to prevent goal

Hustle Board #3 The previous two hustle boards represent individual accomplishments, but some coaches are more interested in team achievements than individual statistics. Here is an example of a hustle board (used by a Division I team in a power conference) that incorporates both individual and team success (table 3.16). The individual offensive board reflects shooting percentages and statistics on free throws, field goals, assists, and offensive rebounds. The defensive board challenges the players with rebounds (five total) and steals (two total), along with going on the floor, getting the charge, and blocking the shot (one each).

The two-team hustle board incorporates six different components. Probably the most important aspect of this concept is that it depends on team accomplishments and motivates all the players to pull together to meet the standards. The coaching staff determines the shooting percentage, and all other components—rebounds, steals, blocked shots and charges—depend on the opponent.

Table 3.16   Hustle Board #3

All of the following goals are to be charted and reviewed at the half, at the end of the game, or at practice the following day.

INDIVIDUAL HUSTLE BOARD	
Offense	**Defense**
Must hit 80 percent of free throws (minimum of 5 attempts).	Must have at least 5 defensive boards.
Must have at least 4 assists (might be necessary to reduce to 3).	Must get 2 steals.
Must have at least 2 offensive rebounds and 1 put-back.	Must get 1 charge.
Must hit 50 percent of field goals attempted.	Must go on the floor for the ball 1 time.
Cannot have more than 2 turnovers.	Must block 1 shot.
TEAM HUSTLE BOARD	
Rules	**Goals**
All team categories depend on defensive work.	Must hold a team to predetermined, realistic field-goal percentage. Set a goal that challenges the team.
Each player gets an award when all 5 goals are accomplished.	Must outrebound opponent.
When subs play, their contributions count the same as starters. This encourages all players to pull for each other.	Must get more steals than opponent.
This builds good team awareness and support.	Must block more shots than opponent.
	Must get more charges than opponent.

This chapter has discussed fair and consistent evaluation procedures. The hustle board is used to help motivate and recognize players by rewarding both their individual effort and their team effort. The hustle board is a useful tool, but it does not replace the player rating system, which converts statistics into a PR production number, giving players input into policy and rule regulations, emphasizing team success over individual accomplishment, and illustrating some of the areas to consider when analyzing and scouting players. The PRS can be one of the best tools for building strong, positive relationships between coaches and players.

AP Photo/Alonzo Adams

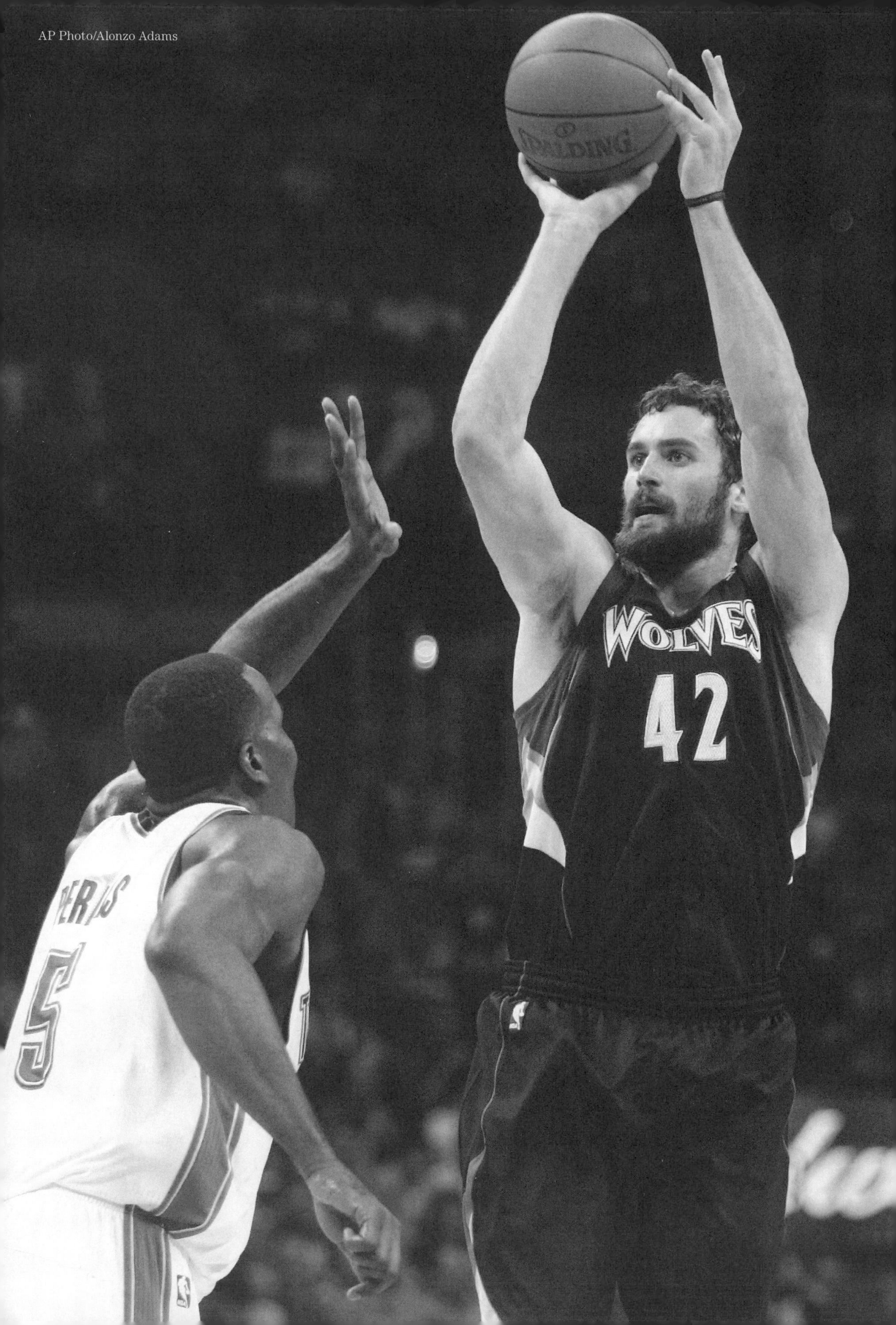

CHAPTER 4

Individual Offensive Skills

Players bring different levels of skill to the court. The coach's goal is to help players develop their skills to the highest level possible. The status quo is rare in basketball, because players usually improve or fall back in each practice. No magic is involved; each player must seize the opportunity through hard work. Pragmatically, the important thing for players is to be confident in their game and positive in their approach when they receive constructive criticism.

Most players enjoy fast-paced offenses, and the wise ones soon realize that scoring is a by-product of executing sound fundamentals. Basketball teams that insist on player and ball movement on offense are extremely hard to guard because the constant movement can cause a defense to break down, thus creating excellent scoring opportunities. Good offensive players spend hours practicing such skills as ballhandling, passing, screening, and shooting. In addition, they learn to balance the court and use good spacing to make themselves and their teammates more difficult to guard. Add the important element of good decision making, and chances are that players will be on the right track toward improvement.

Even if a player doesn't have all the skills, he should never give up. For instance, a player who is big but not fast can find a place if he has good instincts, knows how to set screens, and has passing skills. An athletic rebounder with good speed who doesn't shoot well can complement team defense. A small guard who has limited rebounding or low-post defensive ability but who is able to make good playmaking decisions is ideal on a pressing team. Coaches need be flexible when considering players and positions, especially when it comes to scoring. Regardless of size, shooters are always in demand. Remember, the stereotypical pieces sometimes don't fit, and on most levels of play below the professional level, you work with the skills that your players have.

Let's first examine the more general athletic tools that players can improve on and the offensive fundamentals necessary to play the game. We'll then add decision making, that all-important intuitive quality, as we work our way to completing the process by building an offense.

ATHLETIC TOOLS

Many factors go into determining athletic success—talent, genetics, mental attitude and desire, and even access to facilities and training. To a large degree, genetics determines some part of success in many sports. Jockeys and female gymnasts are small, whereas sumo wrestlers are large. Sprinters have a high ratio of fast-twitch to slow-twitch muscles, a composition needed for explosive power. In contrast, marathon runners have a high ratio of slow-twitch muscles so that they can sustain long periods of energy production. Of course, basketball players are typically tall. According to NBA.com, the average height of an NBA player in 2010 was 6 feet, 7 inches.

Genetic factors may be set, but one cannot categorically say that something or another is in the genes and that nothing can be done. Training can have a tremendous effect on shaping body type. For example, marathon runners become leaner over time, weight lifters bulk up and gain definition, and speed skaters develop massive legs. Some coaches and athletes believe that speed, quickness, and jumping cannot be improved, but that is a myth. The fact is that players can improve all three of these factors through proper techniques and training.

Speed

Players can improve their speed with the eighths program explained in chapter 1. Basketball players intent on increasing their speed need to start early with weight-training programs. Muscular power largely determines an athlete's speed; the athlete cannot develop his highest level of speed without developing peak power performance. Athletes have the potential to improve speed in two major ways: by increasing the frequency of the stride or by increasing the length of the stride. Both occur when the player trains the body beyond its normal capacity—that is, by applying the overload theory.

Overload training depends on implementing a concentrated program including warm-ups, strength, power, endurance, flexibility, and speed techniques. Today's college and professional teams support their coaching staffs with weight-training and conditioning coaches. High school coaches looking for the best results should explore recent trends and research in speed training.

Players need to understand that speed is a great asset for any team. When coaches have the opportunity to select players with speed, they will. Teams with speed have unlimited possibilities on offense and defense. A fast, well-conditioned offensive team can keep the pressure on an opponent's defense by pushing the ball on every possession. On defense, speed permits a team to press, overplay, and create turnovers, which they can turn into easy baskets.

Quickness may separate two players with equal speed. Good quickness enables a player to create space or blow by a defender. It gives the player a chance to break down the opponent's overall defense. In addition, when a defender learns that he is at a quickness disadvantage versus the opponent, a demoralizing factor enters the equation. A quickness advantage allows the offensive player to change sides of the court to initiate the offense without being vulnerable to a five-second count or the possibility of having to pick up the dribble. Developing a playmaker with size (to see over defenders) and quickness (to elude defenders) is sound basketball strategy.

SPEED WITH THE BALL

Focus

Teaching players to create space with ballhandling.

Procedure

Players begin at the left-side hash line. Follow these steps:

1. The coach is the passer. O1 starts on the left-side hash line, closely guarded by X1. O1 dribbles with speed and quickness toward the opposite sideline, free-throw line extended. While continuing to dribble, O1 must create space between himself and X1 by quickly backing up or sliding to one side (figure 4.1)

2. After shedding the defensive pressure, O1 reverses the floor and establishes a new position on the right side of the court to begin the offense.

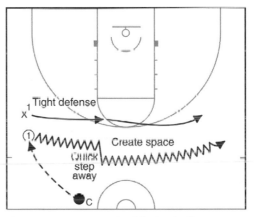

Figure 4.1 Speed with the ball.

This drill concerns ballhandling, foot speed, and the ability to elude a defender and take the ball to a different position on the court. The drill is useful for evaluating ball handlers. The diagram shows the drill on the half court, but it is also an excellent full-court drill.

Hands

Another valuable attribute, especially for inside players, is soft hands, or the ability to catch the ball in traffic. Being big and strong can make a player a prospect, but if the player can't catch the ball, his basketball future is limited, and so is the coach's inside attack. Colleges desperately looking for big players sometimes gamble that they can develop big players who have weak hands. To varying degrees, improvement is possible. One way to accomplish this is by doing daily hand and finger ball drills and by squeezing a rubber ball for finger flexibility. Three major factors—motivation, concentration, and practice—are necessary for improvement.

Soft hands in this context refers to the player's ability to catch the ball without bobbling it, mishandling it, or turning it over. Players who have this skill do not require every pass to be perfect for them to receive it. Then there's the distinction between catching the ball while stationary, such as in direct post-ups, compared with catching the ball on the move or in traffic. In a half-court offense, cross screens, pin-downs, slips, step-ins, and pick-and-rolls all necessitate movement. Executing these techniques can be difficult for players with poor catching skills.

Early in the developmental phase of a young player's career, the coach can determine whether the player needs to be stationary on post-entry passes. If a player must use two hands to catch the ball, the passer needs to be more deliberate and exact. The passer should use the receiver's chest as the target for pass entry, and the receiver should have both arms up, elbows extended, and hands open to receive when calling for the ball. Teams trying to establish a good inside attack know the importance of having post-up players with soft hands.

SOFT HANDS

Focus

Improve the ability to catch the ball and develop soft hands.

Procedure

Players begin on the half court. This drill requires three players and two balls. Follow these steps:

1. O1 lines up under the net with a ball, O2 lines up on the left elbow without a ball, and O3 lines up on the right elbow with a ball.
2. Players fire two-handed chest passes back and forth as quickly as possible for 15 seconds without dropping the ball. On all misses, they start over. O1 is on the hot spot and must keep two balls going. As O1 passes to O2, O3 passes to O1. O1 returns O3's pass, catches a pass from O2, and immediately passes back to O2 (figure 4.2).

3. This cycle continues until the drill is completed. After completing the chest pass, players practice the two-handed bounce pass, the overhead two-handed pass, and right- and left-handed passes.

This drill is excellent for improving eye–hand coordination. As players become proficient, the coach should move to some one-on-one drills.

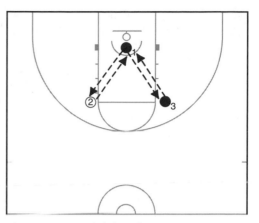

Figure 4.2 Soft hands.

Jumping

The ability to jump is one of the most important components of a basketball player's set of skills. We have seen in chapter 1 that a player can increase vertical jumping ability through improved techniques, desire, and a strenuous plyometric jump-training program. But the significance of being able to jump is another matter. Basketball is a game that is all about jumping.

Players with pronounced jumping skills can have a dynamic effect on many aspects of the game. Jumping shot blockers shock opponents by swatting away what look like guaranteed layups. Dominating offensive rebounders explode with thunderous dunks as they punctuate their power. Three-point shooters who fluidly stop, rise, and sink a 25-footer (7.5 m) over a tightly guarding defender make the game special. Successful coaches understand that developing their players' jumping ability allows them to elevate quicker and get rebounds, to intimidate shooters and change the direction of a shot even without blocking it, and to have a greater effect on the game.

The benefits of working on jumping include more than just attaining greater height; timing is also important. Players who can anticipate, accelerate, and elevate in a timely manner are a step ahead of the competition. Top coaches understand how a jump-training program helps maximize players' skills. Players with amazing jumping ability find basketball a natural fit. In the NBA, an outstanding example is Eddie Robinson, formerly of the Charlotte Hornets and Chicago Bulls. A 6-foot-7 (201 cm) small forward, Robinson scored higher than any other Hornet on fitness tests. He could tip out at 12 feet, 4 inches (376 cm), had a standing vertical of 31 inches (79 cm), a one-step vertical of 36 inches (91 cm), and a running vertical of a phenomenal 43 inches (109 cm). Eddie combined world-class speed with great jumping ability and was one of the most exciting players in the league when running the wing on the fast break looking for a lob.

JUMPING TO IMPROVE TIMING

Focus

Increase strength, explosion, and timing.

Procedure

Players end practice with this jumping drill. Players line up under the backboard and, one at a time, follow these steps:

1. The player extends both arms above the head, bends at the waist (figure 4.3*a*), jumps, and slaps both hands on the backboard (figure 4.3*b*).

2. The player lands on the balls of both feet and immediately explodes, repeating the jump while keeping the arms and hands extended. He does all this in a continuous motion. The player is not allowed to stop, gather, and then jump.

3. The player continues this process for 30 seconds with a coach and a recorder. Only two-hand touches count.

Figure 4.3 Jumping to improve timing: *(a)* bending at the waist; *(b)* slapping the backboard.

Through this drill, players also develop stamina. For high school players unable to touch the backboard with both hands, a piece of tape on the wall measured in inches (or centimeters) will serve the same purpose.

In summary, players can improve three extremely important attributes—speed, soft hands, and jumping ability. The amount of improvement depends on motivation, dedication, and the coach's innovation. Finding the right training programs for players lacking speed, jumping ability, or the ability to catch the ball is up to the coach and the player.

OFFENSIVE FUNDAMENTALS

In addition to the athletic tools just described, basketball specific fundamentals can also be developed to improve individual offensive skills. This section focuses on a variety of teaching techniques for shooting, passing, and dribbling. Critical areas are identified, and a blueprint on how to build a correct foundation for what well-rounded players need to know is provided.

Shooting

Kareem Abdul-Jabbar once said that the greatest thing that ever happened to him was the banning of the dunk when he was in college. Why? Because it forced him to learn how to shoot. In fact, Abdul-Jabbar went on to become the NBA's all-time leading scorer. Shooting should be an integral part of every offensive drill. Players must use proper shooting technique on every shot they take in practice, whether in drills, in half-court work, or in full scrimmages. Let's begin with the three essentials of the jump shot: proper base, visualization, and self-confidence.

Base, Visualization, and Confidence

When shooting, players begin by establishing a solid base with good body balance, feet approximately shoulder-width apart, and shoulders squared to the basket. The ball should rest in the shooting hand, and the fingers should be on the seams for proper rotation (sometimes, in the heat of action, it is not possible to get the fingers on the seams). The shooting elbow should be close to the body, anticipating the lift and shot (figure 4.4a). Players develop this technique only through long hours of practice. With ball support from the off, or nonshooting, hand, the player protects the ball and takes it to a shooting position above and in front of the head (figure 4.4b). The player should stabilize himself and avoid jerking his head, which would distort his aim. In taking the shot, the player begins to release the off hand and allows the shooting hand to do all the work (figure 4.4c), holding the follow-through (figure 4.4d).

The arm, wrist, hand, and fingers work cooperatively to release the ball in a smooth, fluid motion. Shooters should understand that the rim is twice the diameter of the ball and that the object is to shoot the ball in an arc, not with flat trajectory or as a line drive, to permit the ball to drop into the basket. A good shooter has the arm, wrist, and fingers all extended on the follow-through. The proper extension involves the wrist being loose, relaxed, and extending forward as though the shooter is picking fruit from a bushel basket above his head. The index finger points directly at the basket as if it's a trigger finger pointing at a target.

Besides establishing a good base, shooters must also use visualization. Whether catching the ball on the move, off a screen, or pulling up off the dribble, players

Figure 4.4 Shooting: *(a)* establishing a solid base; *(b)* moving to shooting position; *(c)* allowing the shooting hand to do the work; *(d)* holding the follow-through.

have to focus on the target as they are preparing to release the ball. As an assistant coach with the Charlotte Hornets for five years, one of my duties was to work with our players in pregame shooting drills. Dell Curry, one of the best NBA three-point shooters of all time, was on the Hornets team when I was there. Dell and I had many conversations about shooting techniques; where to aim the ball was one of many topics we discussed. He said that he always aimed for the hole just beyond the middle flange (the hooks that hold the net) facing him and over the lip of the rim. Great shooters are able to see through the rim and concentrate on the hole between the front and back of the rim as their target. In pregame warm-ups, good shooters begin their workouts close to the basket and work their way out to the three-point line. This approach helps them create an easy, fluid motion for a shot and helps them to focus visually on the basket.

The third component of shooting involves maintaining confidence. Success in shooting depends on belief in one's abilities. Self-confidence is at the core of sport performance and is based on how the player interprets his experiences. When the brain experiences positive input, a positive response is likely. The more shots a player makes, the more confidence he has. Effective leaders understand that repeated encouragement, confirmation, and support result in positive-in, positive-out experiences. The same experience occurs when players shoot the ball: The more shots they make, the more shots they expect to make. Good teachers develop shooting drills that consider the players' strengths and work at building a confident foundation.

Confidence is earned, not ordained. To tell players to play with confidence is wasted energy; you don't hand out confidence as you do water at a practice break. Success, repetition, concentration, competition, and plenty of practice create the environment to develop confidence. Goal-oriented shots during competitive drills that simulate win-or-lose situations can be great confidence builders. Self-motivating shooting drills that require players to make five shots from one spot or three in a row before moving on are also highly effective. Such drills have concentration, repetition, and success built in. The addition of a player or group and the declaration of a winner add a competitive element that energizes the experience.

Former Clemson University and Charlotte Hornets player Elden Campbell, who stood 6 feet, 11 inches (211 cm), shot 47 percent from the field during his NBA career. He had an effective warm-up shooting drill that helped build his confidence. After a few minutes of close-in shooting, Elden would move out to 15 to 18 feet (4.5 to 5.5 m) from the basket and shoot from five spots—the baseline, the left elbow, a step inside the top of the key, the right elbow, and the right baseline. He had to make five in a row before he moved to the next spot. After he made five in a row, he would continue shooting to see how many he could make consecutively before moving on. On some nights, he would hit 15 straight, and the drill came easy. On other nights, nothing went in, and only his goal of hitting five straight made him concentrate and complete the task.

Off the Dribble

One of the skills that separates good players from great players is the ability to shoot the pull-up jumper while on the move. Players who can do this have a mid-range game—a rare quality in this day of the three-point field goal. Most players can hit the spot-up, long-range jump shot or a driving layup but have difficulty making the in-between 10- to 15-foot (3 to 4.5 m) shot. Players cannot hit shots in that gap for several reasons: lack of ballhandling skills, poor balance on the pull-up, and lack of body control after beginning the dribble move. Players often resist change, not wanting to move beyond their comfort zone. As a result, they don't work on certain aspects of their game and lack confidence in areas such as shooting off the dribble.

Another reason for the scarcity of the midrange game is that coaches don't emphasize it. The best way to approach these issues is to design shooting drills that require all players to dribble and pull up for jump shots, especially midrange shots. The following drills provide an excellent way to develop and improve shooting off the dribble.

SHOOTING OFF THE DRIBBLE, RIGHT HAND

Focus

Shooting technique with movement, right hand.

Procedure

Divide the team into two groups of six. Run this drill on both ends of the court simultaneously. Coaches (marked as Cs in the diagram) or chairs indicate where players take shots. Follow these steps:

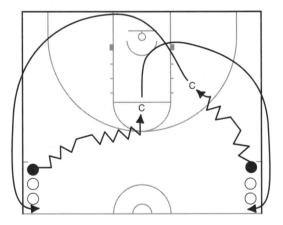

Figure 4.5 Shooting off the dribble, right hand.

1. On each side of the court, players form two groups of three and line up behind the hash line.

2. Players on the right side use a right-foot pivot, switching from a left-handed to right-handed dribble with a crossover step. They then dribble toward the wing position at the free-throw line extended. Players stay low as they drive middle, using two dribbles before shooting a pull-up jump shot.

3. Players on the left side execute the same right-foot pivot technique, switching from a left-handed to right-handed dribble, going middle, and shooting a pull-up jump shot (figure 4.5).

4. Each player retrieves his rebound and rotates to the back of the opposite line.

A second crossover dribble to the left hand on the pull-up shot adds more difficulty to the drill.

SHOOTING OFF THE DRIBBLE, LEFT HAND

Focus

Shooting technique with movement, left hand.

Procedure

Divide the team into two groups of six. Run this drill on both ends of the court simultaneously. Coaches (marked as Cs in the diagram) or chairs indicate where players take shots. The drill is like the previous one, except that the left hand is the focus of the dribble action. Follow these steps:

1. On each side of the court, players divide into groups of three and line up behind the hash line.

2. Players on the left side use a left-foot pivot with a crossover dribble, switching from a right-handed to left handed dribble and moving toward the wing position at the free-throw line extended. Players should stay low as they drive, taking two dribbles before shooting a pull-up jumper (figure 4.6).

3. Players on the right side execute the same pivot technique to the middle with a crossover, switching from a right-handed to left handed dribble and shooting a pull-up jump shot.

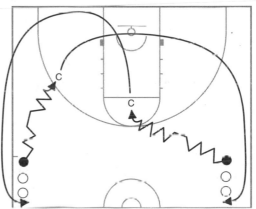

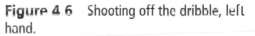

Figure 4.6 Shooting off the dribble, left hand.

4. Each player retrieves his rebound and rotates to the back of the opposite line.

Again, a second crossover dribble increases the degree of difficulty of this drill.

FULL-COURT SHOOTING

Focus

Shooting technique off the dribble, full court, right-handed dribble and left-handed dribble.

Procedure

This continuous full-court running and shooting drill will improve players' mobility, ballhandling, and ability to shoot off the dribble. The drill is six minutes in duration. Divide the squad by having six players at each end of the court, each with a ball. Then follow these steps:

(continued)

Full-Court Shooting *(continued)*

1. Three chairs, marked as Cs on the diagram, are placed at the far end opposite the players. Each chair indicates a shooting spot. Players take the shots in order: first from the middle of the floor, then from the wing, and last from the baseline.

2. The first player in each line starts at the same time, dribbling forward with the right hand. The drill is then follow the leader; players keep a space of two or three dribbles between themselves. After shooting from behind the first chair, players retrieve their own shots and move to the line in the opposite corner from where they started (figure 4.7).

3. On the second trip, they shoot from behind the second chair and so on until they have completed the entire cycle.

4. Should players finish before three minutes are up, they start over at the first spot and continue the drill. After three minutes, they start over at the first spot, dribbling with the left hand.

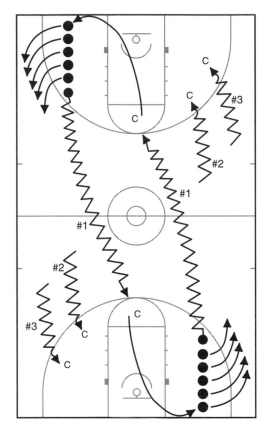

Figure 4.7 Full-court shooting.

Step-Back Move

Every coach looks for the player who has the skills to beat opponents in one-on-one situations. Several skills are associated with good one-on-one moves. Great players possess some, but not necessarily all, of the following skills: a quick first step, an unstoppable crossover, a quick release on the jumper, and a step-back move that creates space between them and the defender. Although Michael Jordan had tremendous skills in all phases of the game, his trademark ability to create space for himself was his most outstanding skill.

Getting the ball at the midpost, he could go baseline or middle with one dribble, separate from the defender, create space, and get an open look at the basket. During his prime, Hakeem Olajuwon had the same ability. Defenders could be all over him, but with his back to his man, Olajuwon could take one quick step, disengage, and shoot an open shot. Jamal Mashburn of the NBA's Miami Heat and Charlotte Hornets was one of the best at executing this skill, and Dirk Nowitzki and Kobe Bryant are two of the best in today's game.

The step-back move involves good pivoting, footwork, proper balance, and head and shoulder fakes. The offensive player must have a good feel for where the defender is and be able to elevate as he disengages from the defender. Leg strength is also important. Step-back moves can come from anywhere on the court. For teaching purposes, however, the midpost to low-post area is ideal. The following drill is helpful in teaching this technique.

SHOOTING OFF A STEP-BACK MOVE

Focus

Separation moves to create space.

Procedure

Divide the team into two groups of six. Groups work simultaneously on both ends of the court. Players rotate offense to defense, defense off. Follow these steps:

1. This drill is a one-on-one in the mid-post on the right side. To emphasize the offensive move, the defender plays behind and permits the entry pass from the coach (figure 4.8).

2. On the catch, the offensive player gets a feel for the defender. With a preshot head fake, the offensive player determines his route. Quick step-back dribbles help build rhythm.

3. To turn middle, the offensive player must step back into the defender with the right leg to eliminate any space and then use a left-leg power step-away while turning, elevating, and shooting.

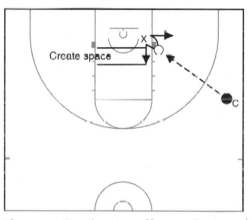

Figure 4.8 Shooting off a step-back move.

4. To turn baseline, the offensive player must step into the defender with the left leg to eliminate any space and then use a right-leg power step-away while turning, elevating, and shooting.

Draw-and-Kick

The further a team goes in state competition, NCAA tournaments, or the NBA playoffs, the more important it is that its players are able to shoot the ball off dribble penetration. By the time the regular season ends, sophisticated advance scouting enables teams to know opponents' offensive sets, taking away the first and second options of plays that have been successful throughout the year. Thus, players in the half court must be able to put the ball on the floor either to improve shooting or passing angles or to drive to the basket. In other words, they must be able to improvise if the set is well defended.

The draw-and-kick maneuver can be a defined offensive set such as the dribble-drive offense, or it can be built into any offense as a last resort when the offense breaks down and the team must improvise. In the draw-and-kick, the ball handler makes a drive to the middle. As the dribbler penetrates and the defense sags to support, the dribbler passes (or kicks) to a teammate, ideally for a catch-and-shoot jump shot. The three-man draw-and-kick is an excellent drill for teaching dribble penetration while also testing decision making.

SHOOTING OFF A DRAW-AND-KICK

Focus

Create shots off dribble penetration.

Procedure

Divide the squad into groups of three and use both ends of the court. Teams with more than 12 players will go from offense to defense, defense off. This is a continuity drill where the offensive set is a spread with two wings and one player with the ball in the middle. Follow these steps:

Option 1

1. The middle player with the ball (O1) passes to the player on the right wing (O2) and either cuts middle or screens away to begin the drill. In the first option, O1 passes, dives to the middle, and then moves to the right corner (figure 4.9).

2. If O2 can beat his opponent to the middle off the dribble, he does. If X3 cuts O2 off, he looks to pass to O3 for a shot. If O3 doesn't have a shooting opportunity, he drives middle, continuing the sequence.

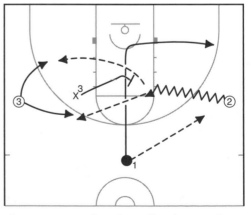

Figure 4.9 Shooting off a draw-and-kick, option 1.

Option 2

1. As a second option when running this drill, O1 passes to O2 and screens away for O3, who rotates to the top of the key (figure 4.10).

2. At the same time, player O2 attempts to beat his man middle and is cut off by X1.

3. After drawing in X1, player O2 kicks the ball to O3 for a catch-and-shoot jump shot or dribble drive. If neither is available, he can pass to O1 and dive to the middle or screen for O2.

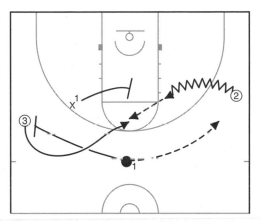

Figure 4.10 Shooting off a draw-and-kick, option 2.

Play each possession until the defense captures the ball or the offense scores. Make sure that both guards and posts practice at each position, so that the big men also work on their ballhandling and decision-making skills.

Passing

Good passes lead to assists, and bad passes cause turnovers. When I was an assistant at the University of Cincinnati, Coach Adolph Rupp of the University of Kentucky was the headliner at our annual Bearcat clinic. Coach Rupp, who won four NCAA championships at Kentucky, made a statement that stuck with me throughout my career. He said that passing was a lost art and that coaches should work diligently to help young players master that skill. For a man who spent more than 40 years coaching, this was a strong statement.

Consistently successful basketball teams pass the ball well, yet passing might be one of the most neglected of the three primary offensive skills (shooting, dribbling, and passing). Turnover differential is a stat that many coaches look at first when evaluating a team's execution. For example, according to the *2012 Official NBA Guide*, in 2010–11 the Minnesota Timberwolves had a ratio of 20.1 assists to 17.0 turnovers and an overall record of 17-65. The Cleveland Cavaliers had a ratio of 20.9 assists to 14.2 turnovers and a record of 19-63. Both team finished in last place in their respective conferences.

Pass Selection

On the half court, the two-handed chest pass, the overhead two-handed pass, and the bounce pass are the safest and most fundamentally sound. One-handed passes, especially off the dribble, should be discouraged because the pass is not as easily pulled back or controlled. The passer can hold back a two-handed pass if a defender steps into the passing lane or if the offensive player runs away from the spot. Speed and accuracy are important elements in passing, and bad passes are more often the fault of the passer than the intended receiver. Coaches should emphasize and encourage good habits in this area by implementing sound passing concepts with fundamental passing drills.

Among the variety of passes in basketball, three of the most common are the chest pass, bounce pass, and overhead pass. Each has a different technique and a different application in the game.

Chest Pass   When executing the chest pass, keep your elbows in close to the body and your hands on both sides of the ball. The ball is held chest high. As you step in the direction to which you intend to pass, push the ball forcefully away from the body and snap the thumbs down on the release. The chest pass is a safe pass and can be paused, unlike a one-handed pass that cannot be pulled back. The chest pass is commonly used in the passing game, specifically on the dribble drive, draw and kick, and whenever fast ball movement around the horn is emphasized. Chest passes are also frequently used as outlet passes when initiating the fast break and at the end of the break when passing to the shooter.

Bounce Pass   As in the chest pass, when executing a bounce pass keep your elbows in close to the body and your hands on both sides of the ball. The ball is again held chest high. As you step in the direction to which you intend to pass, push the ball forcefully down and away from the body, snapping the thumbs down on the release. Aim for a spot on the floor about two-thirds the distance to the receiver. The bounce pass is primarily an offensive half-court pass. It is used to feed the low post and, when attacking the basket, to drop the ball off to a teammate making a backdoor cut. It is also an effective pass when executing a pick-and-roll because you can slip it under the defender to the picker. The bounce pass should be used sparingly on the fast break because the receiver must look down to see the ball, catch it, refocus to find the basket, and then make the shot.

Overhead Pass   In the two-handed overhead pass, keep the ball high overhead with a clear vision of where to pass. Your hands should be on either side of the ball, with fingers spread. As you step in the direction to which you intend to pass, do not bring the ball behind your head where the defense can steal the ball from behind. Release the ball in front of your head, pushing the ball forcefully away from the body and snapping your thumbs toward the receiver. The overhead pass can be soft or thrown with speed. It is a much safer pass than the one-handed pass. The overhead pass is excellent for feeding the low post, reversing the ball, throwing lobs, and executing long outlet passes.

Incorporate passing drills into daily practice to work on the two-handed chest pass, the fake-up-and-pass-down maneuver, or the fake-down-and-pass-over technique. Teach passes that your team needs for their particular style of play. Teams need different kinds of passes depending on whether they use the fast-break style or slow it down and run a half-court offense. Teams that fast-break often use long outlet passes to players streaking down the court to initiate their attack. A half-court offensive team, on the other hand, emphasizes high-post, midpost, and low-post entry passes.

The type of pass called for also depends on where the ball is put in play. For example, are you inbounding the ball in the backcourt, on the sideline, or underneath the basket? The type of pass to be used also depends on what's happening in the game at a particular time. Are you executing against strong pressure, against zones, or against presses? Against presses, are you working against a half-court press, three-quarter-court press, or full-court press?

After a thorough study and years of observation, I've concluded that passing depends on skill, instincts, and basketball IQ. Good passers are blessed with peripheral awareness and take great pride in getting the ball to the right player at the right time. Coaches should do what they can to eliminate passing responsibilities for players with poor passing skills.

The following two-man drills incorporate dribbling, passing, layups, timing, and decision making. All are important, but the key point is to execute a proper pass each time.

INSIDE PASS

Focus

Execute two-man passing, dribbling, and shooting.

Procedure

Players begin on the half court and follow these steps:

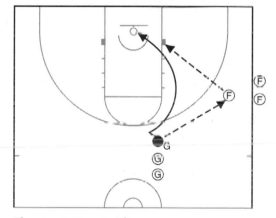

Figure 4.11 Inside pass.

1. A guard (G) with the ball lines up 6 feet (2 m) beyond the top of the key in direct line with the right elbow. A forward (F) lines up 3 feet (1 m) inside the sideline, even with the free-throw line extended.

2. The guard makes a two-handed chest pass to the forward, who prepares to receive the ball by taking a hard jab step toward the baseline and stepping to the passer with both hands up, ready to catch.

3. Using an inside jab step, the guard makes a hard speed cut to the basket. The forward receives the pass and immediately returns the pass to the guard.

4. The guard receives the pass and, depending on his floor position, either dribbles in for the layup or shoots it without the dribble (figure 4.11).

5. The forward rebounds and passes it back to the guard. Players then rotate to the left side of the court and repeat the drill.

6. After the guard has shot on both sides of the court, the players change positions. The forward becomes the shooter, and the guard becomes the passer.

OUTSIDE PASS

Focus

Execute two-player passing, dribbling, and shooting.

Procedure

Players begin on the half court and follow these steps:

1. On the right side, a guard (G) with the ball lines up 6 feet (2 m) beyond the top of the key in direct line with the elbow.

2. The forward (F) lines up 3 feet (1 m) inside the sideline boundary, even with the free-throw line extended.

3. The guard makes a bounce pass to the outside leg of the forward. The guard follows the pass and receives a return pass from the forward. The guard then attacks the basket with no more than two dribbles and shoots a layup.

4. After passing to the guard, the forward continues to the elbow, executes a reverse pivot off the right leg, and gets the rebound (figure 4.12).

5. The forward passes back to the guard, and the players rotate to the left side of the court to repeat the drill.

6. After the guard shoots on both sides of the court, the players exchange positions. The forward becomes the shooter, and the guard becomes the passer.

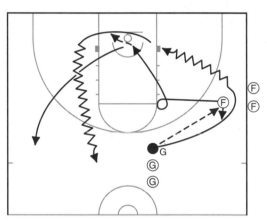

Figure 4.12 Outside pass.

Vision and Angles

A real asset for passers in basketball is good vision. Everyone has heard coaches say of an excellent passer, "He sees the floor well." This means that the player, with his head up so that he can see the court, has good passing instincts. Besides good instincts, exceptional passers like John Stockton, Rajon Rondo, Derrick Rose, Steve Nash, and Chris Paul have excellent peripheral awareness. (Stockton, who retired from the NBA in 2003, is still the all-time leader in assists with 15,806 according to NBA.com.) Jeff Meyer, one of my former assistant coaches at Purdue and South Florida, and currently an assistant at the University of Michigan, put it this way: "Vision on the court is not just for sight, but for insight." Good peripheral vision helps a player see teammates in the outer part of his vision. When a team runs its offensive plays, the designated receiver of the pass may often appear to be open, but when the passer delivers the ball, a defender intercepts it. The interception occurs because the passer is focusing only on the receiver, not on the nearby defenders. Such a passer has narrow vision; good passers see the receiver and everyone nearby. Good passers understand three important factors—angles, space, and timing. In considering angles, certain areas of the floor make passes difficult and should be avoided.

Trying to pass from the top of the key to a stationary low post is extremely difficult, because a pass from that angle must go through too many defenders with active hands. When attempting a direct pass to the low post, having the proper passing angle often eliminates an unforced turnover. Instead of passing from the top, the player should dribble to the wing position at the free-throw line extended, clear out a teammate (which eliminates a defensive helper), and then enter the ball from the wing. Designed offensive plays with slips and step-ins are different because of the deception. Direct passes from the wing, however, are safer and better.

Another extremely dangerous pass occurs when a team attempts either to reverse the ball or to pass to the top of the key for a shot. The passer is at a tremendous disadvantage when he dribbles too low on the wing, thus permitting the weak-side defender an opportunity to shoot the gap. This play calls for the receiver of the pass to recognize the problem and relocate higher out on the court to ensure the safety of the pass. Coaches must constantly remind players to meet all passes.

Offensive plays should always be designed to eliminate as many defensive obstructions as possible.

PASSING ANGLES TO THE LOW POST

Focus

Teaching entry-pass technique, being conscious of angles and floor balance.

Procedure

Visualize and comprehend the proper passing angle.

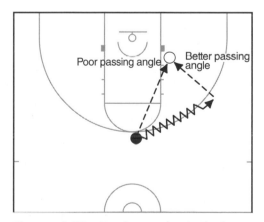

1. This diagram shows a common occurrence. Quite often, a player tries to pass from the top of the key directly to a low post. In this position, the passer must pass through multiple defenders.

2. Instead, the player should adjust the passing angle by dribbling to the wing to make the pass (figure 4.13).

3. Before making the pass, the passer must clear out any other players in the wing area.

Figure 4.13 Passing angles to the low post.

PASSING ANGLES TO THE TOP OF THE KEY

Focus

Teaching passing angles to the top of the key.

Procedure

Visualize and comprehend the proper passing angle.

1. This diagram shows a common occurrence. When a ball reversal occurs off half-court sets, such as pick-and-rolls, horns, zippers, passing games, UCLAs, or weak-side pins-downs, players rotate the ball to the top.

2. If the passing angle is poor, the receiver is giving the defense an opportunity to steal the middle-of-the-floor pass. Instead of stopping, the receiver should continue to the top of the key, or farther if necessary, to receive the pass (figure 4.14).

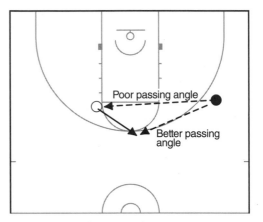

Figure 4.14 Passing angles to the top of the key.

3. The ball handler must remember not to pick up the dribble. He should keep the dribble alive until an opportunity to pass is available.

Dribbling

Dribbling is a special skill, and more coaches have begun to place most of the dribbling responsibility on the team's point guard. Even so, other players will have to dribble at times. Therefore, all players must work daily to improve their dribbling skills. Coaches at all levels need to explain and emphasize ballhandling and dribbling right from the start. First, explain to players that when they dribble, they should do it for a purpose—to take themselves and the ball to another spot on the court that is more advantageous for the team. If a player has no purpose in dribbling, he should look to pass the ball.

Here are six situations when the player with the ball is allowed to dribble:

1. Advancing the ball on the fast break
2. Moving the ball in the backcourt against certain presses
3. Following steals when there is a direct line to the basket

4. Attacking the basket off the dribble in the half court
5. Moving to create a better passing angle
6. Eluding a defender

Ball handlers often make the mistake of picking up their dribble without having a passing outlet. The player has become paralyzed, because he cannot move with the ball after ending the dribble. By picking up the ball, the player invites the defense to employ hard overplays to cut off passing lanes. Successful coaches discriminate between those who are adept at handling the ball and those who are dribble happy and prone to making turnovers. Nothing is more frustrating to a coach than seeing one of his players pound the ball on the floor at the top of the key with no purpose. All that does is stagnate the offense and discourage player movement. Not much defensive skill is required to stop it. As a coach, you have to instill in players the concept that the dribble must take them someplace.

Position-Specific Requirements

Every position on the basketball court has a different set of ballhandling requirements. Guards need to be able to take the ball from A to B: from the backcourt against pressure to the frontcourt to set up a half-court offense; from a defensive steal, rebound, or outlet pass to attack the defense in the middle of the court and make good decisions on finishing the fast break; to improve passing angles; and to elude an aggressive defender.

Forwards must clear defensive rebounds and, when possible, take it with a speed dribble to half court. Exceptional ball handlers may go all the way and attack the basket. In the half court, forwards should be able to improve a passing angle and attack the basket from the wing position. Excellent ball handlers are a must to elude pressure defense.

Centers, at a minimum, should be able to clear defensive rebounds and outlet the ball. In the half court, they should be able to make their own moves with a one- or two-dribble attack. Post players are seldom required to dribble. Nonetheless, those who can dribble bring a unique asset to their team. They can clear rebounds, ignite the fast break, trail the offense, and swing the ball comfortably. Centers can also step out on high-post sets as passers, be available as an outlet against full-court pressure, and be difficult to defend when they make their own moves to the basket. Being big does not eliminate the need to learn how to be an effective dribbler and ball handler. Developing those skills just takes practice.

Point guards are the primary dribblers for most teams. Some coaches are satisfied to keep the ball in one player's hands, but other coaches work at developing several ball handlers, knowing that a team that dribbles efficiently will have an advantage.

Technique

How should players dribble the ball? The preferred dribbler's stance is to have the knees bent and the feet shoulder-width apart, the head up, the eyes forward, and the dribble hand on top of the ball to eliminate palming. The player uses the off arm (nondribbling hand) in a protective mode and dribbles the ball no higher than the knees. Having the hand in a protective mode means that it should be waist high with the elbow bent to ward off any defensive attack. Young players need to work on technique—developing the weak hand, ballhandling control, and change-of-pace action. Coaches should teach these principles, but good ball handlers will seek their own comfort level.

Some great players have different approaches to dribbling. Oscar Robertson, arguably the greatest player ever, said that when he dribbled he liked to get down low, at the same level as his defender. Magic Johnson, on the other hand, was an exception to the standard rule about keeping the dribble low. At 6 feet, 9 inches (206 cm), he liked to bounce the ball high so that he could see over his defender.

Dribble work should begin on the first day of practice. The following drills are designed to improve players' ballhandling skills and reduce their weaknesses. The daily repetition of these basic dribble drills provides a solid base and helps immeasurably when players perform more difficult drills that incorporate pivoting and shooting. Building a solid basketball foundation is like building a stairway in a beautiful house. Each step, each fundamental, takes the player closer to the ultimate goal. The first step in this process is learning to dribble correctly, and the second step is combining dribbling with pivoting and layup shooting.

STRAIGHT-LINE DRIBBLE

Focus
Dribble with right, left, and alternating hands.

Procedure
Follow these steps:

1. Form three groups and begin on the baseline with five in each line—guards are group A, forwards are group B, and centers or big men are group C.
2. All players assume proper dribble stance—knees bent, head and eyes up, and hand on top of the ball.
3. On the "Go" command, group A dribbles full court using a right-handed dribble. Group B begins when group A gets to midcourt, and group C begins when group B gets to midcourt.
4. When group C gets to the end line, group A begins the return, and the drill continues in the same manner, using the right hand only to complete one trip down and back.
5. On the second trip down and back, players use a left-handed dribble, and on the third trip down and back, players alternate hands on each dribble.

DRIBBLE PIVOTS

Focus

Execute proper pivots while dribbling, alternating between the right and left hand.

Procedure

Follow these steps:

1. Form three groups and begin on the baseline with five to a line—guards are group A, forwards are group B, and centers or big men are group C.

2. All players assume proper dribble stance—knees bent, head and eyes up, and hand on top of the ball.

3. On the "Go" command, group A dribbles (with the right hand) diagonally toward the right sideline, free-throw line extended. After three dribbles, players stop, reverse pivot on the left foot while switching from a right-handed dribble to a left handed dribble, and then dribble three times beyond the top of the key.

4. Following the third dribble to the middle, players stop, reverse pivot on the right foot while switching from a left-handed dribble to a right-handed dribble, and head toward the sideline at midcourt. After the third dribble, players reverse pivot on the left foot and continue back and forth until they reach the end line.

5. Group B begins when group A gets to midcourt, and group C begins when group B gets to midcourt.

6. When group C gets to the end line, group A begins the return, and the drill continues in the same manner.

STOP-AND-GO DRIBBLE

Focus

Execute ball control and body balance with the stop-and-go dribble.

Procedure

The coach needs a whistle for this drill. Follow these steps:

1. Form three groups and begin on the baseline with five to a line—guards are group A, forwards are group B, and centers or big men are group C.

2. All players assume proper dribble stance—knees bent, head and eyes up, and hand on top of the ball.

3. Players in group A begin a speed dribble on the first whistle and stop on the second whistle, keeping a live dribble. They alternately go and stop on the whistle until they reach the end line.

(continued)

Stop-and-Go Dribble *(continued)*

4. Group B begins when group A gets to midcourt, and group C begins when group B gets to midcourt.

5. When group C gets to the end line, group A begins the return. The groups repeat the procedure going back.

For a variation, on each stop, have players alternate hands; back up two steps and then sprint forward; or back up two steps, alternate hands, and sprint forward. Players can also experiment with behind-the-back and between-the-legs dribbles on stops. They then sprint forward on the whistle.

CHANGE-OF-PACE DRIBBLE

Focus

Execute ball control and dribble technique with change of pace.

Procedure

Follow these steps:

1. Form three groups and begin on the baseline—guards are group A, forwards are group B, and centers or big men are group C.

2. All players assume proper dribble stance—knees bent, head and eyes up, hand on top of the ball.

3. Players in group A begin the change-of-pace dribble by sprinting five quick steps, slowing down and coasting for five steps, and then accelerating and alternating speed to the end line.

4. Group B begins when group A gets to midcourt, and group C begins when group B gets to midcourt.

5. When group C gets to the end line, group A begins the return. The groups repeat the procedure going back.

After players master this drill, extend the teaching by having players alternate hands.

Pivoting

An excellent drill for teaching fundamental pivoting is to lineup players on both sides of the free throw line at the elbows, each with ball in hand, facing the baseline. Demonstrate first with a slow walk through. Then have the player dribble under control to the endline. While maintaining balance, he should pick the ball up, bending at the waist while establishing the right foot as the pivot foot. The player, with his back to the players' line, spins half way around, while keeping the right toe or foot in constant contact with the floor. Once he is facing the coach, he steps with the left foot and passes to the coach who is stationed at the side of the drill line. The player follows the pass and on the second trip executes a left foot pivot. Once the players can execute the pivot technique effectively, they move immediately into the following single, double, diagonal and baseline pivot dribble drills.

The ability to pivot is fundamental to the game of basketball because it is used in multiple skills. For example, players must learn to pivot when rebounding, when setting screens, when preparing to pass (especially to the low post), and when driving to the basket while avoiding defenders. Pivoting is also an essential component of boxing out opponents when going for rebounds. And nothing affects the outcome of the game as much as a failure to pivot and box out when going for a missed free throw.

SINGLE PIVOT

Focus

Execute proper pivot techniques with the dribble-drive single pivot.

Procedure

Players begin at the hash line on the right side and follow these steps:

1. Start with a crossover move to a right-handed dribble.

2. Dribble with the right hand to the free-throw line extended.

3. Reverse pivot off the left foot and dribble twice with the left hand before switching back to the right hand (figure 4.15).

4. Attack the basket, exploding with a right-handed layup using the backboard.

5. Retrieve the rebound and go to the left hash line.

6. Repeat the same procedure using the left hand.

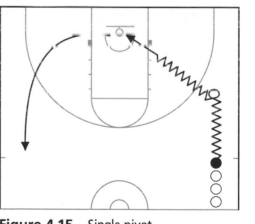

Figure 4.15 Single pivot.

Throughout this drill, prompt players to concentrate and see the ball into the basket.

DOUBLE PIVOT

Focus

Execute pivot techniques with a dribble drive and reverse pivots.

Procedure

Players begin at the hash line on the right sideline and follow these steps:

1. Start with a crossover move to a right-handed dribble.
2. Dribble with the right hand to the free-throw line extended.
3. Reverse pivot off the left foot with a left-handed dribble.
4. Dribble with the left hand to the elbow area of the lane.
5. Reverse pivot off the right foot with a right-handed dribble (figure 4.16).
6. Drive to the basket and shoot a right-handed layup.
7. Retrieve the rebound and go to the left hash line.
8. Repeat the procedure using the left hand.

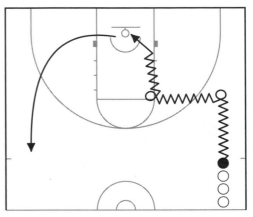

Figure 4.16   Double pivot.

DIAGONAL PIVOT

Focus

Execute a proper dribble, pivot, show ball, and shot.

Procedure

Players begin at the hash line on the right sideline and follow these steps:

1. Start with a crossover dribble to a left-handed dribble in a diagonal to the front of the basket.
2. Come to a complete stop with feet shoulder-width apart and the ball in both hands in front of the chest.
3. Establish balance with the left foot as the pivot foot.
4. Extend the ball upward in the right hand toward the basket with a good ball and head fake.

5. Again, gather balance and then pivot off the left foot for a layup or short right-handed hook shot (figure 4.17).

6. Retrieve the rebound and go to the left hash line.

7. Repeat the same procedure using a right-handed dribble and left-handed shot.

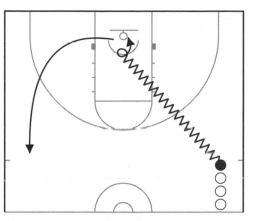

Figure 4.17 Diagonal pivot.

BASELINE PIVOT

Focus

Execute a baseline drive with dribble, pivot, and layup.

Procedure

Players begin at the hash line on the right sideline and follow these steps.

1. Start with a crossover dribble to the right hand and dribble to the corner.

2. Reverse pivot off the left foot with a left-handed dribble (figure 4.18).

3. Attack the basket and shoot a left-handed layup on the right side.

4. Retrieve the rebound and go to the end of the line.

5. On the second time through, shoot a left-handed reverse layup.

6. Retrieve the rebound and go to the left hash line.

7. Repeat the procedure, switching from a right-handed to left-handed crossover dribble and a left-handed layup to right-handed layup.

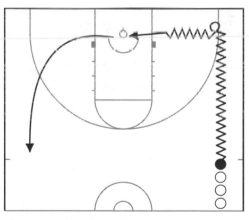

Figure 4.18 Baseline pivot.

Players should always attack the basket, explode up using the backboard, and see the ball into the basket on the layup.

Screening

Screening is one of the most overlooked fundamentals, although it is a teachable maneuver that takes only work and concentration. Players can learn to be good screeners, especially if they are unselfish and team oriented. Many types of screens are used in basketball. Screening usually involves one player screening another player, but in some offensive sets, two or three players set the screen. The most common screens in half-court sets are cross, down, diagonal, and up screens.

The player setting the screen should have the feet shoulder-width apart and the arms down in front of the body with one hand over the other in a protective mode (figure 4.19). The player cannot lean, extend the elbows or knees, or turn into the defender. Technique is important, and in most situations the player setting the screen is responsible for establishing a legal screen, which means being stationary at the time of the screen and making sure that the player being screened is permitted distance and proper vision. For example, a player who screens in front or at the side of a stationary opponent may be as close to the player being screened as he desires because the opponent being screened can see the screener. But if the screen is set behind the opponent, the opponent is entitled to take one normal step before contact. In other words, the screener must give the opponent distance to turn (meaning that the screener cannot touch him), and the screener must allow the opponent who is turning to see him. Thus, the player must give the opponent distance and vision, or he will be called for a foul.

Figure 4.19 Setting a screen using proper technique.

The player using the screen has the responsibility of making sure that the timing is proper; if he moves too soon, an offensive foul occurs. Moving too soon is a fundamental mistake because the player using the screen fails to set up his man properly and moves before the screener can establish a stationary position. Thus, the timing of the screen is a shared responsibility that requires both players to coordinate their movements.

Teaching players how to set and use screens is vitally important to developing an effective offense. To teach proper screening techniques, use a walk-through to show players how to set and use screens. The following drills will help.

DOWN SCREEN

Focus

Screening execution for the down screen.

Procedure

Split the squad into groups of three and use both ends of the court. Begin on the half court, illustrating with no defense, and then go live three on three—offense to defense, defense off. Follow these steps:

1. O1 dribbles to the free throw line extended and prepares to pass to O2.
2. The zipper down screen (a down screen for a player on the low block, who "zips" up off the screen) occurs when O5 at the elbow sets a screen for O2 on the low block on the same side (figure 4.20).
3. To use the screen, the player should jab-step in either direction, trying to get the defender between the screen and himself.
4. If the defender does not go with the jab step, the offensive player goes to the top of the key on the inside, closest to the passer.
5. If the defender takes the fake, the offensive player comes up the middle.
6. Continue live three-on-three play until a shot is made or the defense obtains the ball.

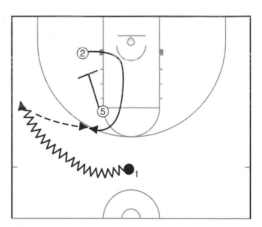

Figure 4.20 Down screen.

WEAK-SIDE PIN-DOWN

Focus

Screening execution and timing for the weak-side pin-down.

Procedure

Split the squad into groups of three and use both ends of the court. Begin on the half court, illustrating with no defense, and then go live three on three—offense to defense, defense off. Follow these steps:

1. On the right side, O1, with the ball, lines up 6 feet (2 m) beyond the top of the key in direct line with the elbow. Use a coach as the middle passer.

2. The play begins when O1 dribbles to the free-throw line extended and passes to the coach at the top of the key.

3. After this ball reversal, player O5 sets a weak-side pin-down screen (figure 4.21; note that weak-side pin-downs can be a single or double screen). The player setting the screen (O5) cannot move on the screen.

4. O2, the user of the screen, must run with a purpose. He should read the defense and go away from or eliminate resistance. If the defender blocks the route, the offensive player must find an alternative.

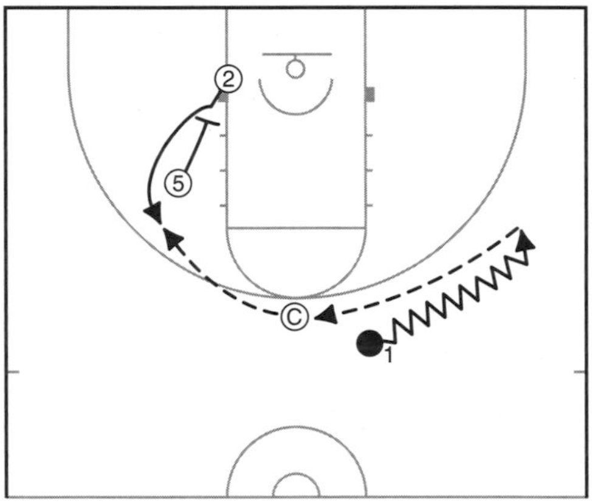

Figure 4.21   Weak-side pin-down.

5. Continue live three-on-three play until a shot is made or the defense obtains the ball.

When players learn to run their routes with a purpose, the offense becomes fluid.

CROSS SCREEN

Focus

Screening execution and technique for cross screens.

Procedure

Split the squad into groups of three and use both ends of the court. Begin on the half court, illustrating with no defense and then go live three on three—offense to defense, defense off. Follow these steps:

1. Play begins on the left side as O1, with the ball, lines up 6 feet (2 m) beyond the top of the key in direct line with the elbow. O1 dribbles to the free-throw line extended, 3 feet (1 m) from the sideline.

2. Player O2 sets a cross screen for player O4 (figure 4.22). Cross screens close to the basket can be extremely physical. Thus, the screener (O2) must be prepared for contact and the big man (O4) cannot move early; otherwise, he will never clear the congested area. Player O4 should wait, move away from resistance, and be quick after starting.

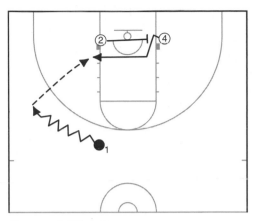

Figure 4.22 Cross screen.

3. After the screen, player O1 looks to pass inside to O4. Player O2 must clear the lane quickly to avoid a three-second violation.

4. Continue live three-on-three play until a shot is made or the defense obtains the ball.

Note that cross screens with a small man screening a big man are excellent for getting the ball on the low post. Defenses seldom switch because of the mismatch. Cross screens are most often used by teams that have good post-up players. Successful teams usually have at least three players capable of posting up.

MULTIPLE SCREENS

Focus

Screening execution and timing for cross screen to up screen.

Procedure

Split the squad into groups of four and use both ends of the court. Begin on the half court, illustrating with no defense, and then go live four on four—offense to defense, defense off. Follow these steps:

1. This play involves two screens—first, a cross screen, and second, an up screen on the player in the free-throw circle for a lob. O1, with no defender guarding him, takes a position at the free-throw line extended with the ball and works on passing.

2. Player O2 first sets a cross screen for player O5. On the cross screen, the offensive big man (O5) takes the opponent baseline because the screener (O2) cannot hold the screen as long.

3. Player O2 quickly turns, gets out of the three-second lane, and sets a second screen for O4, the player in the free-throw circle (figure 4.23).

4. Player O4 must fake the defender with a good jab step left and then look for the lob pass from player O1.

(continued)

Multiple Screens *(continued)*

5. Continue live three-on-three play until a shot is made or the defense obtains the ball.

The first screen is often a decoy that enables the screener to free up the real target for a shot, lob, or strong-side to weak-side rotation pass.

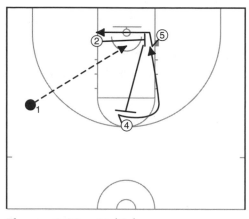

Figure 4.23 Multiple screens.

DIAGONAL SCREEN

Focus

Screening execution and technique for the diagonal screen.

Procedure

The purpose of the diagonal screen is to relocate a big man on the low post, as the Utah Jazz did when John Stockton screened for Karl Malone. The diagonal screen is different because it depends on the strength of the person setting the screen and the player's ability to execute leverage. Split the squad into groups of three and use both ends of the court. Begin on the half court, illustrating with no defense and then go live three on three—offense to defense, defense off. Follow these steps:

1. O1, on the left side with the ball, lines up 6 feet (2 m) beyond the top of the key in direct line with the elbow. O1 begins the drill by dribbling toward the sideline free-throw line extended.

2. Player O2 begins on the low block left side and sets a diagonal screen for player O4, who sets up on the free-throw line right side (figure 4.24). If the screener, O2, doesn't have proper leverage, the big man's defender will power right through.

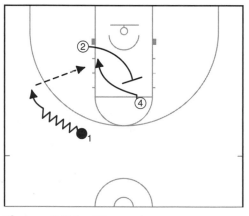

Figure 4.24 Diagonal screen.

3. Player O4 should jab step toward the basket at the point of the screen to establish a good angle for the screener and then make an aggressive cut to the block, looking for the pass from player O1.

4. Continue live three-on-three play until a shot is made or the defense obtains the ball.

Two factors make this screen difficult to execute: The player being screened sees it coming, and the player setting the screen is usually much smaller than the defender being screened.

SCREEN ON THE BALL

Focus

Communications, techniques, and rules for screening on the ball.

Procedure

Split the squad into two even groups and use both ends of the court. Begin on the half court, illustrating the sideline pick-and-roll with no defense and then go two on two—offense to defense, defense off. Follow these steps:

1. The perimeter player, O1, handles the ball on the wing.

2. The big inside player, O5, sets a screen on the ball (figure 4.25). Screens on the ball present different communication issues and screening adjustments. The player setting the screen, O5, must be stationary, and the person with the ball, O1, has the responsibility to make that happen.

3. O1, the ball handler, sees the screen coming, waits until O5, the screener, comes to a complete stop, and then says, "Go!" before making a move. (This sequence is especially important for sideline, corner, transition, and elbow pick-and-rolls.)

4. Continue live two-on-two play until a shot is made or the defense obtains the ball.

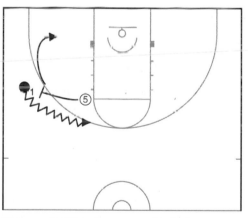

Figure 4.25 Screen on the ball.

Note that in middle pick-and-rolls, the screener is usually set and the ball handler works off a stationary target. For sideline and corner sets, the screener should set the pick on the outside shoulder of the defender, straddle the defender's outside leg with his leg, and then reverse pivot and roll to the basket or pop for the jump shot. Divide the time and exchange the positions so that each player learns to set each screen.

SINGLE AND DOUBLE SCREENS

Focus

Screening execution for running off single and double screens.

Procedure

The single–double offensive set gives the player using the screen the option of using a double screen or a single screen. It requires five position players. Split the squad into even teams and use both ends of the court. Begin on the half court, illustrating with no defense and then working the play into the regular half-court offense. With three teams, go offense to defense, defense off. Follow these steps:

1. The set uses a tight formation with two screeners, O4 and O5, stacked on one side of the basket, and O3, a single screener, opposite. O2 lines up under the rim. O1, in the middle of the court 6 feet (2 m) beyond the top of the key, initiates the play by passing to either side.

2. O2 first breaks as if planning to use the single side. After O2 gets the opponent moving, he pivots or spins and sprints off the double side screens set by O4 and O5, coming as close as possible to the left hip of the first screener and building speed while rounding the second screen (figure 4.26).

3. As O2 clears both screens, he has three options, depending on the defense; he can curl, fade (if the defender tries to shoot the gap), or pop out for a jump shot. At the same time, player O3 sets a screen for player O4, who brushes past O3 toward the opposite-side wing.

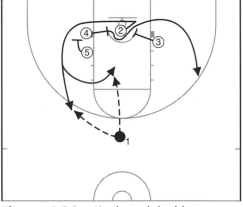

4. If O2, the shooter, uses the single-screen side, the screener, O3, after holding the screen, goes off the double-screen side. One big man, O5, stays, and one, O4, goes opposite to the low block.

Figure 4.26 Single and double screens.

5. Continue live five-on-five play until a shot is made or the defense obtains the ball.

The screeners are stationary because the user of the screens does the work.

BASELINE SCREENS

Focus

Screening execution and timing for baseline screens.

Procedure

This half-court play set requires five position players. Split the squad into even teams and use both ends of the court. Begin on the half court, illustrating with no defense, and then work the set into the regular half-court offense. With three teams, go offense to defense, defense off. Follow these steps:

1. In this formation, two players (O2 and O3) line up opposite each other just off the low blocks. The large inside players (O4 and O5) are wide off the elbows and at an angle, in position for a down screen. Player O1 sets up at the top of the key with the ball.

2. O2, the low man on the left side, moves across and sets a stationary screen for O3, the opposite low man, who jab-steps middle and then uses the screen.

3. O3 then takes a couple of running steps, turns, and uses the second screen set by O5, looking for a catch-and-shoot shot from player O1, while O2, after setting the first screen, immediately uses O4's screen on the opposite side, looking for a jump shot from player O1 (figure 4.27).

4. Continue live five-on-five play until a shot is made or the defense obtains the ball.

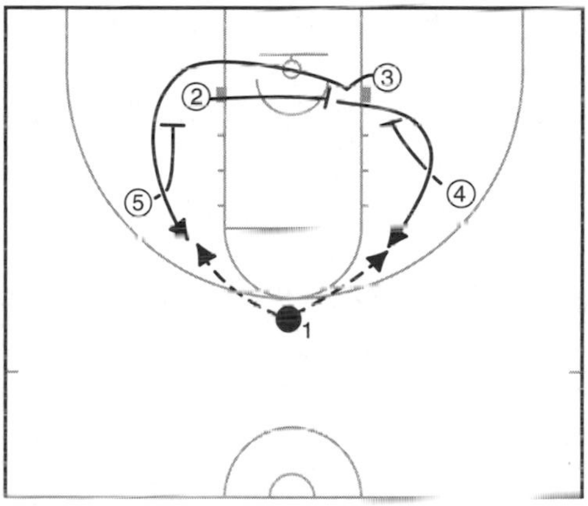

Figure 4.27 Baseline screens.

The emphasis here is getting the angle of the second screen correct and without movement.

Rebounding

Successful rebounding on either side of the ball requires a certain mind-set. Some gifted players naturally have a knack for coming up with big rebounds, but more often than not, good rebounders are successful as a result of hard work and concentration. For players who want to excel in rebounding, the following may be helpful:

Anticipation   Players need to recognize that NBA teams, with the best players in the world, shoot between 44 and 46 percent. This means that more than 50 percent of all shots taken present rebound possibilities. Shooting percentage drops off at the college and high school level, presenting an even greater need for rebounding proficiency.

Aggressiveness   Rebounders compete in the physical dimension of basketball, down where the push-and-shove confrontation is a test of will. The trenches are the place where bodies bang, leapers explode, and the physical power of the game is on display. Rebounding is not for the meek. This is a place where physical players who love contact excel.

Timing   An essential requisite for effective rebounding is timing. Rope jumping (chapter 1), backboard touches (chapter 4), and rebound jumping (chapter 1) drills all increase jumping skills and develop the rhythm necessary for good timing. Players with good timing don't always have to jump high; they just need to get good position and jump at the right time.

Position   Rebounders need to maintain contact with the opponent when a shot is taken, either by stepping back with a reverse pivot or by using the step-through technique. The body should be in a crouched position with hands and palms up, arms spread and lifted to shoulder height, and legs shoulder-width apart for good balance.

Boxing Out   The art of boxing out is a great asset when used properly. Good rebounders are either great jumpers who have excellent timing skills or players who have perfected the art of boxing out. Ask any basketball player about box-out artists, and you'll understand how frustrating it is to play against them. A player who will consistently put his butt in the belly or knees of opponents is one dreaded player. Boxing out requires no magic—just concentration, hard work, and consistency (see chapter 7).

Rims   Smart players always check the rim of the basket before the game. Some rims are lively and provide more bounce to the ball, whereas others tend to soften ball reaction and cause the ball to hang on the rim longer. Lighting and floor surface are not identical in all arenas, and players should factor in the effect of those elements on rebounding.

Many factors, including size, strength, hands, timing, body control, balance, aggressiveness, physical stamina, and jumping ability are important to rebounding effectiveness. Players willing to concentrate and learn the technique of boxing out are important to every team. Rebounding in the trenches is blue-collar work. Any dyed-in-the-wool player willing to work at the fundamentals of rebounding can improve and earn a spot on the team.

The best offensive rebounders depend on movement, which makes it hard for defenders to stay in touch and box them off the glass. Dennis Rodman, one of the most effective offensive rebounders in NBA history, was so good at moving and getting to the offensive boards that his team ran no specific plays for him. He was more valuable to the team when turned loose on the boards. When constructing an offense, the coach needs to build in a triangle concept of putting three players, one being the shooter, on the offensive boards. Teams scoring off offensive rebounds and second-chance points soon find themselves winning games.

Offensive rebounding begins with a concept that is built into teams' offensive sets. When teams run their offensive sets, all five players have designated responsibilities. One is the passer, one is the player back on defense, one is the shooter, and the other two are instructed to go to the boards. Theoretically, one of these players should go to the right-side block, one to the left-side block, and one to the free-throw lane for the long rebound. Of course, everything depends on where and when the shot is taken. To teach assertiveness in rebounding, the following drill was devised.

REBOUND PUT-BACK

Focus

Reacting to the ball, concentrating, quick jumping, scoring, stamina, and perseverance.

Procedure

This drill is usually performed within the first couple of weeks of practice, when stations are done. Players are split into four groups; in each group, all players should basically be the same size and same position. Follow these steps:

1. The drill begins with three players on the court and one player sitting out. Those players participating first surround the basket as the coach throws the ball against the backboard.

2. As the ball ricochets off the board, all three players fight for the offensive rebound and a put-back shot.

3. After a shot is made, the ball is passed back to the coach, who tosses the ball against the backboard again as the drill continues. The first player to score three baskets wins. The winner steps off the court, and the fourth player steps in.

Players should perform three or four rounds of this drill before moving on to the next station.

DECISION MAKING

Basketball players with the right mental fundamentals come to the team with a positive attitude. They are eager to participate and willing to work unselfishly. They agree to support team rules and policies, accept the challenge to improve, and compete in a sporting manner. As for the game itself, no one is perfect, so players must commit to their best effort and welcome constructive criticism. Coaches analyze players' assets and put them in situations where they can succeed. The fewer mistakes a player makes, the greater the playing opportunities become. Players comprehend the game at different levels, and when talent exceeds understanding, the coach must be assertive.

Whether a player makes the right decision is a key consideration when determining a player's basketball IQ. What constitutes making a good decision? For basketball teams, it means doing the right thing at the right time. Coaches need to demand strict discipline, concentration, and focus, which should help the team make fewer mistakes. This concept is not complicated. But to accomplish it, the players must have a thorough understanding of the game; know when to dribble, pass, shoot, or hold the ball; and realize that defense must be fundamentally sound when their opponents have the ball.

A concerted effort by coaches and players is needed to make changes in areas where decision making is a liability. Poor decisions hurt the team in a whole laundry list of areas. These include, but are not limited to, such mental lapses as not getting the ball inbounds within five seconds, being in the lane for three seconds, stepping in too early on free throws, committing technical fouls, jumping too soon on a jump-ball situation, or failing to get the ball across midcourt within the proper time. Other ill-advised acts that hurt the team are game mistakes such as committing charging fouls, making careless passes, overdribbling or dribbling into traps, forcing shots, failing to box out, fouling the jump shooter, permitting coast-to-coast layups, fouling in the backcourt, or gambling at the wrong time.

On the flip side of the coin, success-oriented players don't just beat you in one way; they beat you in many ways. They will do whatever it takes. Smart players get the rebound, block the key shot, dive for the loose ball, and make the big defensive stop. They make the right play at the right time.

The question then becomes whether you can teach players to make good decisions. Coaches can, for example, help players by providing learning situations through drills that put them in decision-making situations. So, yes, coaches can help players improve their basketball IQ if the players pay attention and absorb what they're taught. But if they don't have the natural instincts, lack peripheral awareness, and fail to understand the concept of unselfishness, chances are slim that they will make consistently good basketball decisions.

The individual offensive skills discussed in this chapter—including the athletic tools of speed, good hands, and jumping; the fundamentals of shooting, passing, dribbling, pivoting, screening, and rebounding; and good decision making—are essential for total player development. Players can do only four things with a basketball—dribble it, pass it, shoot it, or hold it. The offensive skills explained here provide players with the knowledge and ability to execute each of those actions.

CHAPTER **5**

Offensive Priorities

The ability of players to perform at a high level is determined by their physical talent, conditioning level, amount and type of practice they've had, competitive experience, focus, and effort. Structuring an offense that takes advantage of the overall talents of the players is not an exact science, but rather a trial-and-error exercise. Of course, players must assume responsibility for working hard on their skills, but the coach is responsible for blending the talents of individual players into a cohesive offense.

IDENTIFYING STRENGTHS AND IMPROVING WEAKNESSES

Talented basketball players have unique skills that provide a basis for a successful offense. Players need to understand their strengths so that they can accentuate them, but they must also recognize their weaknesses so that they can refrain from trying to do things that they don't do well. This is another way of saying that players must play within themselves. Players must take ownership of their own progress. Only by working on their offensive skills can they make significant improvement.

Young players from grade school all the way through college need to have a clear understanding of the basketball fundamentals and ways in which they can improve their offensive skills. Players need to know which drills will help them most and then work tirelessly on them. Playing pickup games without knowing the skills that they need to work on most—for example, passing, rebounding, pivoting, and decision making—probably will not result in success.

One of the greatest endorsements for working on the fundamentals of the game came from the great player Magic Johnson. When he left Michigan State after helping the Spartans win a national championship and joined the NBA, he knew that he had to improve certain aspects of his game. For example, instead of dribbling while facing defenders, Magic became an expert at turning his back to his defender and backing him down to a spot on the court where he could take advantage of his 6-foot-8-inch (203 cm) height, his immense strength, and his ability to score inside or pass to an open teammate.

FIVE FUNDAMENTAL TIPS THAT ALL PLAYERS NEED TO KNOW

Following are five tips that all players need to know concerning the fundamentals:

1. You should work year round to develop your fundamental skills. The off-season is a good time for individual improvement, and dedicated players take advantage of it. Recognize that the people whom you will compete with for playing time are probably working hard; your mind-set should be to work harder than they do. Find a game against the best competition available and then play hard and smart. It's amazing how much young players can improve over the course of one summer if they work at it the correct way.

2. Make sure that you're in top physical condition by the time team tryouts begin. Don't depend on someone else to get you in the best shape possible. It's up to you to be ready for the opening whistle.

3. Few things are more important to winning basketball than good shot selection. Learn what a good shot is and then exercise good judgment. An excellent definition of a good shot is

   a. a made goal,

   b. a shot on which you get fouled, and

   c. an open shot within range, skill, and time.

4. One of the biggest issues on offense at all levels of competition is finishing at the basket. This point applies to layups and offensive put-backs. Make sure that you focus and, most important, see the ball go into the basket. Don't let anything distract you.

5. Keep in mind that a free throw is exactly that—an unguarded 15-foot (4.5 m) shot. As a player, set high goals for your accuracy from the line. Achieving this goal will take concentration, proper shooting form, and hours of practice, and you should master the art of making free throws under pressure if you want to be part of the endgame. Look at these exceptional pro guards, and you can see why coaches love them: J.J. Redick, 99.5 percent free-throw shooting; Jamal Crawford, 94.4 percent; Anthony Morrow, 94.2 percent; Ray Allen, 90.5 percent; Kevin Martin, 90.1 percent; Steve Nash, 87.2 percent; and the NBA's 2011 MVP, leading all the big men, Dirk Nowitzki, 90.0 percent.

As he worked to perfect his dribbling and passing skills, Magic also expanded other phases of his game, such as his outside shooting, which he worked on diligently in the off-season. Johnson, one of the game's greatest players, explained that he picked one fundamental each summer and concentrated on improving that particular area of his game; he said that all players should do the same.

Coaches at all levels of competition should play a leading role in helping players identify and accept their strengths and weaknesses. The player and coach can then work together to develop a plan that can help the player improve his game to become more valuable to the team and ultimately to himself. When this plan is in place, refer to the drills specific to the player's weaknesses in chapter 4.

FITTING INTO AN OFFENSIVE SYSTEM

Besides identifying their own strengths and weaknesses, players need to know how they'll fit into the offensive team concept. Each player brings something different to the offense. Some are scorers, others excel at assists, and some are excellent rebounders and shot blockers. Players need to understand that they are evaluated not only on their physical abilities but also on their mental awareness, which includes both their understanding of how winning basketball is played and their attitude. They must realize that they have to take ownership of these two important elements.

Players' understanding and acceptance of how, when, and where they fit into a particular offensive situation plays a major role in their success. For example, Chris Paul has excellent talent, competitive skills, and the all-important mental acumen to use them in a fashion that best benefits himself and his team. He has been an excellent point guard in the NBA, and when it was evident that the New Orleans Hornets were willing to trade him, many vied for his skill and talents. Eventually, he was traded to the Los Angeles Clippers, who have been a perennial loser. In 2011 the Clippers were 13th in the Western Conference with a record of 32-50. But with the arrival of Paul and his outstanding point guard skills in 2012, the Clippers had a much stronger year, ending the regular season with a 40-26 record. For the 2011-2012 regular season, Paul averaged 19.8 points per game, with a 47.8 field goal percentage, an 86.1 free-throw percentage, and averaged 9.1 assists per game. The Clippers made it to the NBA playoffs for the first time since 2006, beating Memphis 4-3 in the first round and losing to the San Antonio Spurs 0-4 in the second round. The reason for this is that their new point guard understood his role on his new team, turning the Clippers around with his passing and shooting skills, as well as his leadership qualities.

Like Paul, all players need to understand their strengths and the contribution that they can make to winning. After all, coaches are looking for winners. Not everyone is a scorer, a tenacious rebounder, or a great passer, but most players excel in one phase of the game. As a player, you have many options. Find the one or two things that you do better than anyone else on the team and let those become your contribution to winning. Make your skills stand out to the point that they cannot be ignored. The coach will notice, believe me.

DESIGNING AN OFFENSIVE SYSTEM

Building a winning team involves blending the available talent in the best way possible. The coach sees a group of athletes—all with various skills—and then blends those skills to form the best offense possible.

RAYMOND FELTON

Leadership is important to all successful teams. Football requires a quarterback, baseball must have pitchers, and basketball depends on the player with point-guard skills.

Raymond Felton was the point guard for the Charlotte Bobcats from 2005 through 2010, and when the team didn't renew his contract he signed with the New York Knicks. Raymond took many assets to his new team. When the Bobcats failed to re-sign him, they lost a real competitor and their team leader. Felton is mentally tough, extremely coachable, and able to serve as a coach on the floor by knowing and carrying out the coach's game plan. He knows who the shooters are and gets them the ball at the right time in the right spot. Felton had 17 assists in one of the Knicks' wins. He was an unselfish leader for Charlotte and was the same for the Knicks—a great team player all the way. Felton was later traded to the Denver Nuggets and now plays for the Portland Trailblazers.

Being a leader and coach on the floor, similar to Felton, is another way for a player to fit into the offensive team concept.

Let's look at three different offensive schemes and see where your players best fit in. In each offensive set we will emphasize a different position-specific skill set. Both the coach and the players need to understand how they will contribute and fit into the following overall offensive schemes. The team, the coach, and the players will all benefit by recognizing how the parts come together and the role that each person plays, regardless of whether it's a guard-, forward-, or center-oriented offensive strategy based on the talent available.

The following three specific offensive sets will directly affect your coaching philosophy. We will look at each offensive set in terms of its setup, procedure, and advantages.

Guard-Oriented Attack

When a coach has a team in which the best ball handlers, shooters, and decision makers are all guards, then a guard-oriented offense is the best plan. The 2012 Golden State Warriors present a perfect example.

Two very young guards, Monte Ellis and Stephen Curry, carried the load for the Warriors until Ellis was traded and Curry was injured. Ellis averaged 21.9 points per game while hitting 43 percent of his two-point field goal attempts, 36 percent of his three-point shots, and 81 percent of his free throws. Curry averages 14.7 points per game but shoots better than Ellis does. He is hitting 49 percent of his two-point field goal tries, 43 percent of his three-pointers, and a sizzling 90 percent of his free throws. Both are excellent shooters, ball handlers, and creative passers. Teams that depend solely on their guards seldom win big, but excellent guard play can keep a team in games and occasionally allow them to upset a team with better overall talent.

GUARD-ORIENTED ATTACK

Setup

This set begins in a balanced format with the two guards (O1 and O2) above the three-point line approximately 20 feet (6 m) apart. Two forwards (O3 and O4) should set up at the free-throw line extended and about 3 feet (1 m) inside the sideline. The center (O5) should be at the high post a couple of feet (a meter or so) above the free-throw line. The objective of this set is for one of the guards to get a good shot, dribble-drive attack, pick-and-roll, draw-and-kick, or pass to a forward on a post-up.

Procedure

1. The guard with the ball (O1) passes to the strong-side forward (O3), steps away to the middle, and, when even with the defender, pivots hard off the left foot, making a strong inside shoulder V-cut to the basket. (If O1 is on the left side of the floor, he plants the right foot and makes the inside shoulder V-cut to the basket.)

2. If O1 is open, O3 makes an inside return pass for a layup or a personal foul (figure 5.1). If O1 is not open, he stops at the ball-side block.

3. On the initial pass, the opposite guard (O2) dives straight to the weak-side block.

4. Next, the forward with the ball, O3, looks guard O1 through (watches O1 as O1 cuts to the basket) as the center, O5, fakes a basket cut, reverse pivots, and sprints to the top of the key.

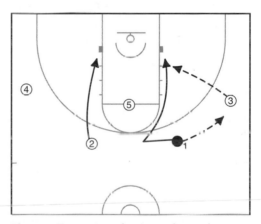

Figure 5.1 Guard-oriented attack: Set up the defender.

5. O5, now at top of key in the middle of the court, receives a pass from O3.

6. Following O3's pass, immediate down screens are set on both sides for the guards, O1 and O2, coming off the blocks (figure 5.2). Guards must let the down screeners, O3 and O4, come to complete, legal stops before working off their screens. This action permits the guards to work off the proper angle.

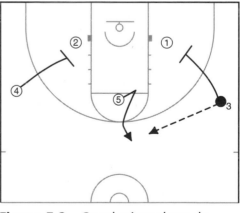

Figure 5.2 Guard-oriented attack: Set screens.

(continued)

Guard-Oriented Attack *(continued)*

7. If a medium jump shot is the goal, the screens will be set deep, but if the screens are for a three-point field goal, the screens will be set farther out on the court. The shot will be determined by the players' skill, the coach's desire, and the team's ability to execute.

8. O5 has the option to dribble handoff or pass to either guard O1 or O2 (figure 5.3) and then screen away or run a pick-and-roll.

9. The pick-and-roll can be set for both middle and baseline drives. If the screen is sideline for a middle drive,

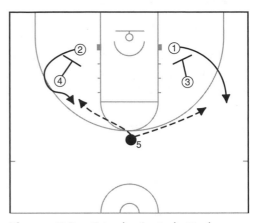

Figure 5.3   Guard-oriented attack: Read the play.

O5 pops to the corner. If the screen is on the baseline side, the center pops toward the free-throw line on the same side of the court.

Multiple Screens

In this setup, the guards, O1 and O2, are on opposite blocks, and either a call or a read can produce a cross screen in preparation for the down screens by the forwards (wing players).

1. If the cross screen is called, the ball-side guard, O1, takes two steps into the free-throw lane and sets the screen. The opposite guard, O2, works off the cross screen first and then the down screen by forward O3. The point guard, O1, who initiated the play, sets the screen and then works off O4's down screen (figure 5.4).

2. Forwards who screened down, O3 and O4, now have the option to post up or screen across and post up. O2, who now has the ball from a pass by the center, O5, looks for the shot, drive, or post feed.

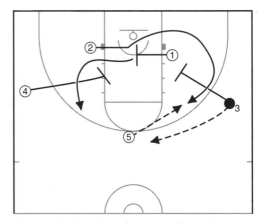

Figure 5.4   Guard-oriented attack: multiple screens.

In this particular set, other options are also possible, including a dribble drive to create a foul and baseline screens for medium and three-point shots.

Advantages of the Guard-Oriented Attack

This guard-oriented offense is a great set for creative guards and does not depend on any one skill. Flexibility is built in for three-point shots, catch-and-shoot short jumpers, the dribble-drive attack, pick-and-rolls, and a two-player game with the post-up forward (wing player). Coaches can run this set knowing that the ballhandling, shooting, and decision making will ultimately be in the hands of the guards.

Forward-Oriented Attack

Identifying the dominant point guards and centers on NBA teams is easy. Forwards, or wing players, can dominate as well, but the best ones like, Kobe Bryant, Dirk Nowitzki, LeBron James, and Dwayne Wade, usually play multiple positions and take advantage of mismatches. Therefore, discerning when a forward-oriented attack may work for your team is sometimes more difficult.

After you have determined that your forwards are your most versatile players, the offense must be designed to take advantage of their skills. When it's obvious that the scoring must come from your forwards, everyone must work to get them open for good shots. Player movement with team and individual screens is important in doing this. The objective of this set is to take advantage of superior forward play by getting them open looks at perimeter shots, dribble-drive opportunities, layups, post-ups, and good three-point spot-up shots.

FORWARD-ORIENTED ATTACK

Setup

In this particular play, the coach focuses on a balanced offensive set. Two guards, O1 and O2, are above the three-point line, approximately 20 feet (6 m) apart; two forwards, O3 and O4, are at the free-throw line extended; and the center, O5, is at the high post. The play can go to either side depending on the ability of the guards to manipulate their dribble.

Procedure

1. The forward on the strong side, O3, must get open above the center, O5, and closer to midcourt for the first pass. After making the pass, guard O1 makes a hard two-step drive toward the basket and then immediately goes behind O3 for a quick outside handoff return.

2. O5 moves to the strong-side elbow, preparing to set a screen for O3.

3. O3 must take the opponent higher out on the court toward midcourt to get the opponent above O5 so that he can use the center player's screen to rub the defender off on a basket cut.

(continued)

Forward-Oriented Attack *(continued)*

4. O3 has the option of a buttonhook by going beyond and around O5, turning quickly, and ducking back toward O1 or an inside dive cut to the block (figure 5.5). If O3 gets his head and shoulders in front of the defender on the basket cut, O1 should deliver the pass for a layup or foul.

5. If a pass is not made to O3 on the initial basket cut, the play continues.

6. After clearing the center area without getting a pass from O1, O3 immediately posts up strong.

7. If open, O1 passes to O3 on the post-up and runs a split action with the second guard, O2, who has rotated to the top of the key (figure 5.6).

8. After setting a stationary screen for the strong-side forward, O3, on his dive to the block, when there is no pass to O3 on a post up, O5 turns and sets the staggered double screen with O2 on the opposite forward, O4, who flashes to the top of the key (figure 5.7).

9. The strong-side guard with the ball, O1, looks deep first and, if O3 is not open, passes to the weak-side wing, O4, who is looking for the pass and a shot.

10. After passing to O4 at the top of the key, O1 slides to the corner to clear the floor and give O4 room to operate.

11. O3's next option is to run the baseline and use the same staggered double screen set by O2 and O5 to get open on the weak side.

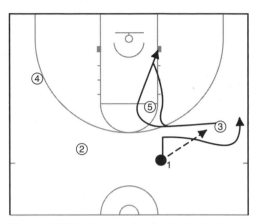

Figure 5.5 Forward-oriented attack: Use center's screen.

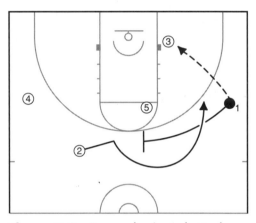

Figure 5.6 Forward-oriented attack: Run split action.

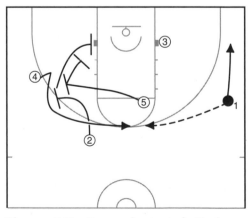

Figure 5.7 Forward-oriented attack: Set staggered double screens.

12. O2 sets the first screen just outside the free-throw lane, turns and clears straight to the far corner. O5 sets the second screen about 6 feet (2 m) behind O2's screen for O3. This action permits O3 to either curl for a short jumper or fade for a three-pointer (figure 5.8).

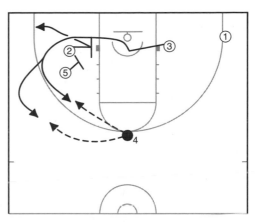

Figure 5.8 Forward-oriented attack: Make the move.

Advantages of the Forward-Oriented Attack

This offensive set is designed to take advantage of a situation in which the team's best players are forwards; it is geared for them. This set of maneuvers depends on reading, timing, taking proper angles when making basket cuts, and setting legal screens. If players are able to make good decisions about when to pass and when to shoot off post-ups, face-up jumpers, top-of-the-key dribble drives, or three-point field-goal attempts when coming off the staggered double screen, this set can be successful for a team with strong forwards.

Low-Post-Oriented Attack

A good low-post attack is the best of all three offensive strategies. The L.A. Lakers' return to the top of the NBA is a great illustration of this concept. The Lakers had last won the NBA title in 2001–2002, going six straight years without winning the championship. Everything changed in 2007–2008 when they picked up big man Pau Gasol from the Grizzlies. Gasol is highly skilled; extremely intelligent; and an excellent shooter, passer, and decision maker. He was the missing piece of the puzzle that the Lakers needed to play for championships again. They won two straight titles in 2008–2009 and 2009–2010. In 2008–2009, Gasol's statistics were 18.9 points, 9.6 rebounds, and 3.5 assists per game, and in 2009–2010, he had 18.3 points, 11.3 rebounds, and 3.4 assists per game. His production and all-around stellar play helped put the Lakers back on top.

When you have a strong center, you should have an inside-out offensive philosophy. The team needs to be able to deliver the ball to the low post when the center has balance and position. For a low-post offense to work effectively, a team must have good passers, and they must be able to read defenses and know when to cut through, hold (stay put), or move to an open spot. Teammates also need to be active and alert to counteract double teams, because crowding the big player will restrict his moves.

Big players must learn how to establish position with a balanced and wide base. The feet need to be wider than the shoulders, and the knees must be bent in a crouched position when necessary to maneuver. They must give their passer a good target by having arms and elbows up, always adjusting to get open while waiting for the ball to be delivered.

After receiving the ball and before making the move, the post immediately identifies where defensive help is coming from. Only when that has been determined does the player make a decision. He could pass to a feeder or cutter, pass out to a stationary spot-up shooter whose defender doubles down, or pass to a weak-side cutter whose defender has momentarily lost visual contact with him. Or, at this point, the center might choose to face up and look for a short jumper, a hook shot, a show-and-go (in which the ball handler shows the ball as if to shoot, fakes the shot, and, when the defender jumps, goes to the basket), or a quick attack to the basket.

POWER DOWN ATTACK

Setup

Having a good center and knowing how to get the ball inside are two entirely different things. Depending on your players' passing skills, many good entry pass methods can be used to get the ball inside. Rather than start the low post on the block and make a direct pass inside where the defense can immediately double-team the center, player movement should first occur both inside and out, and the center should proceed to a spot where a pass inside becomes less dangerous and where the low-post play can be most effective.

To teach low-post play, we begin in a high double post, or what is commonly called a 1-4 box set. The 1-4 techniques must be taught and practiced daily. Forward O4 and the center, O5, set up at the free-throw line high on the elbows. Guard O2 and forward O3 are on the low blocks, and guard O1 is above the circle in the middle of the floor ready to begin the play set. After the guard determines a side, the play begins.

The more play sets that a team can execute, the better prepared they will be. Showing various looks with a 1-4 set and then changing at time-outs to a screen-the-screener alignment can provide an effective means for keeping the opponent off balance. The offensive set can change, but keeping the passers, shooters, and low-post point producer in their most effective and advantageous positions is the goal.

Procedure

1. The point guard, O1, dribbles to the same side as the center, O5, free-throw line extended, while keeping the dribble alive.

2. O5 turns strong side and sets a down screen for guard O2 on the low block, and O2 moves to the top of the key (figure 5.9). After O2 clears O5, O5 immediately executes a reverse pivot and posts up, spreading the legs for balance and showing a big target while looking for the pass.

3. At this point O1 must make the decision whether to pass inside to O5 or pass to O2 at the top of the key.

4. If the pass is made to O5, O1 sets a split-action screen (one player passes to another and immediately screens another teammate's defender) for O2, who becomes an outlet in case there is a double team on O5 (figure 5.10).

5. When the pass to O5 is made, the post decides whether to make a move, but if O5 does not have a shot, he passes to O2, and the play continues.

6. The requirement now is for quick passes around the horn. After O5 outlets the ball to O2, O2 quickly passes to O1, who has relocated to the top of the key off the split-action screen, and O1 rotates the ball to forward O4 at the free-throw line extended.

7. Forward O3 on the left block pops toward the corner as O4 delivers the ball to him (figure 5.11). O4 then screens away for O1, who seeks the ball.

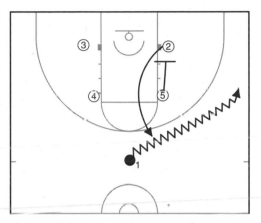

Figure 5.9 Power down attack: Set down screen.

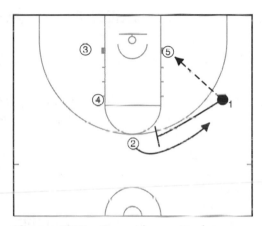

Figure 5.10 Power down attack: Set split-action screen.

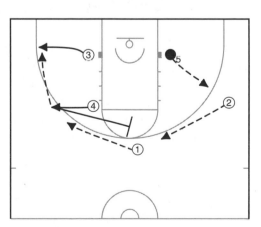

Figure 5.11 Power down attack: Make quick passes.

(continued)

Power Down Attack *(continued)*

8. When O5 sees O2 pass the ball to O1, O5 follows the ball across the lane and establishes a strong post-up position.

9. After the floor is properly spaced and balanced, O3 should be able to get the ball into O5, where he can make a move (figure 5.12).

10. For continuity, if O3 cannot get the ball to O5, the next option is to pass to O1 coming off O4's screen. O1 then looks for the dribble drive or a good shot.

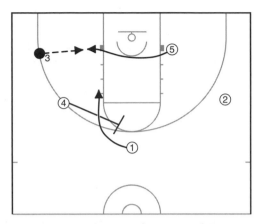

Figure 5.12 Power down attack: Follow the ball.

Advantages of the Power Down Attack

The power down attack is purposely designed to take advantage of an outstanding big player. To run this set effectively, the team needs proper spacing, good ball movement, willing passers, and the patience to do it right. The coach wants to get the low-post player in a one-on-one situation and at the same time build in options, as we've done, to keep the ball moving and the defenders occupied. Kareem Abdul-Jabbar, the NBA's all-time leading scorer, was perfect for this offensive set.

Another advantage of the power down attack is that players can execute it at the junior high, high school, and college levels; it is not complicated or difficult.

POWER CROSS ATTACK

Setup

Getting the ball to a low-post player may take longer because of two major factors. First, rather than making a direct pass to the center, the player will more likely have to make an indirect pass, taking a circuitous route with three or four passes. Second, defenses will come to recognize the patterns, so screens, passes, and decoy moves must be made with precision.

After spreading the floor with the power down attack, the power cross set can be used. It starts within the free-throw box and depends on cross screens and down screens. This set realigns player positions. The forwards, O4 on the left side and O3 on the right side, are opposite each other on the blocks. The center, O5, sets up a little above the free-throw line, guard O2 takes the position on the left-side free-throw line extended, and guard O1, with the ball, lines up above the top of the key in the middle of the court.

Procedure

1. As guard O1 dribbles to the free-throw line extended on the right side, guard O2 remains set up at the free-throw line extended on the left side. Meanwhile, forward O3 sets a cross screen for forward O4, who then moves to the low post on the right side.

2. As soon as O4 uses O3's screen, the center, O5, screens the screener and O3 pops to the top of the key, close to the free-throw line if possible (figure 5.13). O5 immediately posts up strong on the left block.

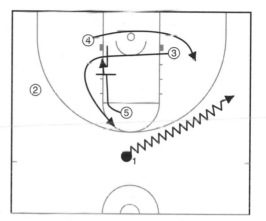

Figure 5.13 Power cross attack: Screen the screener.

3. While this screen-the-screener technique is taking place, O1 surveys the situation. O1 has two basic options: pass to O4 on the right block or pass to O3 at the top of the key.

4. When O1 passes to O3, the ball is quickly passed to O2 on the weakside left wing. O2 makes the play possible with a good pass into the low post, where O5 should be in a good low-post position (figure 5.14).

5. After the pass to O5 is completed, the offensive players can do a number of things to keep the defense occupied.

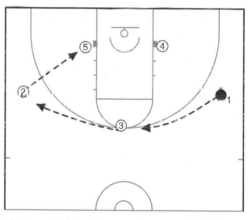

Figure 5.14 Power cross attack: Make indirect post-up.

6. After O2 inserts the ball to O5, O2 runs a split-action screen with O3. As this is taking place, O4 moves in behind O2 and sets a back screen on O2's defender (figure 5.15). This is another screen-the-screener action as O5 keeps an eye on O2, who is diving to the basket.

(continued)

Power Cross Attack *(continued)*

7. At this moment, O5 is in complete control of the offense and has the following options: first, O2 on the dive; second, an opportunity for a one-on-one low-post move; and third, a pass to forward O3, who has rotated to the free-throw line extended for a jump shot.

8. The peripheral players must keep the defenders occupied and away from O5 when and if O5 decides to make a move.

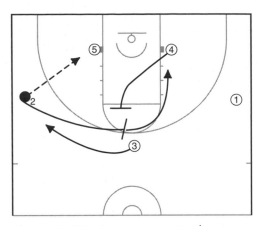

Figure 5.15 Power cross attack: Keep the defense busy.

Advantages of the Power Cross Attack

To be successful, a post player must have the proper skill set. In addition, having a coach who understands how to get the ball inside to the low post is invaluable. For the power down attack to be its most successful, teammates must understand floor balance, spacing, passing angles, and spot-up positions for kick-outs when double teams take place.

MAKING FREE THROWS

Some may look on free-throw shooting as an easily taught fundamental. But teaching the correct technique for free-throw shooting is anything but easy and must be addressed as an everyday challenge. The crucial point is to establish a uniform, consistent attitude toward that one shot that is open and uncontested—the unguarded free throw. The very act of shooting an unguarded free throw places the entire focus of the game on that single event. The shooter has no place to hide; players are completely exposed and must deal with the physical, emotional, and confidence-related factors present.

Free-throw shooting is one of the most important strategic points that coaches can convey to their players. Developing and teaching the appropriate method is a test for every coach, and everyone has a favorite procedure. I found that three things must occur for a player to improve and progress when working on free throws:

1. All players must display proper shooting mechanics with balance, grip, aim, release, and follow-through.
2. Players must concentrate.
3. Players must learn to overcome pressure.

The first two factors, mechanics and concentration, are relatively easy compared with the third, pressure. Several coaches I observed left it up to the players to practice on their own, others kept daily charts on hits and misses, and still others played games in practice to simulate pressure.

It has often been said that if you want to play—whether on your middle school, high school, college, or professional team—you need to be a good free-throw shooter. Every coach should know the importance of having good free-throw shooters in close games; the coach must know the players and which ones are dependable. Some players can hit free throws in the first half or when they are up 20 points with a minute to play, but the question is whether they can hit under pressure. Players can bring many important skills to their team, and when the scored is tied with three minutes to go, being a good free-throw shooter ranks right at the top.

Even Dr. James Naismith, the inventor of basketball, must have thought that the free throw was important because originally he assigned 3 points as the value of each made free throw. In addition, it was originally a 20-foot (6 m) shot instead of the 15 feet (4.5 m) that we use today. The past two years of the NCAA tournament, 2010 and 2011, reveal the value of this free and unguarded 15-foot shot. Statistics show that good teams fell by the wayside because of their inability to hit those free and open shots. Table 5.1 reflects those results.

No one is exempt from having a poor night at the free-throw line, and when it comes, it appears to be contagious. Take, for instance, the University of Kentucky's game against West Virginia in the 2010 NCAA tournament. Kentucky lost their biggest game of the year by 7, 73-66, while hitting only 55 percent of their free throws. UK missed 13 free throws, hitting just 16 of 29, as their starting guard combo went 5 for 14, missing 9 free throws. The Wildcats followed this up in 2011 with a disappointing 4 of 12 from the free-throw line in losing to Connecticut by 1 point.

Even when having an off night, though, a team that has more opportunities at the line has more opportunities to score. As a young coach I attended basketball clinics and listened to the theories of great coaches like John Wooden, Adolph Rupp, and Dean Smith. When asked about his offensive philosophy, Coach Smith said that he wanted to accomplish three things:

1. Score
2. Get fouled and score
3. Get a good shot

He said if he had to choose among the three, he would prefer to get fouled while scoring.

Scoring the basket and getting a free throw usually comes from a jump shot, a drive to the basket, a post-up, or an offensive put-back. The concept of getting fouled is the reason that many coaches subscribe to the inside-out strategy (meaning that before they shoot an outside jumper, they get the ball inside on the block; then, after they get the ball inside and have no scoring opportunity, they pass it back outside). Table 5.2 shows some teams from the 2009–2010 season that profited greatly by getting to the free-throw line. Look at their free-throw attempts, their free-throw percentages, and their win-loss records; these are definitely inside-out teams.

Table 5.1 Free Throws in Postseason Play, 2010 and 2011

NCAA YEAR 2011			
Team	**Lost by**	**Free throws missed**	**Free throws made and attempted by team**
Louisville	1	9	7-16
Kentucky	1	8	4-12
Pittsburgh	1	6	12-18
Texas	1	4	18-22
ODU	2	6	21-27
Vanderbilt	3	9	14-23
UCLA	8	9	16-25
NCAA YEAR 2010			
Team	**Lost by**	**Free throws missed**	**Free throws made and attempted by team**
Texas	1	13	20-33
Vanderbilt	1	12	17-29
South Florida (National Invitation Tournament, home game)	1	10	21-31
New Mexico St.	3	9	13-22
Texas A&M	2	7	10-17
Pittsburgh	3	7	11-18
Wofford	4	7	6-13
Murray State	2	7	5-12
Kansas	2	5	13-18
Kentucky	7	13	16-29

Table 5.2 Correlation of Free Throws to Team Wins During the 2009-2010 Season

Team	Record	Made	Attempted	Free-throw percentage
Kansas State	29-8	668	1,005	66.4
Morgan State	27-10	667	963	69.2
Vermont	25-10	634	920	68.9
North Texas State	22-9	639	890	71.7
Seattle	17-14	563	872	64.5
Tulsa	22-12	606	858	70.6
Washington	26-10	622	855	72.7
Detroit	19-14	556	849	65.4
Oakland (Michigan)	24-9	606	844	71.8
Texas	24-10	536	845	63.4
Kansas	33-3	591	843	70.1
Kentucky	33-3	572	841	68.0
Vanderbilt	23-9	572	826	69.2
Wofford	25-9	547	817	66.9
Butler	32-4	573	766	74.8
Duke	33-5	568	748	75.9

SIX-BASKET FREE THROWS

Focus

Add a little incentive to hitting those important free throws.

Procedure

This drill can be used in high schools and colleges where there are six baskets around the court.

1. Split the squad into groups of two and three players and instruct them that each player must make 5 or 10 consecutive shots before moving to the next basket.

2. Each player shoots until he misses; if the shooter doesn't miss, he rotates to the next basket. A miss puts the player at the back of the line.

Assistant coaches are assigned baskets to rebound and oversee the process. Reward players for success—perhaps getting to leave practice early—and penalize them for failure—such as having to stay late and complete the cycle. Coaches must be careful when setting a number to make because one or two poor shooters can have problems making even five free throws in a row.

TWO-BASKET FREE THROWS

Focus

Create pressure that helps players concentrate on making free throws.

Procedure

When a coaching staff has to work with only two baskets, as is usually the case with game-day practice or shoot-arounds, a few different free-throw games can be used.

1. As an alternative to Six-Basket Free Throws, use both ends of the court and split the team into two groups—good shooters and not-so-good shooters—keeping each group at one end of the court. Each player shoots until a miss and then rotates to the end of the line. This method gives the coach the latitude to assign different designated goals. Each player must make 5 or 10 consecutive shots.

2. This drill focuses entirely on individual players. Line up all the players on either side of the free-throw lane and have them all make one with no misses and then make two with no misses.

3. Divide the team into two groups. Put the first team at one basket and the second team at the opposite end. Players then have to make one, followed by two, and then three free throws—all in a row. The reward and punishment in this case is bragging rights reflected in who wins.

USING THE THREE-POINT SHOT

One of the most interesting offensive trends that has seemed to have a significant effect on playing and coaching basketball in the 2009–2010 and 2010–2011 seasons is the number of three-point shots attempted. The three-point shot was implemented in 1987, and only 9.2 three-point shots were taken per game that year. Teams added one additional shot for each of the next seven years, reaching 16.3 attempts per game in 1994.

When the shot was first introduced to college basketball, two highly successful college coaches—Terry Holland and Denny Crum—vowed that their teams would not shoot three-pointers. Of course, they changed their philosophy as the three-point shot became increasingly prominent.

An average of 17 three-point shots per game became the standard for the next seven years until 2001. The three-point field-goal percentage remained basically the same at 34 percent until the jump to 18 shots per game became the norm, bringing us up to 2009. The only exception was in 2008, when teams launched 19 three-pointers per game to set a new attempt record. The number of individual games played (29.6 to 32.1) did not vary much, but 43 more teams attained Division I status. (There were 290 teams when the three-point shot came to college basketball in 1987, and this number rose to an all-time high of 330 Division I teams in 2009.)

Table 5.3 shows this year-by-year information, including the number of Division I teams, the yearly average of games played, and the three-point averages for attempts, makes, and field-goal percentage.

The 2010 NCAA tournament Elite 8 and Sweet 16 team statistics provide excellent information on the increasing use of the three-point shot (see table 5.4). All the records were rewritten, including three set by Cornell (see table 5.5): three-point field goal percentage, 42.9 percent; total three-point field goals made, 9.5; and three-point field goals attempted, 22. That same year, Butler and West Virginia took 20 three-point shots per game, and midmajor Eastern Kentucky averaged taking 24 three-point shots, making 10 per game. The Virginia Military Institute, which ran a rapid-fire offense much like Paul Westhead's Loyola of Marymount team, led the nation with an average of 35 three-point attempts per game and 11 makes. VMI also led all teams for single-game three-point shots by attempting 63, 49, and 44 on different occasions.

This comparison between the 2009–2010 season and the previous 22 years reflects a major shift in the emphasis placed on the three-point field goal. Although a new distance of 20 feet, 9 inches (6.3 m) was declared for the three-pointer during the 2008–2009 season, the number of three-point shots being launched doesn't seem to be declining. Teams are consistently averaging 18.0- to 19.0-point attempts per game and making them at an average of 34 percent while designing offenses that encourage a faster transition attack. Many teams push the ball down the sidelines looking for quick three-point shots. Instead of sprinting to the paint to find their opponent and begin defensive coverage, now even the big

Table 5.3 NCAA Division I Men's Basketball Three-Point Field-Goal Trends, 1987–2010

Year	Number of teams	Games	Three-point FG made	Three-point FG attempted	Three-point FG percentage
1987	290	29.6	3.5	9.2	38.0*
1988	290	29.6	4.0	10.4	38.4
1989	293	29.6	4.4	11.8	37.2
1990	292	29.6	4.7	12.8	36.7
1991	295	29.6	5.0	13.8	36.2
1992	298	29.5	5.0	14.0	35.7
1993	298	28.6	5.3	14.9	35.5
1994	301	28.7	5.7	16.5	34.5
1995	302	28.7	5.9	17.2	34.3
1996	305	28.7	5.8	17.1	34.1
1997	305	28.9	5.9	17.3	34.1
1998	306	30.2	5.9	17.3	34.1
1999	310	29.0	5.9	17.7	33.3
2000	318	29.9	6.1	17.7	34.4
2001	318	29.8	6.1	17.7	34.4
2002	321	30.1	6.3	18.2	34.6
2003	325	29.6	6.2	18.0	34.4
2004	326	29.6	6.3	18.2	34.6
2005	326	29.9	6.3	18.3	34.4
2006	326	30.0	6.4	18.4	34.7
2007	325	31.6	6.6	18.8	35.1
2008	328	31.9	6.7*	19.0*	35.2
2009	330*	32.1*	6.3	18.3	34.4
2010	334	32.2	6.2	18.2	34.3
2011	335	32.3	6.2	18.1	34.5

*Records up to the 2009–2010 season.

players, centers, and power forwards must move out on the court and cover their opponent. In addition, a belief in basketball is that long shots mean long rebounds, and teams on the move believe that their opportunity for getting an offensive rebound is much better when fast breaking than when running a half-court set. It will be interesting to see how many teams will adapt, adjust, and employ this innovative scoring method in the near future.

Table 5.4 2010 NCAA Three-Point Statistics, Sweet 16 Teams

Three-point field-goal shots based on field-goal percentage.

Team	Games	THREE-POINT SHOOTING		
		Three-point FG attempted	Three-point FG made	Three-point FG percentage
ELITE 8				
Duke	40	19	7.4	38.4
Baylor	36	18	7.0	38.5
Kansas State	37	19	6.8	35.9
Michigan State	37	14	5.0	34.4
Butler	38	20	6.8	34.1
West Virginia	38	20	6.7	33.7
Kentucky	36	18	6.0	33.1
Tennessee	37	18	5.9	32.0
SWEET 16				
Cornell	34	22	9.5	42.9
Ohio State	36	18	7.4	41.3
St. Mary's	34	20	8.3	40.6
Syracuse	35	17	6.9	39.1
Xavier	35	18	7.1	37.6
Washington	36	15	5.3	33.6
Purdue	35	16	5.3	31.8
Northern Iowa	30	19	5.8	29.9

Table 5.5 2010 NCAA New Three-Point Records

Name of record	Old record	New record	Team
Three-point FG made	6.7	9.5	Cornell
Three-point FG attempted	19	22	Cornell
Three-point FG percentage	38.4	42.9	Cornell

THREE-POINT SHOOTING

Focus

Improve three-point shooting with practice.

Procedure

The five key spots when practicing three-point shooting are both corners, both wings, and the top of the key. Split the team into three groups of four or five, depending on the size of the team. Follow these steps:

1. Two teams begin on one half of the court, while the third team warms up on the other half.
2. This drill is competitive. Each team selects one of the five three-point shooting spots. The goal is to make 5 (or 10) shots.
3. One ball is used per team. This puts pressure on making the shot, getting to the rebound quickly, and then making a good pass to the next player in line. Teams call out their makes.
4. The first team to make the required number of shots stays. The team that loses rotates out, and the third team rotates in.

MAKE 'EM TO MOVE

Focus

Accuracy when shooting threes.

Procedure

Divide the squad into three equal teams. This drill is conducted on the half court. Follow these steps:

1. To begin the drill, each team selects from one of five three-point shooting spots: both corners, both wings, and the top of the key.
2. This is a team effort, and the objective is for each player to hit one three-point shot before the team can rotate to another shooting spot.
3. One ball is used per team. Making the shot, rebounding (following the shot), and making a good pass to the next shooter is critical. Players are not allowed to touch the opponent's basketball.
4. When all players on a team have hit their shots, they immediately rotate to an open shooting spot and begin again. The first team to complete the five-spot shooting cycle wins.

Ask anyone who has ever coached what the most difficult thing is in basketball, and chances are they will say, "Manufacturing an offense." Why is this? Offense is all about finesse, and although some players appear to be born with this ability, most players must work hard at it, spending hours on offensive fundamentals. Knowing how to pass is one thing, but knowing when to pass is another. This same thing applies to understanding floor balance and how and when to set screens.

If you are currently on a team, you should meet with your coach and discuss your strengths and weaknesses. Obtain a good understanding of how you can, or will, fit into the team's offensive system. Then outline a program for improvement that you can work on in the off-season. Establish goals and chart your improvement. When you see an outstanding player perform, you can be sure that time, effort, and commitment are part of his work ethic.

CHAPTER 6

Team Offense

Many factors affect the choice of an offensive system, but the foremost aim is always to create an attack that gets maximum production from the players. Preferences as to how the game should be played develop early in a basketball career and can be shaped by unexpected influences. It could be something that you recall from your playing days on your junior high or high school team. Or it might be a style of play that you saw a favorite college or pro team adopt and use with much success. Such impressions do not provide a blueprint for implementing an offense, but they begin the formation of the architecture. And that's a good start.

Back when I was in school, one of my coaches decided that he wanted to use a 2-2-1 full-court zone press. He put the guards up at opposite elbows, two forwards at midcourt, and the center back at the free-throw line to protect the basket. His theory was this: When the pass came in from out of bounds to an offensive player, the guard defending that side of the court was supposed to push the ball handler toward the sideline midcourt and double-team the ball with the forward when the dribbler got to midcourt. He explained it by saying, "Give the ball handler one step on you and then trap him at midcourt."

But there was a problem. Implementing the scheme was physically impossible. If the offensive guard was given one step, there was no way to trap him at midcourt. In this situation, driving a player toward a teammate occurred when we played tough defense and forced the opponent toward the midcourt trap area, rather than when we gave him a one-step advantage. In this situation we learned in spite of the instruction.

As with the 2-2-1 full-court press, coaches learn and adapt their approach by trial and error. Many things are gained from observation, common sense, and practical application. What I came to label the LA offense evolved from both the insights obtained from the work of three of the game's all-time great coaches and a lot of hard knocks from testing what would work and what would not.

During a coaching career that spanned 50 years, I had many opportunities to learn new approaches and philosophies, but the most effective were clinics in which game films were studied and discussed from all angles. A sort of coaching heaven came during the NCAA Final Four, when coaches from all over the country gathered to discuss their sport and talk basketball. Distinguished coaches with sparkling resumes shared their philosophies and concepts. Three of them had a particularly strong influence on my philosophy: UCLA's John Wooden, North Carolina's Dean Smith, and Kentucky's Adolph Rupp.

Of course, Rupp, Wooden, and Smith greatly influenced basketball strategies and the way that the game was played, but more important was the influence that these coaches had in terms of their respect for the game and their integrity in dealing with players. They never embarrassed players in public as many coaches do today, and they maintained a calm, controlled countenance throughout the game. These three coaches epitomized the behavior that should be reflected by a coach, particularly those who coach at an educational institution.

LA OFFENSE

The LA, or all-purpose offense, is a combination of some of the best plays in basketball. The offense requires guards who can handle the ball, attack the basket, pass to designated shooters, and make good decisions. Forwards must set good screens, hit the perimeter jump shot, pass to moving targets, and maintain half-court balance with proper spacing. The center plays both the low post, with his back to the basket, and the high post, facing the basket to have both passing and shooting opportunities.

My idea in developing this offense was first to take a specific concept from one coach: the outstanding guard play of Coach Rupp's Kentucky team—their floor balance, their ability to push the ball, and their knack for making quick, hard basket cuts. I then wanted to take a proven fundamental concept from another coach: John Wooden at UCLA was famous for getting the ball to the low post. His was the first team I remember that used the center to pass to the weak-side low post on a step-in power move. His idea that each pass dictated a different play set is a major component of the LA offense. Finally, I wanted to take a strategy from another successful coach and was attracted early on to Coach Dean Smith's style of play and his four-corners offensive control pattern. The more I watched his teams play, the more I appreciated his game management and team approach.

The LA offense is a continuity pattern that combines three major sets in one. Each pass—guard to forward, guard to center, or guard to guard—calls for an entirely different attack. This offensive set is designed to attack pressure in a fluid manner. When entering the frontcourt, the guard can move away from pressure with any of three passes. The LA set is also an excellent pattern from which to attack zone defenses. Rather than calling a specific zone attack, the LA guard-to-forward pass provides enough ball and player movement to detect whether the offense is attacking a zone or a man-to-man. This point is really important when playing a team with changing defenses.

A unique feature of the LA guard-to-forward pass is that as the play develops all five players have a chance to touch the ball and possibly score. The object of an offense is to get a good shot. Some coaches like to dribble, pass, and cut for 30 seconds before even looking at the basket. In most instances that is what you get running the flex, motion, and various control patterns. Contrary to this kind of system is the popular one-and-done mentality. Rather that get trapped into either of these systems—ball control or no control—a coach can choose a happy medium that emphasizes making good decisions and running a play that permits and encourages the team to take the first *good* shot available. With the multiple options built into the LA offense, everyone has a scoring opportunity when we ran our half-court sets.

For further information regarding the LA offense, see the drills beginning later in the chapter.

Coach Adolph Rupp's Influence

The real joy in coaching is to create a system that is successful against opponents with comparable talent. As mentioned earlier, taking pieces of the game from three legendary coaches enabled me to create the LA offense.

Here is how the LA offensive pattern came together. Coach Adolph Rupp always emphasized outstanding guard play. This came easy, because my college coach was C.M. Newton, who played on Coach Rupp's 1951 NCAA championship team. Naturally, we employed Rupp's system of drills and offensive sets, and as point guards on Newton's teams, the guard play became second nature for us.

Coach Rupp was always regarded as an excellent teacher of the fast break. His guard play ranked with the best in the country. Kentucky's excellent movement of ball and players, combined with precise screening and excellent shot selection, all originated with superb play by the guards. Guards liked Rupp's offense because he started from a two-guard front and ran hard horizontal basket cuts to initiate his offenses. Constant player movement was emphasized and taught through drills that my teams practiced every day. Coach Rupp's two- and three-man drills (all-purpose drills) were excellent for teaching ballhandling, passing, pivoting, screening, and decision making. The parts were combined to create our half-court offenses, including the LA offense.

Coach John Wooden's Influence

Coach John Wooden's style of play brought a different emphasis. Always playing to his players' strengths, his teams played from both a one-man and a two-man front. The UCLA one-guard front was the set that worked best in developing the LA offense. Designed by Wooden, it was basically a 1-3-1 half-court set. The beginning of Coach Wooden's 1-3-1 UCLA set had excellent movement that became a major part of the LA offensive set.

Coach Wooden's offenses were designed with good floor balance and passing angles so that each pass led to multiple scoring opportunities. The important lesson learned from Coach Wooden's play that carried over into all our offensive sets is that every time a pass is made, different options develop. Consequently, you don't run just from a one option play; you run a continuity set in which each pass dictates a different cut with multiple options.

For further information regarding Wooden's UCLA offense, see the drill later in the chapter.

Coach Dean Smith's Influence

During the time that my concepts were being formulated, Coach Smith's North Carolina teams were consistent competitors in the NCAA tournament. It was always interesting to see the changes and modifications he made based on the talent of each of his teams. Three things that were dominant with Coach Smith's teams were floor balance, precision passing and cutting, and good shot selection. More than just the Xs and Os, his strategies, especially in the four corners, became a major part of my offensive philosophy.

Dean Smith emphasized three things on offense:

1. **Get a good shot.** This was vitally important in our LA offense. We wanted our players to shoot a disciplined shot that came out of our patterns. We were not a quick one-and-done team. We knew that when shooting a disciplined shot, all our players were in their set positions and we could cover offensive rebounding by sending three players to the board. You can do this with a disciplined offense, and the LA was a disciplined offense. Also, with this disciplined offensive set we were able to maintain our defensive assignments by rotating one player back to protect our basket, and we designated one player always to pick up the ball handler when retreating on defense.

2. **Always finish at the basket.** Many times players get offensive rebounds but fail to score or get fouled. This might appear to be a small thing, but Smith's emphasis on finishing made good sense to all of us in the LA offense.

3. **Take the ball inside.** This goal also had a direct bearing on the LA offense. Any time you get the ball on the low block, you have a chance to profit in three ways: you can score, you can get fouled and score, and you can put another personal foul on your opponent. All three of these offensive traits were paramount in the LA offense.

The LA offense was created by taking offensive concepts and pattern techniques from the best basketball minds of that time. Coaches Wooden, Smith, and Rupp were coaching masterminds. They were exceptional in maximizing the things that their players did best while disguising their weaknesses.

Learning the LA Offense

Most winning basketball coaches would agree with the concept that ball and player movement are essential for good offensive basketball. Having an offensive set that guarantees that all five players are moving and will have a chance for an open shot makes for good team chemistry. Offensive sets that permit two players to do all the shooting generally have three players just standing around, and that approach is not good basketball. Players who are constantly moving come up with loose balls, get long rebounds, and have opportunities for put-backs. The LA offense gets players moving and thinking about spacing, screening, balancing the floor, going to the glass, and looking to make hustle plays. It also teaches players to pass, dribble, screen, and develop into more efficient players. Practicing the following LA offensive options will help players and coaches understand the skills necessary for this offensive set to be successful.

UCLA for Balance and Space

When teaching players about balance and spacing, breaking down the game into smaller areas helps. To underscore the significance of having three players on one side and two on the other, Wooden's UCLA set serves as a great example. When running the initial cut for a layup or post-up, balance and spacing are crucial. Players need to be able to read the defense and respond with the correct offensive strategy. In the UCLA set, if the defensive center drops off to help defend the guard, the post will be open. If the defensive center plays the post tight, the guard is a post-up option. Following a wing pass to the high post and a pin-down, if the play doesn't end with O1's jump shot, many teaching opportunities are available. The UCLA strong-side options provide an excellent drill for teaching balance, spacing, and timing, all of which are used in the LA offense.

Players who understand floor balance and spacing avoid dribbling into congested areas or passing into tight quarters where space and vision are limited. I worked with Del Harris when we were both with the Milwaukee Bucks, and he called it dead baseline if a ball handler tried to attack the basket while a teammate was on the low block on the same side. He gave it that name because the player on the low block had nowhere to go. This common mistake shouldn't happen, and it is easily corrected.

The three-point shot improves floor balance, because the three-point arc gives coaches a marker that players recognize. Players are instructed to clear to the three-point line when running cuts and setting screens. This spacing gives the offensive player room to maneuver when driving to the basket or dribbling to improve a passing angle.

Offensive flow improves when players understand the importance of floor balance and spacing, which are important keys in making effective entry passes to the low post. If a defender drops off the passer into the lap of the intended receiver, a smart player will dribble quickly to establish a better passing angle or pass to a teammate who has better spacing for an entry pass. Players with basketball savvy know not to force the ball into areas where a turnover could easily occur.

UCLA MOVEMENT

Focus

Execute movement, screening, spacing, and timing.

Procedure

Divide the team and run this drill at both ends. Begin with three-on-three; players rotate from offense to defense based on the outcome of each possession. Allow no dribbling or offensive screening on the ball. Players work their way to the basket by executing proper balance and spacing with good screens and passes. Follow these steps:

1. The offense must make five passes before taking a shot, unless they shoot a layup.

2. Begin play with O1 passing to O2 on the wing. O1 rubs off O3's stationary screen, looking to get a layup or quick post-up.

3. After setting the screen, O3 takes two steps toward midcourt and receives O2's pass.

4. O2 sets a down screen for O1, who curls middle or wide looking for a pass from O3 (figure 6.1).

5. At this point, players have made only three passes, and this is where the teaching kicks in. When O1 receives O3's pass, O2 must either up-screen for O3, or O3 must down-screen for O2. This is the decision that assures continuity, movement, and learning.

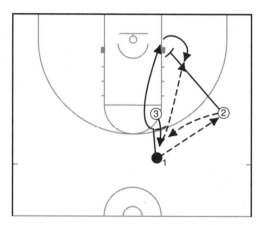

Figure 6.1 UCLA movement.

Coaches need to design sets that emphasize proper floor balance and spacing, and constantly emphasize the importance of each of those elements. The players must then execute the plan and know when to pass and when not to pass. The concept of "sight and insight" is a determining factor for many coaches, and they work to reduce the passing responsibilities of players who can't grasp the concept.

The most enjoyable strategic and tactical aspects of basketball don't involve the separate offensive options, such as backdoors, splits, pop-outs, post-ups, give-and-goes, cross screens, pick-and-rolls, or UCLA variations. Putting those components into a continuity pattern is what makes an offense effective. This pattern should not be complicated or overemphasize one player or position. In the early evaluation process, the goal is to adopt an offensive style that is fair, quickly taught, and effectively evaluated.

LA Offense Options

Players set up this offense with a two-guard front. The two wing players are at the free-throw line extended, and the center plays a high post.

The beauty of the LA set begins by identifying three passes. When the guard enters into frontcourt, he can make three basic passes—to the opposite guard (guard to guard), to the forward on his side (guard to forward), or to the high-post center (guard to center). Each pass requires a spontaneous and different set of offensive maneuvers.

Guard-to-Forward Pass Pattern   As the guard enters the ball into the frontcourt, the forward, at the strong-side free-throw line extended, works to get open. The forward should receive the ball and establish a right-foot pivot. The guard-to-forward pass has three options.

GUARD-TO-FORWARD PASS PATTERN

Focus

All-purpose offense, guard-to-forward pass pattern.

Procedure

Players begin on the half court. Follow these steps:

1. O1 passes to O4, takes a hard jab step to the middle, and tries to get his head and shoulder around the opponent for an inside ball cut. If O1 is open, he gets a quick return pass. If O1 is not open, he continues to the low block on the strong side.

2. As O1 cuts, O5 turns and screens for O3, who relocates to the strong-side elbow looking for a pass and a possible shot.

3. O2 V-cuts to the top of the key and gets a pass from O4 (figure 6.2).

4. O5 relocates to the low post on the weak side. (Options 2, 3, and 4 pick up here.)

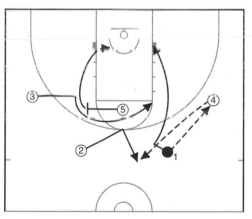

Figure 6.2   Guard-to-forward pass pattern, setup.

(continued)

Guard-to-Forward Pass Pattern *(continued)*

Option 1

5. As O2 receives the pass, O1 turns out off O5's baseline screen. O3 continues toward the basket and relocates to the low block opposite O5.

6. After O4 passes to O2, O4 pins down on O3's opponent and O3 pops out. This puts O4 at the basket for the rebound.

7. O2 takes one or at most two dribbles, looking to reverse the ball. O2 passes to O1, who can shoot, pass to O5, or call O5 out for a sideline pick-and-roll.

8. After O2 passes to O1, O2 turns and screens for O3, who is coming off O4's down screen (figure 6.3).

Option 2

5. Play begins with O2 catching the ball at the top of the key.

6. O4 screens down for O3, and O1 turns out off O5.

7. O2 has the option of starting toward O1, reversing the dribble, and passing to O3 (figure 6.4).

8. If O2 reverses and dribbles toward O3, O5 steps into the middle, looking to post up on X5.

9. This effective counter play can be called at a time-out.

Option 3

5. Another option has O2 with the ball at the top rotating the ball to O1.

6. O2 then reverses and sets a staggered double screen with O4 for O3.

7. O3 works off the screens, looking for a catch-and-shoot (figure 6.5).

8. O5 is a post-up option. O1 can also run a pick-and-roll with O5.

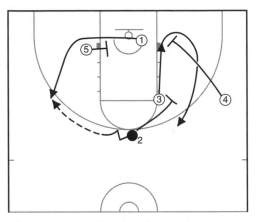

Figure 6.3 Guard-to-forward pass pattern, option 1.

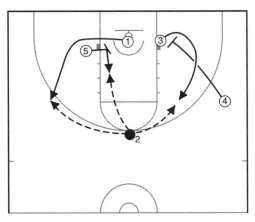

Figure 6.4 Guard-to-forward pass pattern, option 2.

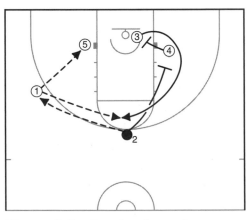

Figure 6.5 Guard-to-forward pass pattern, option 3.

Either guard can start the play to either side. In this scenario, the shooting options went to O1, O3, and O5. If O2 starts the play to O3's side, the scoring options go to O2, O4, and O5.

Guard-to-Guard Pass Pattern In the LA offensive set, either guard can start the play on either side. As the guard enters the ball into the frontcourt, the opposite guard gets parallel, 15 feet (4.5 m) away, with hands up to receive a pass.

GUARD-TO-GUARD PASS PATTERN

Focus

All-purpose offense, guard-to-guard pass pattern.

Procedure

Players begin on the half court. Follow these steps:

1. O1 passes to O2 and sets an inside screen for O3.

2. O3 exchanges position with O1 and receives a direct pass from O2 (figure 6.6).

3. O3 passes to O1.

4. Using a jab step, O3 tries to get an inside ball cut while diving to the block on the strong side.

5. O2 dives to the block on the weak side after seeing O3 pass to O1.

6. O5 watches both O3 and O2 clear the post area and then pops out to receive the pass from O1 (figure 6.7).

7. O5, after receiving the pass, turns and faces the defender, always protecting the ball.

8. As O1 passes to O5, O3 steps up and sets a back pick on O1's defender. An inside cut to the basket is preferred because X3 must loosen up and help should X1 get screened.

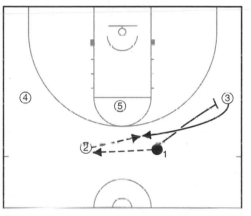

Figure 6.6 Guard-to-guard pass pattern: Exchange positions.

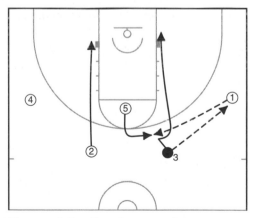

Figure 6.7 Guard-to-guard pass pattern: Dive to blocks.

(continued)

Guard-to-Guard Pass Pattern *(continued)*

9. If O1 is open, O1 is O5's first pass option (figure 6.8).

10. After setting the back screen, O3 takes two steps and opens to the ball, looking for a catch-and-shoot jump shot.

11. On the weak side, O4 pins down on O2, who comes off looking for a catch-and-shoot or a curl to the basket.

12. If O2 pops and catches, he also has a good opportunity for a two-man game with O4. O4 can post up or run a sideline pick-and-roll.

13. O5 must keep the dribble available in case he has to use a dribble hand-off to get out of trouble.

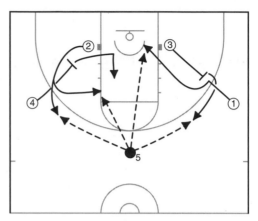

Figure 6.8 Guard-to-guard pass pattern: See the court and make the play.

Guard-to-Center Pass Pattern As the guard brings the ball up the court, the center establishes a high-post position with the hands up and legs shoulder-width apart, looking for a pass. The guard-to-center pass can be initiated any time the offense is set. Whenever there is pressure on the guards, the center must be ready to step out to meet the pass and be an outlet while continuing the pattern. When the defense applies pressure, the play can start from the midcourt area, especially when defensive forwards overplay their opponents.

GUARD-TO-CENTER PASS PATTERN

Focus

All-purpose offense, guard-to-center pass pattern.

Procedure

Players begin on the half court. Follow these steps:

1. O1 makes a post pass to O5 and then sets a screen for the opposite guard, O2.

2. When O5 receives the ball, the strong-side forward, O3, makes a backdoor cut (figure 6.9).

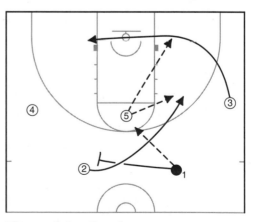

Figure 6.9 Guard-to-center pass pattern: Make backdoor cut.

3. The backdoor cut by O3, the first option, is an automatic timing play that is extremely effective against pressure defense.

4. After looking for the backdoor cut, O5 looks to see whether O1's screen frees up O2.

5. If O2 is open, O5 passes to O2 for a jump shot or a drive. O2 has the entire side of the court to work one on one against the defender.

6. If O2 is not open, O3, the third option, uses the double-stack screen set by O4 and O1, looking for a catch-and-shoot jump shot (figure 6.10).

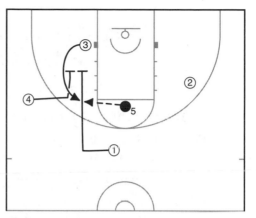

Figure 6.10 Guard-to-center pass pattern: Set double-stack screen.

Releases

All offensive patterns should include releases or escapes. In the event the basic options bog down, the coach should present alternatives. If for some reason the forward backdoor cut, the guard-around, or the turn-out off the double stack all fail, here are suggested releases:

1. When O5 cannot pass to O3, O5 immediately uses a dribble handoff as O3 keeps coming to the ball.

2. O4 dives to the middle off O1, who has the inside lane.

Figure 6.11 Guard-to-center pass pattern, releases.

3. Third, O5 may choose to pass the ball to O2, who has now relocated on the sideline, free-throw line extended, and run a pick-and-roll (figure 6.11).

Remember, in all half-court offensive sets, the coach must designate one player to rotate back to protect the basket and another to contain the ball by slowing down the opponent's outlet pass and dribble penetration.

STRENGTHS AND WEAKNESSES OF THE LA OFFENSE

Strengths

1. LA provides great floor balance.
2. It has built-in opportunities for all five players to score.
3. It includes constant ball and player movement.
4. LA has excellent inside-out possibilities.
5. It is a great counter to teams that switch defenses.
6. It allows the team to control game tempo within the offensive set.

Weaknesses

1. LA needs unselfish players who will share the ball and make good decisions.
2. It needs disciplined players with passing skills and good decision capabilities.

FLEX OFFENSE

As far back as the early 1970s, various coaches believed in what was then called the shuffle-cut. This was an early version of what became the flex offense, and it was acknowledged as a disciplined, controlled offense. The flex, similar to the shuffle-cut in many aspects, added baseline screens and a pick-the-picker option, thus becoming a complete continuity offense. The flex began as a disciplined, inside-oriented offense. It was a ball-control attack that allowed very little individual deviation.

Two highly successful coaches—Gary Williams, winner of the 2002 NCAA championship at Maryland, and Al Skinner, who led Boston College to seven NCAA tournaments—were strong proponents of the flex offense. Coaches are always experimenting with offensive sets in the hope that they can find the answer to their problems. Few coaches have not wrestled with the flex.

The flex offense is a disciplined continuity pattern that emphasizes ball control, timing, and close-range shooting. Player positions are interchangeable and depend on strict adherence to the set. The flex depends on a coach's ability to teach and on the players' ability to execute screens properly. The offense is a three-player system in which two screens are set—one for the baseline cutter and the other a pick-the-picker pin-down on the first screener. Screens are set on the baseline and at the middle of the free-throw lane. Besides requiring the execution of solid screens, the flex depends on mobile big players who can pass, make good decisions, post up, and hit the 15-foot (4.5 m) jumper.

The objective of the flex is to keep a balanced, tight alignment and force a defensive mistake that leads to the offense scoring a layup or getting an open 15-foot (4.5 m) jumper, which certainly qualifies as a good shot. Defenses attempt to disrupt the offense by slowing down the screener, switching, and forcing the big men to make decisions. When defensive teams have trouble fighting through the various screens, they usually resort to a zone defense that takes away the layups and forces the offense to attack more from the perimeter.

A major concern in the flex offense occurs with all the player movement, especially when guards get stuck under the basket or in the corners. Opponents then push the ball in transition looking to score fast-break points. Guards stuck on the baseline are in big trouble when turnovers, deflections, and long rebounds occur.

FLEX OFFENSE

Focus

Learning the flex offense pattern.

Procedure

Players begin on the half court. Follow these steps:

1. Begin with O1 and O2 in a two-guard front. O1 has the ball on the right side, and O2 is opposite O1 outside the three-point circle. Forwards O3 and O4 are in opposite deep corners, and O5 sets up on the strong-side block, in line with O1.

2. Play begins with a pass from O1 to O2 as O3 makes a timed shuffle cut either high to the middle or baseline off O5's screen, looking for a layup or post-up pass from O2. If O3 doesn't receive the pass, he stops on the block, preparing to set a screen as the play continues.

3. After passing to O2, O1 sets a down screen or a screen the-screener maneuver for O5 and relocates immediately to the right deep corner.

4. O5 uses O1's screen to free himself and relocate to the free-throw lane (elbow area), looking for a shooting pass from O2.

5. After receiving the pass from O1, O2 looks first for O3 on the shuffle cut and then for O5 rotating to the elbow at the free-throw line (figure 6.12). O2 passes to O5, and if O5 has an open shot, he takes it. If not, the play continues.

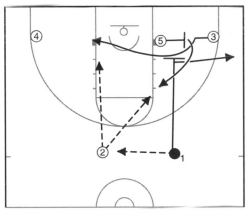

Figure 6.12 Flex offense, cycle 1.

(continued)

Flex Offense *(continued)*

6. After passing to O5, O2 sets a down screen or a screen-the-screener maneuver for O3 and relocates immediately in the left deep corner.

7. O3, on the block, sets a screen for O4 and then uses O2's screen to free himself and relocate to the free-throw lane (elbow area), looking for a shooting pass from O5.

8. When O5 does not shoot, he looks immediately for O4, who uses O3's screen by going either baseline or middle, looking for a pass from O5. If no pass occurs, O4 sets up on the strong-side low block.

9. O5 also has the option of passing to O3 to take an up-the-lane jump shot or continue the play (figure 6.13).

10. After passing to O3, O5 screens down with screen-the-screener action for O4 and relocates in the deep right corner.

11. O3 looks for O1 running the baseline action, seeking a layup or a post-up.

12. If there is no pass to O1, O4 relocates and receives a pass from O3 at the elbow (figure 6.14).

13. After O3's pass to O4, O2 runs the baseline and makes a cut off a screen from O1.

14. O3 continues the play by setting a down screen or screen-the-screener maneuver on O1 and relocating to the deep left corner. O1 relocates to the elbow, looking for a pass from O4 and a shot (figure 6.15).

15. O4 passes to O1, and O5 runs off a baseline screen set by O2, looking for a layup or post-up opportunity.

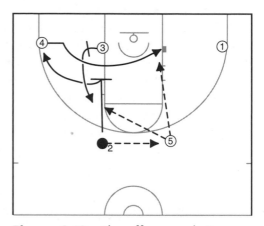

Figure 6.13 Flex offense, cycle 2.

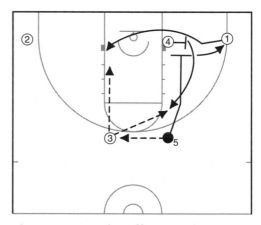

Figure 6.14 Flex offense, cycle 3.

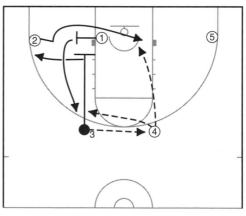

Figure 6.15 Flex offense, cycle 4.

16. After passing to O1, O4 down screens for O2 and slides to the deep right corner. O2 relocates to the right elbow free-throw line extended as O1 surveys the options (figure 6.16).

At this point, all five players have run a complete cycle of all five flex positions.

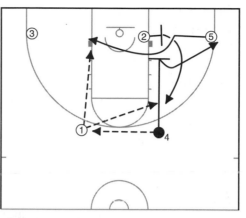

Figure 6.16 Flex offense, cycle 5.

STRENGTHS AND WEAKNESSES OF THE FLEX OFFENSE

Strengths

1. This special type of offense is effective for unique players who have a disciplined coach to direct it.
2. Players who have patience can learn a great deal about screening, timing, passing, making decisions, and shot selection.
3. This offense allows the team to dictate the tempo. It is a methodical offense when properly executed.

Weaknesses

1. A big disadvantage and weakness of this offense surfaces when the team falls behind. The flex is not a catch-up offense because points come at a slow pace.
2. For this offense to be effective, everyone, both coaches and players, must buy into the system. The flex offense requires discipline and accurate execution.
3. Within the system, on long rebounds and turnovers, the guards can be caught screening on the low blocks or deep in the corners, making it impossible for them to get back on defense.

The flex half-court set may not look complicated, but players must master five fundamentals when learning this offense:

1. Precision passing
2. Proper screening techniques
3. Shot selection
4. Patience
5. Most of all, decision making

TRIANGLE OFFENSE

The triangle offense is ideal for coaches who want ball control, floor balance, interchangeable position players, backdoor cuts, pick-and-rolls, splits actions, isolations, post-ups, and continuity that depends on various passes to initiate player and ball movement. The triangle offense begins with a conventional two-guard front, a post player at midpost strong side, and the forwards at the free-throw line extended on opposite sides of the court. In the triangle offense, passing dictates cuts, floor balance, screens, and high-percentage shots.

The triangle is basically one big set of integrated plays all connected and dependent on passes that determine movement, cuts, screens, and shot opportunities. From the outside looking in, the most important thing that players must do is read the defense and react accordingly.

An excellent feature of the triangle set is that it can be initiated from either a two- or three-guard front. By using a ballhandling small forward as the third guard, teams can space the floor and minimize all forms of defensive pressure, especially front-court traps or full-court man-to-man pressure.

Another important benefit and option of the triangle set is that it allows players to start the offense from various floor positions. If the opponent plays a token defense, players can dribble to a normal starting position, approximately 15 feet (4.5 m) into the frontcourt. If the defensive guards apply backcourt pressure, the offensive guards can begin the play from the backcourt with speed cuts into the set formation.

The biggest advantage of the triangle is that although other teams' playbooks contain 75 to 150 plays for their players to memorize, triangle teams work on their timing and execution from an array of play options from one primary set. The core set remains the same and has escapes and releases built in to each of the various movements. For that reason the triangle is easier to teach. Overloading players with too much information and too many plays can be a major problem.

TRIANGLE OFFENSE

Focus

Learning the triangle offense (upper or lower) pattern.

Procedure

Players begin on the half court. Play begins with a token defense with no defensive pressure. Follow these steps:

1. The guard with the ball, O1, enters the front court and passes to O3.

2. O1 then cuts to the deep corner, strong side. O1 has the choice of either making a diagonal cut to the corner or going around O5 if there is defensive pressure (figure 6.17).

Option 1

3. The first option is the corner pass. O3 chooses to pass back to O1 in the corner.

4. After the pass, O3 takes two quick steps toward the middle of the court and then pivots hard on the left foot, trying to get his head and shoulders ahead of the defender.

5. O5 takes a step out and sets a screen for O3 as he cuts baseline (figure 6.18), looking for a quick return pass from O1.

6. If there is no pass to O3, he clears to the far corner. O1 holds the ball and waits for O3 to clear so that O5 can set a pick-and-roll corner sideline screen for O1.

7. O1 moves off O5's screen to go middle, giving O5 an opportunity either to roll or to pop, depending on the defensive strategy.

8. O1 dribble-drives to the middle looking for a layup, a draw-and-kick (figure 6.19), or a pull-up jumper.

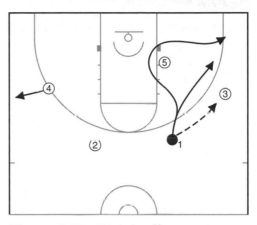

Figure 6.17 Triangle offense, setup.

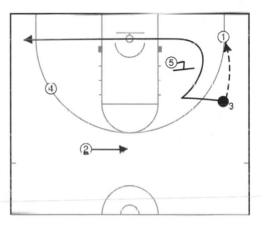

Figure 6.18 Triangle offense, option 1: Make corner pass and cut baseline.

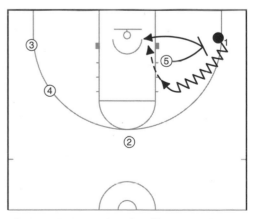

Figure 6.19 Triangle offense, option 1: Perform corner pick-and-roll.

(continued)

Triangle Offense *(continued)*

Option 2

3. As a second option to passing to the corner, O3 passes to O5. This is an automatic backdoor reverse for O1 out of the corner.

4. A pass from O5 to O1 should get a layup or a foul. If there is no pass to O1 and if O5 does not make a quick one-on-one move, the play continues.

5. After the pass to O5, O3 runs a post split action by setting a screen for O2 (figure 6.20). The basic rule to follow is that the passer to the post sets the screen.

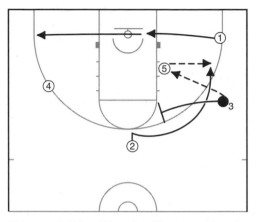

Figure 6.20 Triangle offense, option 2.

6. To prepare for O3's screen, O2 makes a hard, left-footed jab step toward the basket to set up the defender and then uses O3's screen and a pass from O5 for a drive opportunity or an open jump shot.

7. If O2 cannot get a good shot, he maintains the dribble and runs a sideline pick-and-roll with O5. The baseline is clear, so O5 can either roll to the basket or pop to the corner.

Option 3

3. Option 3 is a timing play. O4, on the weak side watching closely, sees that there is no pass to O1 on the baseline cut, nor is there a pass to O5 on the low post for O1's backdoor cut and an O3–O2 post split. O4 makes a hard flash cut to the top of the free-throw circle as O3 delivers him a sharp pass (figure 6.21).

4. O2, beyond the three-point line in the middle of the floor, fakes a quick step as if he is going to catch the pass and then makes a backdoor speed cut, looking for the ball and a layup.

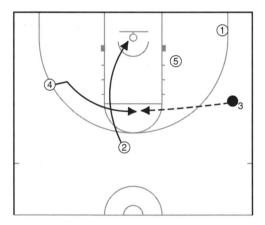

Figure 6.21 Triangle offense, option 3: Make hard flash cut.

5. If O2 does not get the backdoor pass, he can immediately pivot and post up.

6. Now it is up to O4 to make the play. After passing to O4, O3 turns and sets a screen for O1 coming out of the corner toward the ball.

7. O4 has the option to pass to O1, pass to O2 on a post-up (figure 6.22), or look for his shot and make the play.

Option 4

3. As a fourth option, O3 passes to O2 at the top of circle.

4. O4 has the option of setting a back screen or a sideline pick-and-roll screen for O2, depending on where the defender is playing. O2 reads the screening position and runs a two-player game, looking for a good shot (figure 6.23).

5. After passing to O2, O3 turns and sets a screen for O1 coming out of the corner toward the ball. This puts O1 in a perfect position to be the player back on defense.

Isolation

Through practice, the four perimeter positions in the triangle are interchangeable so that when an isolation is called for, the procedure is just another option within the continuity of the offense. Here is one way to isolate player O2:

1. The play begins with O2 and O3 exchanging positions. O4 drops down to the low block weak side. O1 then passes to O2 and goes to the strong-side corner.

2. O2 reverses the ball to O3 and makes a brush cut off O5, who has set up a little higher to help free up O2 as O2 cuts across the floor. O2 sets a down screen for O4, who relocates to the middle of the free-throw circle (figure 6.24).

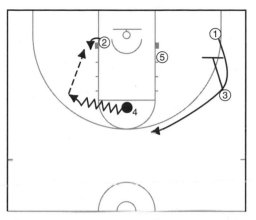

Figure 6.22 Triangle offense, option 3: Make the play.

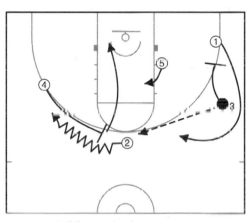

Figure 6.23 Triangle offense, option 4.

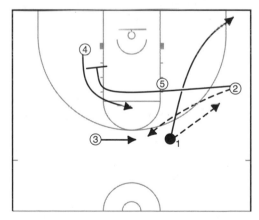

Figure 6.24 Triangle offense, isolation: Brush cut and down screen.

(continued)

Triangle Offense *(continued)*

3. After receiving the pass, O3 dribbles left toward the sideline to get a good passing angle as O2 posts up strong, looking for the ball.

4. O3 looks to insert the ball to O2 (figure 6.25). After the pass is made, O3 clears out so that O2 has the entire side of the floor on which to operate.

5. Depending on where O2 receives the ball, he will have a number of options: a quick post-up move to the basket, a step-back move to create space with, or a dribble out face-up one-on-one dribble drive.

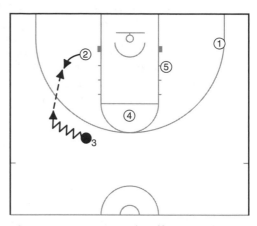

Figure 6.25 Triangle offense, isolation: Post up and isolate.

Transition to Opposite Side

Another reason that the triangle offense is effective is that an easy transition can be made when starting the play.

1. O1 enters the right side of the court but then decides to run the play on the left side. Only a few adjustments need to be made.

2. O1 passes to O2. O2 quickly passes to O4 and relocates to the corner ball side.

3. O5 crosses the lane to the strong side and establishes a midpost position (figure 6.26).

4. O1 and O3 now have weak-side responsibilities, O4 has the four passing options, and the play continues.

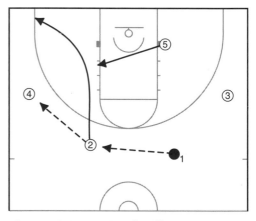

Figure 6.26 Triangle offense, transition to opposite side.

STRENGTHS AND WEAKNESSES OF THE TRIANGLE OFFENSE

Strengths

1. This offense includes baseline backdoors, post-ups, splits, pick-and-rolls, isolations, pin-downs, midfloor backdoors on overplays, and pop-outs for high-percentage shots.
2. It gives a team the ability to attack a weak defender.
3. It is a complete offense, predicated on spacing, shot selection, and offensive sets with passing reads that determine player cuts.
4. It is an understandable offense using four basic plays that are executed by predetermined passes.

Weaknesses

1. The triangle offense, as we knew it under Phil Jackson, always had great players. I doubt that many coaches can get players to buy into the triangle with the focus and determination that his teams displayed.
2. The triangle offense is a great continuity offense that was run with outstanding talent. As Phil Jackson was winning 11 NBA titles executing the triangle offense, no other team incorporated the triangle into their system. Was it lack of talent? Was it their reluctance to conform to the system? Was it the inability of other coaches to teach it?
3. The biggest weakness of this offense may come from the reluctance to risk trying it.

DRIBBLE-DRIVE OFFENSE

Basketball strategies aren't the only things that change over the years—so do the terms that we use to name systems. For instance, what is now called the dribble-drive offense was previously known as the draw-and-kick. This offense features a slasher (or multiple slashers) who drives into the gap of the defense and either attacks the basket or passes to a teammate when another defender has to lend a helping hand to try to minimize the damage created by dribble penetration. The slasher has three opportunities:

1. Get to the rim and finish
2. Pass to an open teammate for a good shot
3. Pull up and shoot a midrange shot

The dribble-drive offense is a specialized offensive set that can be run only with highly skilled players. Dribble-drive teams must possess outstanding dribblers with first-step quickness and the ability to perform change-of-direction crossovers, excellent alley-oop passers, scorers, good free-throw shooters, and players with superior peripheral vision.

All teams would love to be able to penetrate the defense off the dribble. All kinds of good things happen when a crafty ball handler can break down the defense. For one, the defense commits more fouls trying to stop the penetration. And two, as big-men defenders come over to help stop the penetrating offensive players, offensive rebounding lanes open up because boxing out for the defensive big men becomes a major problem. Quick guards who have the ballhandling skills to beat defenders off the dribble are every coach's dream. NBA players who possess all the necessary skills to excel in the dribble-drive offense include the following:

Steve Nash	Chris Paul
Derrick Rose	Dwayne Wade
LeBron James	Monta Ellis
Tony Parker	Rajon Rondo

The dribble-drive offense depends on the offensive player's ability to beat the opponent off the dribble and then make a good decision whether to pass, drive to the rim, or shoot. Quick ball handlers who have excellent peripheral vision can make coaches who use this offense look smart indeed.

Getting the right players in the proper alignment for the ball handler to operate is called "setting the table." This process involves some preliminary passes, player and ball movement, numerous dribble handoffs, and a screen or two until the team gets the ball exactly where they want it to give their ball handler every advantage. We will look at two different ways of getting into the dribble-drive attack.

ONE-GUARD FRONT

Focus

Transitioning into the half-court dribble-drive attack.

Procedure

The decision of whether to attack in transition off made or missed field goals or made or missed free throws depends on the skill of the ball handlers and the confidence of the coach. In the example illustrated here, the team is playing in an open, spread 3 out, 2 in alignment, looking to attack the middle immediately. Follow these steps:

1. Play begins as O1 enters the front court, right side. O2 is above the three-point line, approximately 6 feet (2 m) from the sideline (and basically parallel to O1 when he starts the drive to the middle). O5 is on the left-side baseline 15 feet (4.5 m) from the goal, ready to attack the basket when O1 drives. O4 is on the right-side baseline 15 feet from the basket, and O3 is on the free-throw line extended, 6 feet inside the sideline on the right side.

2. O1 attacks the middle, looking to penetrate and get past the defender. If O1 does, he attacks the basket, looking for O5's defender to challenge. If X5 covers the basket, O1 draws the defender and passes to O5 with a lob or a pass that O5 can dunk. If no one stops O1, he has a good chance of making a layup or drawing a personal foul.

3. If the defense cuts off O1's initial penetration, O1 veers off and runs a dribble handoff with O2. O2 continues the middle attack, working hard to turn the corner. If O2 cannot get middle, he looks to draw and kick to O3. If O2 turns the corner, he attacks the basket, looking to lob or dish off to O5 when and if X5 rotates to protect the basket.

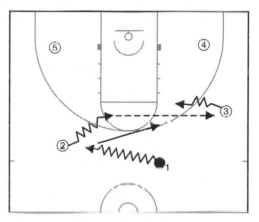

4. If O2 must draw and kick to O3 and O3 cannot get a shot, O3 drives middle and runs a dribble handoff with O1 (figure 6.27). O1 continues the course of action until there is a shot, lob, or drive to the basket. O5 and O4 key off the dribble penetration, looking for a pass.

Figure 6.27 One-guard front.

1-4 FRONT

Focus

Establish balanced alignment while getting the ball to a playmaker.

Procedure

Follow these steps:

1. Play begins when guard O1 enters the front court with the ball. O5 and O4 begin in a high double post on opposite elbows. O3 is on the right-side free-throw line extended about 3 feet (1 m) off the sideline. O2 is set up on the left-side free-throw extended and about 3 feet off the sideline.

(continued)

1-4 Front *(continued)*

2. O1 passes to O3 and dives straight to the right low block. On the pass, O2 dives straight to the left low block. O5 screens for O4 and relocates on the low block left side, where he will set a staggered double screen with O2 about 6 feet (2 m) behind O2. O4 relocates to the top of the key and receives a pass from O3 (figure 6.28).

3. On O3's pass to O4, O2 steps into the middle of the free-throw lane and sets a screen for O1. O5 sets the second screen as O1 sprints off the staggered double screen to the left-side free-throw line extended to receive O4's pass. Meanwhile, after making the pass to O4, O3 moves to the low block right side and sets a screen for O2.

4. At this point, the alignment is set. O5 is on the low block left side. O2 curls off O3's screen and relocates to the free-throw line extended right side. After setting the screen, O3 continues across the free-throw lane and works off O5 to the left corner (figure 6.29).

5. O4 has the ball at the top of the key and can go either way, to O1 or O2, with a pass or dribble handoff. O4 passes to O1 and dives to the low block right side.

6. O1 has the ball, and the middle is clear. O5 and O4 are set up on respective low blocks, and O2 is in good position for a draw-and-kick or a catch and attack on the basket. O1 drives middle and attacks the basket (figure 6.30).

7. If either X5 or X4 steps out to defend O1 as he penetrates, O1 can then dish it to O5 or O4 with either an alley-oop or a lay-off pass. If O2's defender rotates to help, O1 can make a dribble handoff or exercise a draw-and-kick to O2, who, if passed to, can attack off the dribble or shoot an open jump shot.

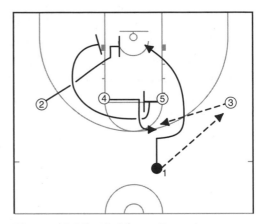

Figure 6.28 1-4 front: Pass to top of key.

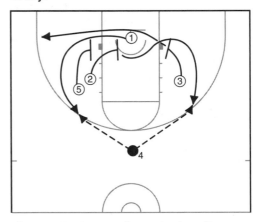

Figure 6.29 1-4 front: Set baseline screens.

Figure 6.30 1-4 front: Drive middle and attack basket.

STRENGTHS AND WEAKNESSES OF THE DRIBBLE-DRIVE OFFENSE

Strengths

1. If you have an exceptional point guard, as you'll need in this offense, you'll have an effective offense.
2. A penetrating and passing point guard makes everyone better.
3. Teammates know that if they get open, they'll get the ball.
4. When guards drive in this offense, big men know to get ready for a lob or a dunk.

Weaknesses

1. If the lead guard has a shooting weakness, the team is vulnerable. Opponents will foul a poor free-throw shooter and back off a poor jump shooter.
2. You cannot stay in this offense for long periods because some players become totally uninvolved.
3. The offense has few set plays—just spacing, attacking the basket, and adjusting to defensive pressure.

MOTION OFFENSE

The motion offense is an effective weapon that every team should consider adding to its repertoire, but it cannot be used as a complete offense because too many players have to handle the ball and make crucial decisions. It should be seen as one set in a team's offensive stockpile. When a team becomes stagnant and a coach wants to get the players moving, the motion offense is an excellent way to create movement.

The motion offense is usually an open offense that has no post player. It relies primarily on player and ball movement within a basic structure. Player decision making is extremely important, as are setting good screens and making good passes. But if a coach doesn't have good decision makers on the court, the motion offense will likely break down. All players need to understand the various positions and be able to execute at a high level. Thus, the motion offense should be run in short spurts rather than for an entire game.

A basic five-player motion produces a constantly moving offense that has the point guard initiating the play with a pass. The point guard either makes a hard cut to the basket or screens away with a teammate, replacing him on the point. Players must be able to read defenses for the motion offense to be effective. Some teams include pick-and-rolls with dribble-drive attacks, looking to draw and kick.

Others like to run a four-player motion game with a stationary post playing either high or low. The rules remain about the same except for the greater use of the post.

Motion can also be run in a more structured way. Purists would contend that this isn't a true motion offense, but providing more structure within the set can be helpful. Purdue could run motion with 7-foot (213 cm) All-American Joe Barry Carroll, but his skills and size allowed him to establish inside position. Being an inside-out coach, my thrust was always to go inside.

A number of precautions need to be understood when running the five-player motion offense. Here are three motion option characteristics that must be implemented:

1. Players must be able to pass and screen away.
2. Players must be able to pass and make hard basket cuts down the middle for layups or corner screens for the power forward or center.
3. Players must be capable ball handlers when dribble handoffs and dribble-drive opportunities present themselves.

All players must be prepared to rotate and relocate within the structure. Because the team employs ball and player movement, the big players rotate and relocate in positions where they handle the ball more. If the big players are not capable of moving out on the court, modification must be built in.

MOTION OFFENSE

Focus

Building in box-and-one options.

Procedure

Motion is an open offensive set with a box-and-one alignment. Follow these steps:

1. O4 and O5 start in the low corners, approximately 6 feet (2 m) off the baseline and 6 feet inside the sideline. O2 and O3 are at the free-throw line extended, approximately 6 feet off the sideline.
2. O1 begins the motion from the middle of the court, 6 to 12 feet (2 to 3.5 m) above the top of the free-throw circle. From here, four motion options can be run, each initiated by a different player.
3. O1 can pass to either side. O1 passes to O3 and has two choices:
   a. O1 can make a quick cut down the middle looking for a return pass or
   b. screen away for O2, who can backdoor cut or replace O1 in the middle position.

4. In the middle drive option, O1 passes to O3, fakes a screen on O2's defender, and then cuts hard (figure 6.31), trying to get head and shoulders inside X1's body and the passer, O3.

5. If open, O1 has a layup, a foul, or both. If O1 is not open and there is no return pass, O1 replaces O4 in the corner.

6. O4 rotates and replaces O3, who now moves out front with the ball to balance the attack.

7. O3, now with the ball, has three basic options:

   a. beat the defender off the dribble,

   b. pass to O4 and make a middle dive basket cut or set a corner screen, or

   c. pass to O2 on the wing and screen away.

8. In the corner screen option, O3 passes to O4 and runs a corner screen for O5 (figure 6.32). O5 uses O3's screen and posts up on the strong side.

9. If there is no pass, O5 continues to the corner strong side, O3 replaces O5, and O4 centers the ball and has the same basic three choices.

10. In the screen away option, O4 passes to O2 and screens away for O1, who cuts hard down the middle (figure 6.33).

11. If O1 is open, O2 looks to deliver the pass for a layup or foul. If O2 cannot make the pass, O2 now moves to the center of the floor, where he again has the same three basic choices. O1 replaces O3, O3 replaces O2, and O4 replaces O1 on the wing. O5 remains in the right corner.

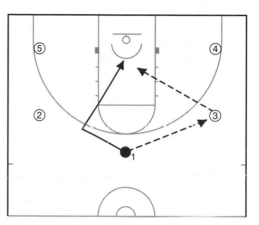

Figure 6.31 Motion offense: Cut middle.

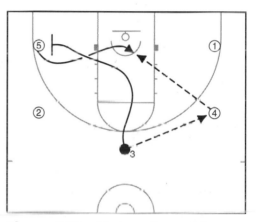

Figure 6.32 Motion offense: Set corner screen.

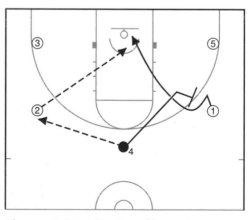

Figure 6.33 Motion offense: Screen away.

(continued)

Motion Offense *(continued)*

12. In the dribble handoff option, O2 dribbles to the right for a dribble handoff to O4 (figure 6.34).

13. O4 then dribbles to the left and executes a dribble handoff with O3.

On each exchange, each dribbler looks for an opportunity to attack the basket. The action is similar to a three-player weave with dribble-drive opportunities. These options continue until a score, foul, missed shot, or turnover occurs.

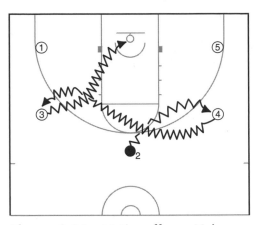

Figure 6.34 Motion offense: Make dribble handoff.

STRENGTHS AND WEAKNESSES OF THE MOTION OFFENSE

Strengths

1. Motion is a good offensive set for a team that does not have an inside game.
2. It provides a control pattern when the team needs to slow down the tempo.
3. It forces opponents to defend out on the court with their big players.
4. Motion is a good offense when the team needs to protect players in foul trouble.

Weaknesses

1. All five players need to handle the ball and make good decisions.
2. Motion leaves the team vulnerable when the big players are away from boards.
3. It can force defensive teams to play zone to try to take away dribble drives and layups.
4. Getting five players to execute motion well is difficult, much less six or eight.

ANALYSIS OF OFFENSES

For seven years I was an assistant coach in college—four at Transylvania and three at the University of Cincinnati. During those seven years, I observed head coaches as they wrestled with complicated coaching issues, including offensive sets. In the eighth year, I became a head coach, and all those issues became mine.

For two weeks I left all distractions behind and began writing down my basketball philosophy and goals. In addition to offensive concepts, my notes included ballhandling and defensive drills, as well as my aims to make sure that players would graduate, that I would never embarrass a player publicly, that I would maintain ethical standards, and so on. And, as the years passed, I learned from Rupp, Wooden, and Smith.

Coaching, and designing an offense in general, is a bit like making vegetable soup. You put in the ingredients that you like—corn, tomatoes, beans, carrots, cabbage, Brussels sprouts, some seasoning, and water—and cook it on the stove. You've created it; it's your soup. I liked Rupp's fast break, Wooden's 1-3-1, and Smith's four corners, but they were not mine. The LA offense was mine—my soup. I designed it. I knew it worked, and I proved it.

The flex offense works for some coaches, but it's not for me. We used a motion set when things bogged down, but not for long. The dribble drive is a great set with the right personnel. The triangle has many of the LA characteristics, which is why I like it. But for me, the LA offense brings together pieces of all these unique offenses. And if I were coaching today, the LA is exactly what I would start with.

TEAM OFFENSIVE DRILLS

Players bring different levels of skill to the court. The coach's goal is to help players develop their skills to the highest level possible. The status quo is rare in basketball, because players usually improve or fall back in each practice. No magic is involved; each player must seize the opportunity through hard work. Pragmatically, the important thing for players is to be confident in their game and positive in their approach when they receive constructive criticism. To gain this confidence, what players do in games they must first learn in practice through drills.

Specifically related to offense, players must first learn how to screen. Offensive screening is a vital fundamental in basketball. Offenses must be able to execute numerous types of screens to combat and react to defensive coverages. Offenses must be able counter and react when defenses go over, go under, hedge, trap, or switch on a screen—all defensive strategies that confuse and destroy timing and execution. Every offensive player should understand how, when, and where to set a screen. Each of the offensive sets discussed in this book relies heavily on setting good screens. An excellent way to teach essential screening tactics is through the following three-player screening drills.

Three-Player Screening Drills

The following three-player drills continue to focus on ballhandling, passing, and shooting layups. These drills also highlight proper screening techniques, which are often overlooked. Players must learn these screening techniques:

1. The screener must know the distance restrictions for front, side, and back screens as they apply to the defender being screened.
2. The screener cannot move or lean to cause contact.

3. Proper body position has the feet spread shoulder-width apart, arms and elbows in (not extended), and the body upright.

All effective half-court offenses depend on proper screening techniques to avoid committing offensive fouls. Nothing hurts a team more than holding for a last shot at the end of the game and then having a player set an illegal screen to forfeit the opportunity to win. Here are four excellent three-player drills that can build a stronger basketball foundation.

SPLITS: GUARD SETS SCREEN

Focus

Three-player drill—screening, passing, and shooting.

Procedure

Players begin on the half court and follow these steps:

1. On the right side, a guard (G) with the ball lines up 6 feet (2 m) beyond the top of the key, directly in line with the elbow.

2. A forward (F) lines up 3 feet (1 m) inside the sideline boundary, even with the free-throw line extended.

3. The guard makes a direct pass to the post (P) and sets a screen for the forward.

4. To set up the defender, the forward uses a jab step to the baseline and cuts to the middle off the screen set by the guard, looking for a pass from the post. This action is commonly known as split action or scissors.

5. In setting the pick, the guard must stop and hold the screen until the forward clears the contact area (to avoid committing a moving screen, which results in an offensive foul). The guard continues to the baseline, looking for a return pass from the post and the opportunity to score.

6. The post decides who shoots the ball. He can pass either to the forward cutting down the middle or to the guard on the baseline (figure 6.35). The third option is to let both teammates clear the area and then make an individual move.

7. Whoever doesn't shoot becomes the rebounder, and the players return to their respective lines.

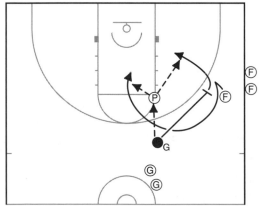

Figure 6.35 Splits: Guard sets screen.

SPLITS: GUARD REVERSES

Focus

Three-player drill—screening, passing, and shooting.

Procedure

Players begin on the half court and follow these steps:

1. On the right side, a guard with the ball (G) lines up 6 feet (2 m) beyond the top of the key, directly in line with the elbow.
2. A forward (F) lines up 3 feet (1 m) inside the sideline boundary, even with the free-throw line extended.
3. The guard makes a bounce pass to the forward, goes behind him, and receives the handoff.
4. The guard makes one or two quick dribbles, stops, executes a left-foot reverse (that is, the left foot is the pivot foot), and passes to the post (P) at the mid-post area. The guard then sets a screen on the forward's defender and cuts to the middle, looking for a return pass and the shot.
5. After the forward hands off the ball to the guard, the forward takes two steps away from the guard. After the ball goes into the post, the forward cuts baseline off the guard's screen, looking for the ball and a shot.
6. The post decides who will shoot the ball and passes either to the forward on the baseline or to the guard cutting down the middle (figure 6.36). The third option is to let both teammates clear the area and then make an individual move.
7. Whoever doesn't shoot becomes the rebounder, and the players return to their respective lines.

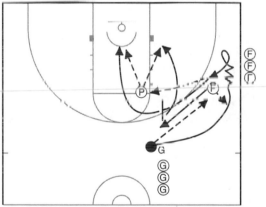

Figure 6.36   Splits: Guard reverses.

SPLITS: GUARD GOES TO CORNER

Focus

Three-player drill—screening, passing, and shooting.

Procedure

Players begin on the half court and follow these steps:

(continued)

Splits: Guard Goes to Corner *(continued)*

1. On the right side, a guard (G) with the ball lines up 6 feet (2 m) beyond the top of the key, directly in line with the elbow.
2. A forward (F) lines up 3 feet (1 m) inside the sideline boundary, even with the free-throw line extended.
3. The guard makes a chest pass to the forward and goes to the ball-side short corner.
4. The forward passes to the guard and takes a couple of steps toward the middle to create space and provide a better passing angle for the guard.
5. The guard then passes to the post (P) and sets a screen for the forward. After the ball goes to the post, the forward uses a jab step and cuts baseline off the guard's screen, looking for a pass and a shot.
6. The post decides who will shoot the ball and can pass either to the forward on the baseline or to the guard cutting down the middle (figure 6.37). The third option is to let both teammates clear the area and then make an individual move.
7. Whoever doesn't shoot the ball becomes the rebounder, and the players return to their respective lines.

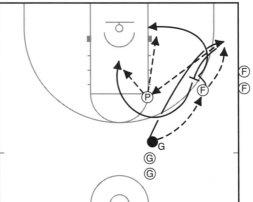

Figure 6.37 Splits: Guard goes to corner.

SPLITS: FORWARD MAKES POST PASS

Focus

Three-player drill—screening, passing, and shooting.

Procedure

Players begin on the half court and follow these steps:

1. On the right side, a guard with the ball (G) lines up 6 feet (2 m) beyond the top of the key, directly in line with the elbow.
2. A forward (F) lines up 3 feet (1 m) inside the sideline boundary, even with the free-throw line extended.
3. The guard makes a chest pass to the forward and goes to the ball-side short corner.
4. The forward passes to the post (P) and sets a screen for the guard.
5. The forward can step through or use a left-footed reverse pivot and cut to the basket.

6. The post decides who will shoot the ball and can pass either to the forward on the baseline or to the guard going to the middle (figure 6.38). The third option is to let both teammates clear the area and then make an individual move.

7. Whoever doesn't shoot becomes the rebounder, and the players return to their respective lines.

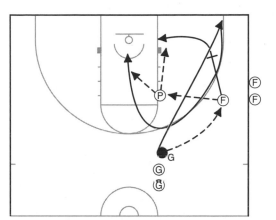

Figure 6.38 Splits: Forward makes post pass.

Full-Court Drills

To execute offensive sets, besides learning how to screen, players must be able to execute passing and layups properly, even when hard on the run. The following three-player full-court drill is different from most three-player weaves drills because it is demanding and requires an all-out sprint. This drill is designed for speed, conditioning, and accuracy. Before performing this drill, players must stretch and make sure that they can run at full speed. A missed layup or bad pass requires repeating the drill immediately.

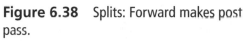

TWO TOUCHES

Focus

Running hard and making those important layups.

Procedure

Players should be warmed up and loose for this full-court fast-break drill. Teach the drill with a one-dribble allowance for the first couple of days and then eliminate dribbling altogether. Two-handed chest passes are recommended. Players form three lines on the end line and follow these steps:

1. Have an even number of players in the three lines with the ballhandling guards in the middle. Centers, forwards, and big guards run the outside lanes.

2. O1, with the ball, begins at the free-throw line, and O2 and O3 are on the end line occupying the running lanes. As O1 throws the ball on the backboard, O2 and O3 sprint toward the opposite goal, staying wide in their lanes.

(continued)

Two Touches *(continued)*

3. O1 throws a lead pass to O2, who catches the ball in full stride and throws a two-handed lead pass to O3, who catches and shoots the layup.

4. O1 must sprint to the basket and catch the ball before O3's layup hits the floor. O2 changes sides of the court by cutting across the top of the circle and taking the opposite lane. O3 shoots the layup and continues running to the opposite lane, looking for a short outlet pass from O1 (figure 6.39).

5. O1 rebounds the made layup and, without dribbling, passes to O3, who clears the area after making the first layup.

6. O2 has changed sides of the court and begins a sprint toward the opposite basket as O1 rebounds and passes to O3.

7. O3 catches the pass and, without dribbling, passes back to O1, who is cutting up the middle.

8. O1 catches on the dead run and, without breaking stride, makes a two-handed chest pass to O2, who is streaking to the basket for a layup (figure 6.40). All passes in this drill are lead passes.

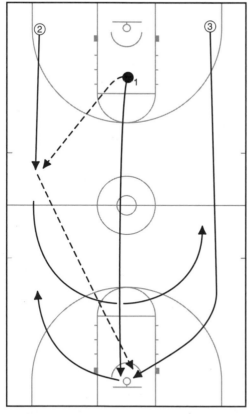

Figure 6.39 Two touches: Catch and shoot first layup.

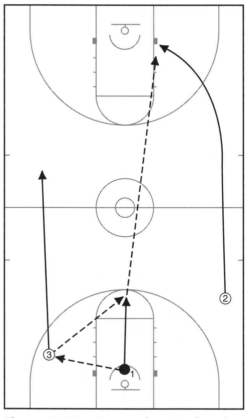

Figure 6.40 Two touches: Catch and shoot second layup.

9. The next three players in line begin as O2 is shooting the layup. The guard in the middle gets the rebound out of the net and, without dribbling, throws a lead pass almost to midcourt to the wing runner, and the drill continues. All players must be alert and ready to run when their time comes.

10. After any missed layups, the group runs again.

This drill builds with repetition. Begin with one, then two, and eventually three times up and down the court for each group. Layups become important, especially when players are running two and three times.

Besides using demanding warm-up drills, professional teams use the entire 94 feet (28.7 m) when they go on the offensive attack. Teams call the secondary break different names, such as early, turnout, thru, or quick, but the strategy is the same: Enter the frontcourt with a scoring plan. On steals, long rebounds, or bust-outs, players automatically attack the basket. The difference is that on normal rebounds, when a big man rebounds and outlets to a guard, most teams have a specific strategy. As the defense retreats in transition, the offense has a planned attack, looking for mismatches, early post-ups, and catch-and-shoot scoring opportunities.

A major benefit of the secondary break is player and ball movement. The offense creates a faster pace and puts the onus on players to make good decisions. In situations in which teaching time is limited, such as the NBA's Chicago Predraft Camp, their summer leagues, or the Portsmouth Invitational Tournament, the thru secondary pattern is perfect because it's not complicated and players can learn it quickly.

The thru set is an excellent offense for coaches to use in evaluating overall player skills. The guards must pass the ball ahead, the inside players must run, screens are designed to free players for shots, pick-and-roll options are built in, and good decision making is essential. The inside big players must run from block to block so that coaches can evaluate how quickly they run in the open court and how fast they can change ends.

THRU

Focus

Proper alignment off the rebound.

Procedure

One team begins on the half court. Follow these steps:

1. Start by defining the routes and roles for each player. O1 handles the ball, O2 and O3 run the wide lanes, and the bigs, O4 and O5, either run to the block or rebound and trail.

(continued)

Thru *(continued)*

2. When O2 or O3 receives the pass, he can drive to the basket, pass to the low post, or pass to the top of the key for ball reversal.

3. Begin the play with O5 rebounding and passing to O1. O1 uses a sideline pass ahead to O3 and cuts through to the low block on the weak side.

4. The first big down the court, O4 in this case, goes to the block on the strong side for a post-up.

5. The second big, O5, becomes the trailer and goes to the top of the key as an outlet. If there is no low-post pass, O5 screens for O2 coming to the top of the key and then pins down for O1 (figure 6.41).

6. O2 catches the ball at the top of the key.

7. O1 pops out off O5's pin-down, receives the pass from O2, and looks for an O5 post-up or calls O5 out for a sideline pick-and-roll.

8. O4 sets an up screen for O2, who cuts to the basket looking for the lob. If there is no pass, O2 continues out the weak side and runs off a staggered double screen by O3 and O4, looking for a catch-and-shoot pass from O1 (figure 6.42).

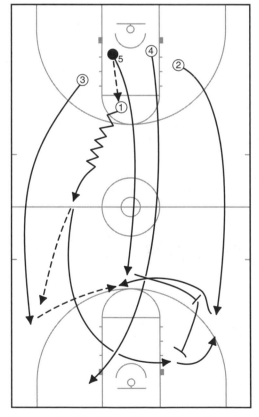

Figure 6.41 Thru: Pass to top of key.

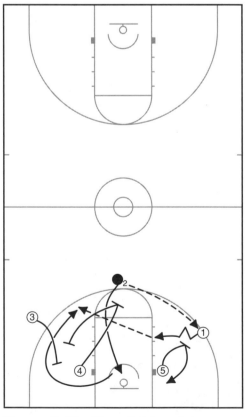

Figure 6.42 Thru: Catch and shoot.

Thru is a continuity pattern run in transition. The pattern has constant movement with post-up opportunities on both sides, up and down screens, and a pick-and-roll and catch-and-shoot option at the end. The pattern requires making decisions on the run and offers an excellent situation for analyzing player skills.

Group Shooting Drills

As players move up the competitive ladder, they must adjust to spending a lot of energy in a lengthy shooting warm-up before their games. They must expect a seriousness of purpose in this warm-up. Coaches go on the floor, especially in pro ball, and work with players during these warm-up sessions. In the NBA, teams require players to be on the floor at a designated time, usually 90 minutes before game time, to participate in group shooting drills. Group shooting drills follow along the lines of the next drill.

PREGAME WARM-UP SHOOTING

Focus

Jump-shot shooting techniques.

Procedure

Each player has a ball. Follow these steps:

1. Divide the team evenly into two groups. One group begins on the left baseline, and the other begins at the hash line on the right side.

2. The first players in line pass to the coaches, who make return passes to those players for shots (figure 6.43).

3. Players follow their shots, get their own rebounds, and return to the end of the lines.

4. The baseline shooters work on the following shots:

   a. Curl: two- and three-point shot attempts

   b. Fade: two- and three-point shot attempts

   c. Up the middle: shot at the free-throw line

   d. Up the middle: shot inside the three-point line

   e. Up the middle: three-point shot

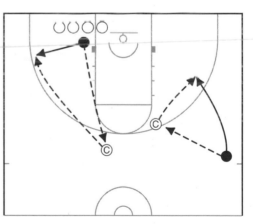

Figure 6.43 Pregame warm-up shooting.

(continued)

Pregame Warm-Up Shooting *(continued)*

5. The perimeter shooters on the right side, with a right-handed dribble, work on the following shots inside the three-point arc (when they switch to the left side, they dribble with the left hand):

   a. Catch-and-shoot with no dribble

   b. Catch-and-shoot with one dribble

   c. Catch-and-shoot with one dribble, bank shot

   d. Catch-and-shoot with two dribbles

   e. Catch-and-shoot with one dribble crossover

6. The perimeter players then repeat the sequence for three-point shots.

7. Coaches have players shoot both inside and perimeter shots on one side and then switch sides of the court.

8. After both sides have finished, the players split up and focus on position-specific shots. One coach works with the inside players on post-up moves.

9. The coach moves to the free-throw line extended and works on perimeter shooting. The players, each with a ball, begin at midcourt and pass to the coach, using the drill sequence that they used for the catch-and-shoot on the sideline.

The two-pass full-court lay-up drill, the transition offense, and the pregame shooting drills are all designed to help players adjust to the speed of the game, adjust to transition possibilities, and develop good shooting habits. Developing proper shooting mechanics with the right form, base, and follow-through is a matter of concentration and practice. Coaches at each level work constantly with players to improve their shooting skills.

An expression often heard at basketball clinics and workshops is this: "Players don't go to the park without a ball to work on their defensive skills." Check it out: Players of all ages go to the park or gym to shoot. Young players grow up thinking that they need a ball to work on their game. But basketball is much more than that, and these past two chapters have provided drills for individual improvement that go beyond just catching and shooting. Defense requires not only a different mind-set but also another person with whom to work on such things as contain, close out, and contest. Chapters 7 and 8 will explore these and many other concepts.

CHAPTER 7

Defensive Skills and Tactics

Basketball is a game in which divergent talents and skills collide. It's a game of finesse versus strength, a game in which athleticism, quickness, and strength can disrupt the flow and rhythm of a silky smooth finesse team blessed with pure shooters. Putting points on the board and defending are equally important to the outcome of games, but those tasks demand different skills. People often say that offensive players are born, not made. The same is not true of defenders. Most players naturally gravitate to scoring and shooting, whereas they must be taught team and individual defensive fundamentals.

Good defenders have several identifiable qualities. They are athletic and quick. They enjoy physical contact, anticipate well, play with reckless abandon, love to take on a challenge, and are usually good team players. They will sacrifice their bodies by taking the charge, boxing out, and defending bigger, stronger opponents. They have a focused mind-set. Defensive-minded players respond well to predetermined goals, for both the team and the individual, and they love to hold teams under their per-game field-goal percentages and keep the opponents' star players under their scoring averages.

Skilled defenders are usually well built and are seldom heavy or overweight. They are well proportioned and strong. Good defenders anticipate well, are quick to get to the ball, and are always thinking one pass ahead. By combining quickness and anticipation, skilled defenders have the ability to show an open area and then close it off before the dribbler can get to it. Another important characteristic of a good defender is aggressiveness. A good defender attacks the offensive player to make him change direction, and the best defenders are able to stay in front of their opponents and deny dribble penetration. Defensive-minded players play hard and get through screens, front opponents, and deny passes one player away.

Defense, when played right, can be consistent every night. Coaches love to say that defense travels, meaning that when the offense fails on the road, the defense will be there to keep the team in the game. Good defensive coaches understand the importance of selling defense. Lip service will not work.

Defense is the emotional part of basketball. Coaches teach players to execute basic individual defensive principles that complement team strategy. Executing the following individual principles is integral to a team defensive philosophy.

DEFENSIVE FUNDAMENTALS

In precise terms, the object of a good defensive team is to reduce opponents' field-goal percentages, free-throw attempts, and second-shot opportunities. Following are 16 defensive fundamentals: 2 guiding imperatives—communication and hustle—that provide the foundation for a sound defensive philosophy, 7 on-ball techniques, and 7 off-ball techniques.

Communication

The ability to communicate, regardless of whether it relates to politics, marriage, coaching, or playing, is vital to a successful team effort. From day one, communication is crucial because players must understand how they fit into the coach's plan, how they must go about preparing, what's expected of them in practice, and how they will be evaluated. Great coaches have the ability to convey their expectations to the staff and to the players' mutual understanding.

Nothing is more important than communicating on defense. For example, teammates must let each other know which way to drive an opponent: middle or baseline. Or, on pick-and-rolls, they must yell, "Over," "Under," "Switch," and so on, so that the player being screened knows how to play the situation. Without an oral warning, the person being screened is vulnerable.

As you will see, there is a great deal of difference in the physical on-ball and mental off-ball concentration required to communicate. For example, on ball, everyone can see when a player fouls a jump shooter, especially a three-point shot, whether it is communicated or not, but a player needs a keen eye to detect whether a defender is providing weak-side help and to communicate that knowledge to teammates.

Designing at least one communication drill for your practices in which players must yell out commands is vitally important to team success.

Hustle

Coaches are responsible for teaching defensive techniques, but players are expected to provide the necessary hustle and effort. This quote is often used to describe the player commitment: "The disappointment in losing is equal to the amount of energy expended in trying to win." Players should begin every practice session with this thought: *No one is going to outhustle me.*

Hustle plays have a way of inspiring players and exciting fans. Coaches need to encourage plays such as taking charges, going to the floor for the ball, and hitting the boards. Each of these reflects alertness, desire, and all-out hustle—and hustle is contagious. When Phil Scott, a 6-foot-6-inch (198 cm) string bean of a small forward with tremendous speed, quickness, and jumping ability, was a freshman at UNC Charlotte, he once blocked three consecutive shots during a single possession and received a standing ovation. That play inspired everyone in the arena—especially everyone pulling for UNC Charlotte!

On-Ball Defense

On-the-ball defense is the term used to define the defender guarding the player with the ball. When coaches make their man-to-man defensive assignments, they must avoid matching up a slow-footed defender on a quick, penetrating offensive opponent. With more teams running motion, passing game, dribble-drive, and pick-and-roll offenses, on-the-ball defenses becomes vulnerable and are more easily exposed. Basketball players over the years have improved ballhandling and dribbling proficiency, so defenders need constant support. Therefore, to be effective, on-the-ball defense requires quick feet, lateral dexterity, and an excellent supporting cast.

Contain the dribbler.   The object is to stay in front of the ball to keep the offensive player from penetrating. The proper stance—bent knees, being balanced, and being prepared to slide or run—is critical. Players must learn to assess their own speed and quickness as compared with that of their opponent. If the defender perceives the opponent to be quicker, then he will have to back up a step because the goal is to avoid being beaten off the dribble. Fundamentally sound defenders do not gamble and reach, thereby putting their teammates at a disadvantage.

Fake at the dribbler.   This maneuver occurs in full-court and half-court situations when two offensive players with the ball attack one defender at the basket. A defender caught in a two-on-one situation must lower his body, fake a jab step at the ball handler, and slide toward the opponent without the ball, looking to deflect or steal the pass. If no pass is made, the defender then challenges the attacking offensive player.

Close out under control.   When an offensive player has the ball within a scoring area and the defender rotates out, the action is called a close-out. The two key aspects to closing out properly are: staying down so that the ball handler can't penetrate to the basket and being under control in a position to direct the offensive player in a predetermined direction, whether to the middle or the baseline.

Contest each shot.   According to Jordan Cohn, long-time NBA scout and statistical analyst, there is a 12 percent difference between a guarded shot and an open shot. Therefore, defenders should contest every shot. The technique is to get the arms up and extended to obstruct the shooter's vision. The defender should use the same-side hand for the blocking procedure. If the shooter is right-handed, the defender's left hand should be to the ball side. If the shooter is left-handed, the right hand should be to the ball side. When low-post defenders find themselves directly behind an offensive opponent, with knees locked and at a definite disadvantage, the important goal is to avoid fouling. Instead, the defender should extend both arms as high as possible and maintain vertical position. This situation often occurs when the defender is rotating to help or when an offensive player gets a put-back.

Don't foul jump shooters.   Good defenders are aggressive in containing the dribbler, closing out, and contesting shots. But sometimes they are too aggressive, resulting in fouls on the jump shooter. Fouling jump shooters is not acceptable, especially on three-point attempts. When practicing close-out techniques, players must stay down with the hands up. If they jump off the floor, they are far more likely to foul the shooter. As the defender runs out to cover an open shooter and closes the distance to the offensive player, he takes smaller steps, drops his body lower, and becomes more under control. This action enables the defender to have complete body balance for contesting the shot or preventing dribble penetration.

Activate the passer.   Anytime the offensive player picks up the dribble, the defender should apply pressure, looking for a deflection or a steal. By picking up the dribble, the ball handler has essentially paralyzed himself. When the defender applies pressure, all defenders who are one pass away should immediately overplay and be in a denial position. The defender on the ball should call out, "Deny" or "Up," communicating to teammates that pressure defense has been activated.

Off-Ball Defense

The defensive imperative is to stop or contain the player with the ball. If one defender can control the player with the ball (which is difficult to do, especially when the defender is not allowed to touch the ball handler), then all other defenders can stay home (meaning that they continue to guard their own opponents). But if two players are needed to control the ball handler, then the defensive team must be prepared to give team support. The closest defender must be in support mode (a position to help), letting the player defending on the ball know that he is there. The following fundamentals will help players do just that.

Maintain ball–you–man position.   This defensive concept applies to the position of the defensive player guarding the weak side. The concept involves three players: the player with the ball, you in the middle, and the player you are guarding. The idea is for the weak-side defender (you) to take a position at the point of the triangle where you see the player with the ball and the player you are defending. The size or angle of the triangle will vary depending on the position of the player with the ball. The weak-side defender should always be in a position of support. This theory reinforces the importance of seeing the ball and teaches players proper weak-side position when providing weak-side help and checking cutters going from weak side to strong side. Ball–you–man is an excellent tool for teaching defensive awareness, body positioning, and player alertness.

See the ball.   Unless instructed to deny and overplay an opponent, defenders should always be able to see the ball. Not keeping the ball in view is one of the most important but most frequently violated defensive principles. Communicating this principle during the game is a full-time assignment for an assistant coach. Seeing the ball requires players to turn their bodies constantly to get into proper defensive position. A common bad habit occurs when a player retreats on defense to midcourt and beyond before trying to see the ball. In practice, constant encouragement, repetition, and sometimes penalties (like running an eighth) are needed to get this point across.

Provide weak-side help. Good defensive teams understand the concept of giving support and help, from both the weak side and the strong side. Playing good defense is about sacrifice and willingness to help a teammate in trouble. Whether it's double teaming, protecting the basket, picking up an open cutter, drawing a charge, rotating to an open shooter, or giving up a foul when necessary, players must be willing to give support. A defense that forces an offense to make the extra pass or throw to a poor shooter is an effective defense.

Overplay the wing pass. The defenders should force the receivers out on the floor to start the opponent's offense. Defenders on the wings should then overplay their opponents, denying the pass. To do this, the defender (for our purposes in this example, on the right side of the court) bends in a crouched position and extends his right arm in front of the receiver to discourage the pass. The defender must also have his left hand on the offensive player's hip in case the player decides to cut backdoor. The defender's objective is to keep the wing from getting the pass. If an opponent receives the pass, the defender uses his body angle to dictate the opponent's direction. (The game plan determines middle or baseline direction.) When the ball handler cannot make the entry pass and the offensive wing decides to reverse, the defender stays focused on the opponent. The defender stays and does not open up, but instead looks for the cutter's reaction to the ball and has the intent to deflect or steal the pass.

Step toward the receiver. Teams that have excellent shooters at the two and three positions like to run them off screens for catch-and-shoot jump shots. When teams are running curls and pin-downs, the defender on the passer should step toward the receiver each time, hoping to disrupt the timing of the play. By stepping with the pass, the defender may distract the receiver for just an instant, giving a teammate an opportunity to catch up. The defender also positions himself as a help-side defender should the offensive player decide to drive the ball middle.

Follow your man. Teams run various baseline action plays with pin-downs, screens, pop-outs, and turnouts. The defender's responsibility is to follow the offensive player as closely as possible (shadow) by trailing on his outside hip and running step for step with him. The defender does not attempt to shoot the gap or avoid the screen by going up the middle; the defender always follows his man.

Protect the basket. Giving up an easy basket is against team objectives. This concept takes root by establishing that each player is responsible for protecting the basket. If players get caught on the weak side, they must give support to the low post. If defenders are beaten, teammates must rotate to prevent a layup. Regardless of the situation, players must always protect the basket.

Box out. The defender can capture rebounds in three distinct ways: box out with a reverse pivot, box out with a step-through pivot, or disregard his opponent and attempt to outjump everyone for the ball. Two of these methods, the reverse pivot and the step-through pivot, depend on teaching and repetition. The third, outjumping opponents, depends on instinct and the player's ability to elevate. The safest and surest method for most rebounders is the step-through because the defender maintains eye contact longer. But today's players are so athletic that they prefer just to go for the ball. Coaches should expose players to all three methods, determine which one suits each player best, and help them develop their technique.

Incorporating these 16 fundamentals into a team concept brings the coach's half-court defensive philosophy into full play and gets to the heart of team defense. Here is where the coach must have a master plan, goals to accomplish the plan, and the ability to execute the plan to achieve those goals.

Choosing the Right Defenses for Your Team

Most basketball teams, from high school to college to the professionals, are built around offensively gifted players. But trying to manufacture offense is the Achilles' heel for many basketball coaches. Consequently, hard-nosed, fundamentally sound, team-focused defense is the obvious alternative. In the 2011 NBA Finals, three great Miami Heat players—Dwyane Wade (25.0 points per game), LeBron James (24.2 points per game), and Chris Bosh (18.5 points per game)—had a combined total of 68 points per game in regular-season play. In comparison, Dallas' top regular-season scorers were Dirk Nowitzki (28.0 points per game), Jason Terry (16 points per game), and Shawn Marion (12.0 points per game), who together put up 56 points per game. This 12-point offensive advantage for Miami made it clear that in order for Dallas, the underdog, to compete, they had to play outstanding defense. And that is exactly what Dallas did as they won the 2011 NBA championship in 6 games, 4 to 2. Dallas kept Miami off balance by playing an unpredictable zone defense and took the decisive final game 105 to 95 in Miami.

LEARNING TO ADJUST

During the early part of Coach Rupp's career, he was a staunch man-to-man defensive team coach. He later added a 1-3-1 half-court zone defense. He probably made the change for several reasons, but he was at least partially influenced by the fact that Ray Mears, the head coach at Tennessee and a Rupp rival, employed the defense with great success. In any event, Kentucky became a much more difficult team to attack after it added the 1-3-1 zone to its repertoire.

During the late 1960s and early 1970s while I was coaching at Transylvania College, we worked on the 1-3-1 and sprung it on a conference opponent. Our new defense was quickly exposed. Transylvania's player on the point of the zone was a 5-foot-8-inch (173 cm) guard, whereas Coach Rupp's defender on the point was 6-foot-6-inch (198 cm) Tommy Kron, who had athleticism and long arms. Small guards had a lot of trouble passing over him, whereas Transy's 5-foot-8-inch defender presented few such problems. The difference was not in the system itself, but in the placement of the players. Without changing the lineup, the players were realigned. Transy moved 6-foot-6-inch forward John Snell to the point and switched the small guard to the baseline, which made the 1-3-1 much more effective.

Coaches have a multitude of defenses to choose from, and in today's game, all teams must be able to play more than one defense. Picking the right defenses for your team is important and can provide more game options. Teams must be able to play man-to-man, play some form of a zone or zones, and press full court either in a zone or a man. Alternating defenses from man-to-man to zone can sometimes distort the opponents' timing and disrupt the flow of their offense. Defenses can be as elaborate as your imagination and willingness to take a risk.

Specifically, coaches must design a defensive plan that covers ways to influence the ball handler, defend against pick-and-rolls, rotate out of low-post double teams, determine where weak-side defense help should come from, and handle a multitude of other strategies that teams employ. Successful coaches reduce these myriad defensive techniques to the smallest common denominator to promote better understanding and eliminate confusion for both players and assistant coaches. For example, a descriptive defensive concept presented to a team might be to eliminate ball penetration. In this proactive, full-throttle defense, coaches continually applaud and encourage deflections, steals, rebounds, taking charges, proper footwork, body angles, and any play that shows hustle. Coaches set goals, and establish standards, and then build on the players' hard work ethic and defensive commitment.

As a head coach, I began by adopting the philosophy that defense was best served by teaching man-to-man fundamentals with zone principles. For me, this meant that even when we played a zone, we would match up with opponents and apply all the principles used in man-to-man, such as forcing baseline, keeping

DEFENDING AGAINST INBOUND PLAYS

While coaching in college, I used the following combinations when our opponents inbounded the ball:

Underneath our basket	2-3 zone
Side court in frontcourt	1-3-1 zone trap
Side court in backcourt	Hard man-to-man
Full court in backcourt	2-2-1 zone press

Three good things resulted from this system:

1. We used a player substitution policy in which players substituted themselves. Each inbounding spot meant different players were inserted into the game. More players got into the game based on their size (zone defenses) and quickness (man-to-man and 1-3-1 zone).

2. Opponents had to prepare for all of these different alignments.

3. Our players responded enthusiastically and competitively in an attempt to disrupt the flow of the opponents' offense.

the ball out of the middle, and not allowing ball-side cuts. Regardless of the specific defensive tactic, we determined that such defensive principles would apply equally to both man-to-man and zone defenses (refer to the defensive objectives beginning later in the chapter.

Coach John Wooden's half-court defense reflected the goals we set out to emulate, so his system was the one that we worked with. Note that this defensive system will not work for everyone; coaches must be creative and see to it that the defensive system fits their players' skills and capabilities.

COACH JOHN WOODEN'S DEFENSE

Coach John Wooden implemented his innovative defense when he coached 7-foot-3-inch (221 cm) Lew Alcindor (now known as Kareem Abdul-Jabbar) at UCLA. Coach Wooden's defense forced everything to the baseline and kept the ball out of the middle. Any time the ball is in the middle of the floor, the offense has the advantage. This advantage exists regardless of whether the ball is at the top of the key, the free-throw line, or on the low post; a player who dribble penetrates and gets into the middle has the option to attack the basket, pass to a spot-up teammate, or drive and kick. Wooden's whole concept was to stop both middle and dribble penetration by keeping the ball on the side. Another important benefit was the fact that this defense cut the floor in half, allowing UCLA to defend only one side of the court. Taking this a step further by dividing the floor into quadrants and forcing the ball baseline, Coach Wooden's teams had to defend only one quadrant of the half court.

To keep the ball out of the middle, players must assume an entirely different defensive mind-set. Instead of playing the opponent head up, the defender overplays him half a man to the outside (toward the middle) shoulder, giving the opponent only one option, to dribble-drive. With the ball on the side, the defender is driving the ball handler baseline toward the low block on the same side. For this to be effective, the center must rotate to the low block and be prepared to get the charge or block a shot if the player attempts a layup.

After the offensive player is forced baseline, a whole set of realignments occurs on defense. As the center rotates to the low block, the weak-side forward now defends the middle area and picks up the center's man. The off-side guard must read the situation and either move immediately to the middle of the free-throw line area to cut off a pass into the middle or drop down and block out the weak-side forward.

With Alcindor as the defender on the low block, the consensus was that this defense was innovative and effective. Although coaches may like the philosophy, rarely do they have a player of that caliber and size to defend the goal. Therefore, the challenge is to take the basic principles and apply them to an average team. Keeping the ball on the side, forcing the ball handler baseline, and rotating the weak-side players takes practice, reaction, and concentration.

But the success of this defense begins and ends with the concept of keeping the ball out of the middle. The team must defend the flash post and the ball at the high-, mid-, and low-post areas. Doing this against superior players is a difficult assignment, and teams must give to get. The defense must give up something—such as a guard dropping to protect in the middle or a center that must front, knowing that weak-side help is present. This is the creative part that must be employed for this defense to be effective.

For my players and assistant coaches, Wooden's defense was a complete change in their defensive thinking and foreign to their defensive comfort zone. It was different and it is risky, and without a full commitment, a team cannot be successful. That said, after using this defensive configuration to keep the ball out of the middle, I would never go back to another defense.

DEFENSIVE OBJECTIVES

A defense such as Wooden's that eliminates ball penetration breaks down into five key team defensive objectives. Coaches must identify those objectives and apply them from the beginning of practice or training camp. Here are the five key half-court team objectives, the foundation for an effective overall defense:

1. Keep the ball out of the middle.
2. Allow no middle-dribble penetration.
3. Permit no ball-side cuts.
4. Allow no second shots.
5. Contest all layups.

MY DEFENSIVE SELECTIONS

Following are the various defenses that I used with my teams. Consider these different examples and how you might apply Coach John Wooden's five basic defensive objectives to them.

1. 2-3
2. 3-2
3. 1-3-1
4. 1-3-1 half-court trap
5. Box-and-one
6. Triangle-and-two
7. 2-2-1 full-court press, trap at midcourt
8. 1-3-1 three-quarter court press, trap at midcourt and corner
9. Man-to-man full-court press, run and jump

These five objectives all lead back to the underlying goals of playing good defense: Keep the ball out of the middle, eliminate ball penetration, and force opponents to shoot from the outside. Coaches and players soon discover that these five team defensive objectives incorporate three important features:

1. They are easily understood.
2. They offer consistent objectives with teachable techniques.
3. They apply equally to man-to-man and zone coverages.

Following are these five objectives, along with drills to improve each of them.

Objective 1: Keep the Ball Out of the Middle

This defensive system combats two major offensive strategies: getting the ball into the middle of the court and reversing the ball quickly to the weak side. The key is preventing post-entry passes, whether it's to the high-, mid-, or low-post area. Is this difficult? You bet. Impossible? No, but it takes a lot of work and concentration. The following focuses on the three post areas and offers strategies for keeping the ball out of the middle. We will break the concept down by looking at each defender on the floor.

Defending the Post

The position of this defender is determined by where the ball is. The defender needs to be ball side in a three-quarter defensive position (figure 7.1). The arm closer to the ball is up in a denial position, and the leg to the ball side is slightly in front of the offensive player, almost in a hugging position. The opposite arm is bent at the elbow, and the palm is open, maintaining contact with the opponent's

Figure 7.1 Defending the post using proper technique.

hip. This contact permits the defender to know when the offensive player attempts to reverse to the basket. No excuse is acceptable for failing to execute the proper stance. Proper footwork is critical, and working individually with players so that they can find a comfort zone is helpful.

DEFENDING THE HIGH POST

Focus

Keeping the ball out of the middle while defending the high post.

Procedure

Players begin five on five on the half court. Follow these steps:

1. A coach or one of the guards begins the drill by passing to either O3 or O4, both of whom are set up at the free-throw line extended on the wings.

2. X3 has his hands up to discourage a post pass and his body down, preparing to force baseline.

3. X5 is in a three-quarter denial defensive position. His left arm is on the ball side, and his legs are straddling O5's leg on the strong side. X5's primary function is to keep the ball out of the middle. X4 is responsible for protecting the basket.

4. X1, one pass away, drops to the lap of (in front of) O5 to discourage a pass.

5. X2, two passes away, drops two steps toward the free-throw line and two steps to the ball to support weak side. X2 takes X4's position if X4 goes to trap.

6. X4, three passes away, is in a weak-side support position and has basket-protection responsibilities.

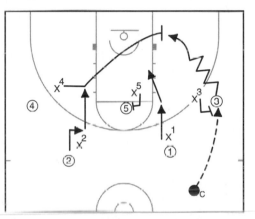

Figure 7.2 Defending the high post.

7. If O3, with the ball, drives baseline, X4 rotates to the strong-side block and stops dribble penetration (figure 7.2). X2 drops (sinks and fills) and is responsible for keeping O4 off the boards. X1 drops to the middle, looking to intercept a pass from O3 to the middle, or rotates out and covers the first pass out if a double team occurs.

DEFENDING THE MIDPOST

Focus

Keeping the ball out of the middle while defending the midpost.

Procedure

Players begin five on five on the half court. Follow these steps:

1. O3 has the ball at the free-throw line extended, by dribble or pass. X3 has his arms extended to deflect a pass and straddles O3's outside leg, forcing the baseline drive (figure 7.3).

2. O1 (or any offensive player) occu-pies the strong-side corner. X1, one pass away, drops a full step to the middle, in support position for X3, and looks for the charge or a pass to the corner.

3. X5 is in a three-quarter deny defen-sive position with his left arm ball side and his legs straddling O5's leg on the strong side. X4 protects the basket.

Figure 7.3 Defending the midpost.

4. X2, one pass away at the top of the key, drops to discourage a post pass and supports X3 in case of a middle drive. As the ball drops toward the basket, so does X2, sinking, filling, and looking for the rebound. O2, normally a spot-up shooter, is X2's primary concern. If O2 cuts to the basket or moves away, X2 maintains distance and vision to contain a pass or contest the shot.

5. X4, two passes away, is in total support mode, has basket-protection respon-sibility, and must guard against all lobs to O5.

DEFENDING THE LOW POST

Focus

Keeping the ball out of the middle with the low-post defender.

Procedure

Low post-ups come off direct passes to the post and after turnouts. Players begin five on five on the half court. Follow these steps:

1. O2 has the ball at the free-throw line extended, by dribble or pass.

2. Defensively, X2 keeps the ball on the side by forcing his opponent baseline with an exaggerated over-play, straddling the outside leg of O2 (figure 7.4). X2 must maintain ball pressure, with hands up, to eliminate an easy lob to O5. X5 plays three-quarter topside.

3. X3, at the top of the key, steps toward the ball and provides weak-side support. If the ball rotates to O3, X3 closes out under control and applies pressure to eliminate a lock-and-lob to O5.

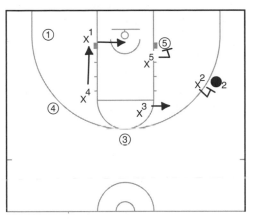

Figure 7.4 Defending the low post.

4. X1 is now the primary weak-side supporter and has the responsibility of protecting the basket, including guarding against the lob to O5.

5. X4, two passes away, must sink and fill as X1 vacates, and must be alert for O4's flash to the post area or flare screen for O3.

Defending the Ball Handler

The defender on the ball handler plays a major role in keeping the ball out of the middle. He is the first line of defense. When the ball handler picks up the dribble, the defender plays a cat-and-mouse game—first closing and then retreating with arms up and hands extended, trying to deflect, discourage, or steal the pass. Will the guard get an open look at the basket when the defender retreats? Possibly. But by knowing the tendencies of the opponents' personnel, the coach can better gauge how far the defender should be from the offensive player. The policy here is to prevent inside passes; it's better to give up a three-point attempt.

DEFENDING THE BALL HANDLER

Focus

Keeping the ball out of the middle when the ball handler picks up the dribble.

Procedure

Divide the squad evenly and work on both ends of the court. Have two players on offense and one on defense on each side of the basket. Follow these steps:

1. On the right side, O5 is at midpost when the ball handler picks up the dribble. X2 must defend with the in-and-out technique (figure 7.5).

(continued)

Defending the Ball Handler *(continued)*

2. X2 is tight defensively until the ball handler picks up the ball. X2 then retreats immediately, with hands and arms up, dropping directly to the lap of the center.

3. On the left side, O4 is on the low post when the ball handler picks up the dribble. X3 must defend with the in-and-out technique.

4. X3 is tight defensively until the ball handler picks up the ball. X3 then retreats immediately, with hands and arms up. X3 drops a couple of steps toward the low post but makes sure that he can get back and contest the offensive threat.

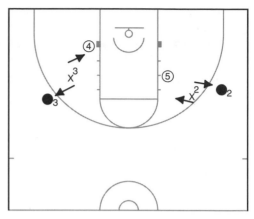

Figure 7.5 Defending the ball handler.

The defensive philosophy is to defend the inside first. Defenders need to make every effort to prevent the ball from getting to the post. If the defense must give up a shot, play the percentages and make opponents hit the outside shot. Alternate players at various positions.

Defending Weak Side

Players on the weak side provide support and must always be aware of lobs to the low post and midpost. They are also responsible for weak-side rebounding and, in most situations, have basket-protection responsibilities on baseline drives. The defender positioned on the weak side below the free-throw line, in the low corner and farthest from the basket, drops to the paint, looking to help with steals, deflections, charges, or rebounds. To communicate support to the post defenders, he is drilled to call out, "I've got the basket," or simply, "Basket."

DEFENDING WEAK SIDE

Focus

Keeping the ball out of the middle, weak-side defender, low post.

Procedure

Players begin five on five on the half court. Follow these steps:

1. O1 begins with the ball, looking to pass to O5 posting up. X5 plays three-quarter topside aggressive on the opponent.

2. X1 forces the opponent baseline or, if a pass to O5 is successful, drops down to disrupt O5's dribble (figure 7.6). When going to help, X1 still has responsibility for O1.

3. X3, at the top of key and one pass away, provides help against the middle drive and drops to discourage a weak-side flash post. X3 also has rebounding responsibilities at the free-throw line.

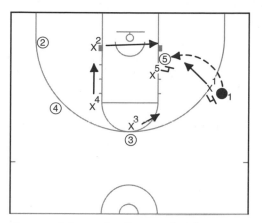

Figure 7.6 Defending weak side.

4. X2, three passes away, has basket-protection responsibilities. X2's area extends across the free-throw lane to the opposite block to stop spin drives and lob passes.

5. X4, two passes away, drops to the ball and into the weak-side paint, ready to relocate and replace X2 if X2 vacates. X4 also has weak-side rebounding responsibilities.

The major concerns in this drill should be the lock-and-lob from the side or the top of the key and the direct pass from the wing.

Defending Ball Side, One Pass Away

The defender one pass away will constantly change as the ball moves from player to player. Players should understand that after the ball enters one side of the floor, they should make a supreme effort to keep it on that side. Defenders must constantly work to push the ball to a wing position and then establish an angle that will force the ball handler baseline.

DEFENDING BALL SIDE, ONE PASS AWAY

Focus

Keeping the ball out of the middle on the ball side, one pass away.

Procedure

Players begin five on five on the half court. Follow these steps:

1. With O1 with the ball on the wing, two players are one pass away—one at the top of the key, X2, and one in the strong-side corner, X3.

(continued)

Defending Ball Side, One Pass Away *(continued)*

2. To discourage penetrating passes and give support on middle or baseline drives, X2 and X3 should move two steps from their opponents, O2 and O3, and slide one step to the post player, O5 (figure 7.7). Depending on their quickness, X2 and X3 could move closer to or farther from their opponents.

3. X4 must keep O4 in his line of vision and be ready for a lob or baseline drive by O5. X2 keys off X4 and should be ready to rotate and screen out O4 if X4 goes to help X5.

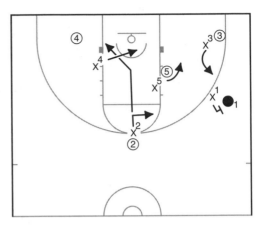

Figure 7.7 Defending ball side, one pass away.

The goals here are to prevent middle drives, keep the ball out of the post, prevent a weak-side flash post, and force the dribbler baseline, where weak-side help is waiting.

Defending the Ball in the Middle of the Court

The issue is team support when the ball is in the middle of the court, at the top of the key, in a 1-4 spread offense with no post player. In this open offensive set, the defense is at risk because of the one-on-one dribble action. The team goal is to eliminate drives to the basket and stop dribble penetration. A drive to the hoop leaves the defense vulnerable to the draw-and-kick perimeter jump shot. Here's where run-and-jump defensive principles can maintain pressure on the shooter. Let's look at a drill to practice defensive alignment and coverages when the ball is entered into the frontcourt from the top of the key.

DEFENDING THE BALL IN THE MIDDLE OF THE COURT

Focus

Keeping the ball out of the middle against a 1-4 spread or open set.

Procedure

Players begin five on five on the half court. Follow these steps:

1. O1 begins with the ball at the top of the key. X1 must contain O1 and not permit a dribble drive. After O1 passes to O3 at the wing, X1 drops toward the basket and looks to support. If O1 passes and screens away, then X1 drops and follows or switches on a predetermined call.

2. After O3 receives the ball, X2 immediately drops a step and slides to the middle for support. Should O1 and O2 exchange positions, X2 reads the situation and adjusts. If no switch occurs, X2 goes with his opponent while being conscious of middle support.

3. X3 straddles O3's outside leg and forces baseline with help from X5 (figure 7.8).

4. X5 supports X3 by dropping two steps to the middle, preventing a dribble drive. Should O5 vacate the corner, X5 calls, "Clear," and trails O5, always watching O3 and ready to double-team if O3 attacks the basket.

5. X4, two passes away, has basket-protection responsibilities and watches O3, anticipating a drive. X4 rotates across the lane looking for a charge, deflection, or steal.

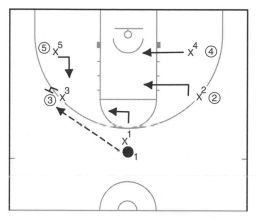

Figure 7.8 Defending the ball in the middle of the court.

Objective 2: Allow No Middle-Dribble Penetration

Most defensive objectives discussed thus far can be readily accepted, but the issue of keeping the dribbler out of the middle is not often practiced, much less subscribed to. This philosophy is contrary to the commonly held notion that the dribbler should be forced to the middle rather than to the baseline. The no-middle-dribble-penetration defense is a system designed to direct the offense rather than allow the offense to dictate the flow of the game. This aggressive defense acts on predetermined principles instead of reacting to a multitude of offensive sets. To teach this concept, begin with the most basic drills and build on them daily.

IDENTIFYING FLOOR AREAS

Focus

Defining no-middle-drive areas.

Procedure

The court is divided into six basic areas, and players' responsibilities are defined by the position on the floor. Players begin five on five in the half court. Follow these steps:

1. Practice defensive responsibilities in each of the floor areas shown.

(continued)

Identifying Floor Areas *(continued)*

2. Alternate positions so that every player has a chance to defend each floor area (figure 7.9).
3. After each player has experienced each position, ask players to concentrate on their specific position.

This drill should help all players appreciate each of the different floor responsibilities.

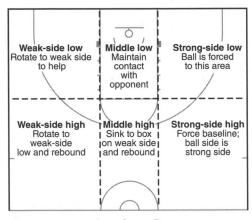

Weak-side low Rotate to weak side to help	Middle low Maintain contact with opponent	Strong-side low Ball is forced to this area
Weak-side high Rotate to weak-side low and rebound	Middle high Sink to box on weak side and rebound	Strong-side high Force baseline; ball side is strong side

Figure 7.9   Identifying floor areas.

Cutting Off the Angle

To eliminate middle drives, guards should funnel or, as coaches like to say, influence the ball handler to the side court as the ball enters the frontcourt (figure 7.10). After the ball handler declares a side, the defender must keep him on that side. The defender must understand angles, the relative speed and quickness of the opponent, and positioning.

Figure 7.10   Cutting off the angle using proper technique.

CUTTING OFF THE ANGLE

Focus

Techniques on how to cut the angle off and prevent middle penetration.

Procedure

Players divide into pairs on the half court. Follow these steps:

1. A coach makes a pass to O, the offensive player, to begin the drill.
2. After making a V-cut to get open, O faces X, the defender, with a live dribble.

3. X permits the catch and cuts the angle off to prevent the middle drive. X straddles O's body with his outside leg closer to midcourt. X's body position has his back at an angle slightly toward midcourt and at a safe distance, disallowing a blow-by.

4. O attempts to drive middle as X contains and overplays. X forces O baseline with X trying to catch up and cut off the baseline drive (figure 7.11). The idea is to show baseline and then beat the dribbler to it and cut him off.

5. O attacks the basket or pulls up for a jump shot, as X defends through the possession.

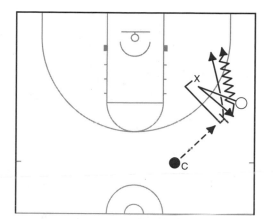

Figure 7.11 Cutting off the angle.

Players rotate from offense to defense. After they play defense, they step off the court to the rear of the line.

Closing Out

When an open opponent has the ball, the defender must close out (run out), typically over a distance of 12 to 30 feet (4 to 9 m), to contest the shot. The key here is control. The defender should sprint for about three-quarters of the distance (figure 7.12a) and then drop, bend down, and take short, choppy steps (figure 7.12b), making sure to be well balanced with the arms up when approaching the ball handler (figure 7.12c). The defender must avoid taking the ball fake and jumping off the floor, which permits the ball handler to blow by and get to the basket.

Because our goal is to prevent the middle drive, we must add another element. The defender must execute the close-out technique in a way to get the angle that forces the ball handler baseline. The concern is not to block the shot but to be under complete control and give the offensive player only one option—to drive the ball baseline, where help is waiting. Here we begin working on the team concept by building in a weak-side baseline rotation. This player is in a sink-and-fill support position, looking to protect the basket and rebound weak side.

Figure 7.12 Closing out: *(a)* sprinting three-quarters of the distance; *(b)* taking short, choppy steps; *(c)* maintaining a low, well-balanced stance.

In general, the following drills are a solid way to reinforce the four Cs of individual defense. These four factors come into play each time the defender guards the player with the ball. When a defender moves out on the floor to challenge an opponent with the ball, the following is the proper sequencing:

1. Close out under control.
2. Contain by staying in front of dribbler.
3. Contest by getting the hand on the ball side up.
4. Clear the rebound aggressively.

CLOSING OUT

Focus

Closing out so that no middle penetration occurs.

Procedure

Players begin on the half court. Split the team into two even groups. Begin with the understanding that the offensive player has the advantage because the defensive player is going to close out to the high side. Relative distance, speed, and size put the responsibility of getting to the offensive player in time to contest a shot squarely on the defender. Follow these steps:

1. To start the drill, a coach can pass the ball to O. Alternatively, X, starting under the net, can speed roll the ball to O.

2. X begins in an all-out sprint and then slows down for control, balance, and proper close-out angle.

3. X should get to O in time to contest (not block) a jump shot, be down and under control to prevent a middle drive, and in proper position to force a baseline drive (figure 7.13). X is not giving up the baseline but rather is driving O with pressure.

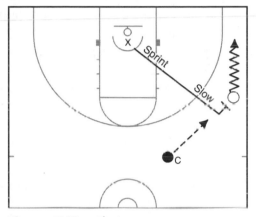

Figure 7.13 Closing out.

Players rotate offense to defense, defense to offense. The objective of the drill is to teach the defender how to get the correct angle and force a baseline drive. Coaches must constantly emphasize good footwork. As players learn to close out properly, adding a come-from-behind, shot-blocking feature enhances the drill.

CLOSE, CONTAIN, AND CONTEST

Focus

No-middle emphasis for close-out, contest, and contain techniques.

Procedure

Players begin three-on-three. Follow these steps:

1. A coach begins the drill by passing to O2. X2 yells loudly, "I've got ball!" while rotating to close out and force O2 baseline.

(continued)

Close, Contain, and Contest *(continued)*

2. X4, defending low on the weak side, must read, anticipate, and yell (so that all can hear), "I've got baseline!" X4 then sprints across the free-throw lane, clearing it, and establishes position with both feet on the opposite block. X4's call tells X2 that he has support. X4 looks to double-team the driver, block a shot attempt, or get the charge.

3. X3, defending at the top of the key, sees the drive and then yells, "Basket!" while sinking and filling, telling everyone that the basket is protected (figure 7.14). If O2 shoots a quick baseline shot, X3 must zone up and go for the weak-side rebound.

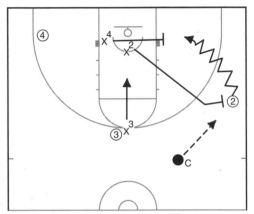

Figure 7.14   Close, contain, and contest.

4. The drill continues until the offense scores, the defense steals the ball or captures the rebound, or the ball goes out of bounds. On defensive fouls, the offense retains the ball and repeats the drill. On offensive fouls, teams exchange positions.

Defenders rotate and play all three positions. After they've completed the cycle, another group of three steps in. The emphasis in this drill is on technique, spacing, communication, weak-side rotations, basket-protection responsibility, and weak-side rebounding.

Objective 3: Permit No Ball-Side Cuts

A ball-side cut is any cut by an offensive player that puts the player between the defender and a teammate who has the ball. A good ball-side cut results in a layup for the offense or establishes a good low-post position for a player coming from weak side to strong side. Properly defended ball-side cuts prevent straight-line layups and weak-side post flashes to the elbow and low block.

The concept of eliminating ball-side cuts, the third objective of this five-part defensive philosophy, ties in with the goal of keeping the ball out of the middle. When the offensive player cuts to the basket (figure 7.15*a*), the defender must get between the ball and his opponent (figure 7.15*b*). Not defending ball-side cuts, a seemingly simple offensive maneuver, will give the offense easy baskets. The defender who permits the offensive cutter to get ball side puts the team in jeopardy for two reasons. First, the defender is vulnerable to being scored on because the opponent can get his head and shoulders in front of him, where a good pass by the player with the ball produces a layup. Second, even if the opponent does not

Figure 7.15 Permit no ball-side cuts: *(a)* offensive player initiating cut to the basket; *(b)* defender getting ball side.

score but catches the pass, the defender's only alternative is to foul and prevent the easy basket. Even worse, the opponent can make the basket and draw a foul.

The proper defensive technique for avoiding this situation is first taught in two- and three-player drills. The technique demands concentration, alertness, anticipation, quickness, and strength. The following diagrams illustrate the ball-side cut areas and how to defend them.

Guard, No Ball-Side Cut

To defend against a guard cutting to the middle, the player must slide, or jump to the ball, two steps on the cut to prevent the opponent from getting inside (between the defender and the ball). The defender should have his arms up to discourage a pass and should focus on the opponent's eyes, anticipating a pass as they clear through the free-throw lane area. In most cases when the defender slides to the ball and the opponent makes the cut, incidental contact will occur as the defender denies the opponent the easy route inside.

The following drill provides practice at the defensive guard's position as O1 makes a basket cut on the strong side of the court.

GUARD, NO BALL-SIDE CUT

Focus

Footwork execution and jump-to-the-ball techniques.

Procedure

Split the team into equal groups. Players begin two on two on the half court. Follow these steps:

1. X1 begins the drill in a normal defensive position on O1, who has the ball at the top of the key.

2. O1 passes the ball to O2 on the wing and makes a cut to the basket. X1 slides to the ball with two steps as O1 makes the cut, relocating inside O1 while defending the cut to the basket.

3. X1 should have his arms up to discourage a pass as O1 clears through the free-throw lane (figure 7.16).

4. After O1 clears the rim, X1 turns and finds the ball. Offense then moves to defense, and defense rotates off.

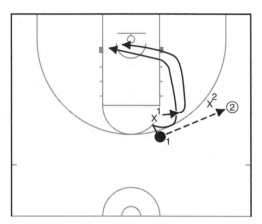

Figure 7.16   Guard, no ball-side cut.

Post, No Ball-Side Cut

A quick post flash from the weak side is one of the most difficult moves to defend in basketball. Even fundamentally solid defensive teams have difficulty guarding this move because, besides defending the flash, they have two other key weak-side responsibilities—protecting the basket and boxing out. To execute all three coverages simultaneously requires total concentration; thus, working on this defensive move is mentally demanding. If the offensive player gets his head and shoulders in front of the defender, the defender is beaten. Ideally, the defender should be a step off the offensive player and shading two steps to the middle in a normal weak-side defensive position. The player is bent in a crouching position, with arms at shoulder height, focusing on the ball–you–man theory and anticipating a cut to the basket.

FORWARD, NO BALL-SIDE CUT

Focus

Technique to defend the weak-side flash.

Procedure

Players begin on the half court. Split the team equally and follow these steps:

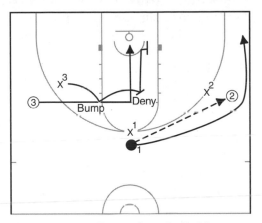

1. O1 passes to O2 and cuts behind O2 to the corner.

2. O3 makes a ball-side cut from the weak side to the strong side.

3. To defend, X3 must be positioned to the middle and able to see O3 making the ball-side cut.

Figure 7.17 Forward, no ball-side cut.

4. X3 steps in front of O3, makes contact at the elbow, and reroutes O3 down the middle of the free-throw lane (figure 7.17). X3 has his hands up and watches O3's eyes for a possible pass from the strong side.

LOW POST, NO BALL-SIDE CUT

Focus

Denying the ball-side cut in the low-post position.

Procedure

Divide the squad equally for this three-on-three drill. Players begin on the half court. Follow these steps:

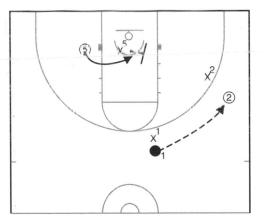

1. O1 begins the drill by passing to O2.

2. O5 makes a ball-side cut from the weak side to the strong side.

3. To defend, X5 is off O5, shading two steps to the ball.

Figure 7.18 Low post, no ball-side cut.

4. As O5 moves across the lane, X5's job is to deny the cut, the position, and the ball (figure 7.18).

5. X5 steps in and makes hip contact with his lower body, holding his arms up to discourage a pass.

6. The offense moves to defense, and the defense rotates off.

This drill teaches low-post footwork and positioning to prevent the low post from getting strong-side position.

Objective 4: Allow No Second Shots

One of the hardest things that a coach has to deal with is watching his team play solid defense throughout a possession but then give up an offensive put-back because someone failed to block out. All that hard work of keeping the ball out of the middle, eliminating weak-side flashes, denying weak-side cuts, and keeping the ball on the side goes for naught if someone fails to block out. Coaches must emphasize the importance of defensive rebounding by using box-out drills and giving regular reminders. They may find this a difficult job because many players would rather use their jumping skills to rebound instead of putting a body on the opponent.

Players are willing to work on their shooting skills and ballhandling, but they neglect the art of boxing out. Not surprisingly, players often fail to box out, and the result is that their teams lose games. Nothing is more demoralizing than watching an opponent get an offensive rebound off a missed free throw and convert it into a basket. Teaching the correct box-out techniques should begin early, in junior high school at the latest, and coaches should constantly reinforce the techniques at all levels. Regardless of their jumping ability, all players should learn two basic box-out techniques—the reverse pivot and the step-through. Let's look at these techniques.

Box Out With a Reverse Pivot

Players box out for a simple reason: to reduce the number of shot attempts by the opponent. Permitting the offense to get tip-ins, put-backs, and second-chance points is a surefire way to lose the game. Teaching proper box-out techniques should be a high priority and come early in the teaching phase of practice. Coaches must worry about two categories of offensive players—shooters and nonshooters. Boxing out the shooter is easy because the shooter is concentrating on the shot and the defender is within touching distance. On the other hand, a defender on a nonshooter is generally several steps away from the opponent, looking to give support, so the job is more difficult. The box-out technique is the same for shooters and nonshooters, and the reverse pivot is the basic move.

In this move, the defender must make contact with the offensive player as soon as possible after the shot. The defender is down, ready to rebound (figure 7.19a). If the offensive player goes to the defender's right, the defender pivots on the left foot (figure 7.19b) into the offensive player (figure 7.19c). The defender is in a crouched position, bent at the waist, elbows shoulder high, arms up, legs at least shoulder-width apart, and solidly balanced. If the offensive player goes to his left, the defensive player pivots on the right foot into the offensive player's belly (using the body mechanics already mentioned).

The biggest issue that most players and coaches have with this technique is the fact that the defender loses sight of the ball when executing the pivot. Executed properly, however, this technique neutralizes the offensive player.

Figure 7.19 Box out with a reverse pivot: *(a)* preparing to rebound; *(b)* pivoting; *(c)* boxing out.

BOX OUT WITH A REVERSE PIVOT

Focus

Reverse pivot technique on the box out.

Procedure

Three offensive and three defensive players pair off approximately 15 feet (4.5 m) from the basket. Follow these steps:

1. The drill begins with the coach passing to one of the three offensive players, who shoots the ball.

2. The defenders must execute the reverse pivot, box out, and capture the rebound.

3. If the offense gets the rebound, the defense stays on the court. The coach determines how many stops the defense has to get before the next group participates.

Box Out With a Step-Through

The major difference between the step-through and the reverse pivot box-out technique is footwork; in the step-through the defender never loses sight of the offensive player. The step-through, or front pivot, is a classic case of face guarding; the player may lose sight of the ball but never the opponent because his only responsibility is to keep the offensive player off the boards. This technique is often successful in keeping great offensive rebounders in check.

To execute boxing out on a step-through, the defender maintains eye contact with the opponent (figure 7.20*a*). When the shot is taken, the defender steps out, initiating contact with a front pivot. If the offensive player goes to the defender's right, the defender, while maintaining visual contact, pivots on the right leg (figure 7.20*b*) and steps in front of the offensive player (figure 7.20*c*), using the left leg and shoulders to block the offensive player's path to the basket. If the offensive player goes to the defender's left, the defender, while maintaining visual contact, pivots on his left leg and steps in front of the offensive player, using the right leg and shoulders to block the offensive player's path to the basket.

When the offensive player is far from the basket, the step-through is the most effective maneuver. The reverse pivot is more effective closer to the basket. Thus, coaches must teach both techniques. Inside players can quickly pivot, maintain contact, and keep the opponent away from the ball. Out on the court, however, defenders must use the step-through, with visual contact, to keep athletic players from using a running start to crash the boards from the weak side. Note that the step-through technique leaves the defender vulnerable because he loses sight of the ball.

Figure 7.20 Box out with a step-through: *(a)* preparing to rebound; *(b)* stepping through; *(c)* boxing out.

BOX OUT WITH A STEP-THROUGH

Focus

Step-through rebound technique and footwork on box-outs.

Procedure

Three offensive and three defensive players pair off approximately 15 feet (4.5 m) from the basket. Follow these steps:

1. The drill begins with the coach passing to one of the three offensive players, who shoots the ball.
2. The defenders must execute the step-through, box out, and capture the rebound.
3. If the offense gets the rebound, the defense stays on the court. The coach determines how many stops the defense has to get before the next group participates.

Objective 5: Contest All Layups

The fifth objective of a hard-nosed defense is to prevent easy layups. Fouling a player who is shooting a layup means that the player must hit two free throws from 15 feet (4.5 m) to earn those 2 points. A smart defensive team will use fouls only in the paint, using an approach called fouling for profit. Teams that foul out on the court or in the backcourt are not playing smart basketball. Players will have plenty of opportunities to use fouls in an intelligent, constructive way. Any time a player drives for an open layup or an offensive player gets an offensive rebound and is looking at a point-blank dunk, giving up a foul makes sense.

Easy scores off layups should be hard for the offense to come by. The best way to eliminate them is to stress their importance by keeping a statistic demonstrating the differences between how many layups your team gets and how many your opponent gets. This statistic is one that coaches think about but that you won't hear or read about. Keeping an account of layups and whom they were scored against can be extremely useful in certain game situations. Team and individual charts showing game-to-game totals can be a tremendous motivator.

This drill teaches proper fouling techniques when trying to prevent layups.

CONTEST ALL LAYUPS

Focus

Giving a foul at the basket.

Procedure

Players begin on the half court. Divide the team into two groups and run the drill on both ends. Os form a single line just beyond the three-point arc. This distance may vary depending on the speed of the players. Follow these steps:

1. The drill begins with the coach passing to the first player in the O line. O must attack the basket and shoot a layup.

2. X, the defender, begins under the basket. On the coach's pass, X sprints and touches the intersection of the free-throw lane and the free-throw line with his foot. X then turns and sprints back to prevent the layup by O (figure 7.21).

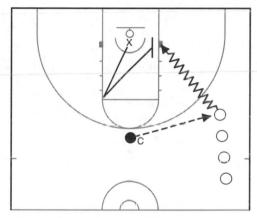

Figure 7.21 Contest all layups.

3. X should go for the ball first (to block the shot) and the offensive player's wrist second before he gets airborne. This foul should not be a hard foul, but an intelligent foul.

4. After defending three attempts, X rotates out and O becomes the new X to defend against the next O in line.

The idea is to teach players how to foul properly, using the same strategy as giving a foul when the clock is short and pressure is on the offense to score.

This chapter is a road map for both coach and player, offering a thorough explanation of what it takes to play good half-court defense. The 16 half-court individual defensive fundamentals provide greater appreciation of what it takes to play man-to-man defense. Coaches looking for a sound half-court defensive system can profit by implementing the five basic objectives discussed in the no-middle defensive strategy. The next step is to put the individual fundamentals and no-middle objectives together to build an effective half-court defense. Chapter 8 does just that.

Team Defense

Defense is the solid base on which coaches should contemplate building their teams. Defense is the steady, reliable building block on which a dependable team effort can be united. Offense, on the other hand, is like a house built on sand; it is elusive and unpredictable and can come and go on any given night or in any given moment. A few missed free throws, botched wide open shots, and unforced turnovers can turn the offensive tide quickly. In chapter 7 we discussed the individual priorities that coaches should consider when building a solid defense. In this chapter we integrate those individual priorities into teachable drills as we build a cohesive team defense.

TEAM DEFENSIVE ALIGNMENTS

To build a solid defensive foundation, coaches must be sure that players understand the individual priorities discussed in chapter 7. An excellent method to teach these fundamentals is to select four each day, establish four stations (two on each half court), and have the players rotate through them. On the second day, refresh players by going over the drills from the day before and then teach a new priority. Repeat this process until all the principles are covered. This way the players are introduced to all priorities. From here you can move into teaching the all-purpose shell described next and begin building a cohesive defensive unit.

Shell

The shell is an active defense taught on the half court using four players on defense in a box set—two guards out front (called perimeter players) and two big players (called bigs or inside players) who slide from the baseline (deep and wide) to the elbow area, free-throw line extended. Shell work begins with a review of footwork, spacing, proper angles on close-outs, floor alignment for support, and body movement as the ball is passed.

When the four-on-four shell drill first came into play in the early 1990s, most coaches were hesitant to use it because it was new and different. As coaches experimented and shared their findings about the defensive shell drill, however, their confidence grew, and soon everyone was teaching their own version of this defensive technique. Initially, the four-on-four shell drill was used for teaching the mechanics for ball-side cuts and weak-side post flashes. As time passed, many versions of the shell drill were created.

Shell work in this chapter features two passing drills—around the horn and diagonal. For the purpose of these drills, players will be designated as Xs and Os rather than by position, because all positions are interchangeable in this drill. Begin each drill with a token defense or no defense, just slides. The coach determines when to initiate live action.

Defending Passes Around the Horn

This drill is a position and support help drill that teaches players the importance of floor balance and weak-side or off-the-ball support; it leads right into close-out, contain, and control features. All these options merge into an excellent teaching drill for footwork, balance, and not getting faked off the floor on perimeter shots. The run out to contain a player with the ball has to be quick, but not so fast that the defender gets beaten off the dribble. In this way, passing around the horn is also a useful method for teaching individual defense.

This drill begins with the coach defining the body angle, stance, slide, and support responsibilities for all four defenders as the offense moves the ball from the right corner to the right wing, from the right wing across to the left wing, and from the left wing to the left corner. The defender rotating to check the offensive player receiving the pass must execute the proper close-out technique. To save time and confusion, have at least three teams with different-colored scrimmage jerseys.

DEFENDING PASSES AROUND THE HORN

Focus

Around-the-horn passing for defensive slide techniques and stance.

Procedure

Players begin in the half-court, four-player shell set. Follow these steps:

1. Begin in a box set. Two perimeter players are at the elbow extended, beyond the three-point line. The two big men are wide and deep on the baseline.

2. On a pass from perimeter to baseline, all four defenders move in unison with slides and close-out techniques. X1, guarding the ball, drops down two steps and slides one step toward the ball, protecting against the middle drive. X2 drops to the middle of the free-throw line, discouraging middle passes. X3 closes out under control, influencing the shooter baseline. X4, in the weak-side corner, rotates to the block, looking to help (figure 8.1). If an offensive player drives baseline, X4 continues to the strong-side block for a double team.

3. After the four defenders make their slides, the offense should pass the ball back out to the strong-side perimeter player, who passes to the weak-side perimeter player. He then passes to the weak-side corner player.

4. At each passing interval, the defensive players slide and rotate either to cover the ball or to be in a help position (figure 8.2).

5. The drill ends when the ball rotates from one corner to the opposite corner and back. The offense then goes to defense, the defense steps off, and four additional offensive players come to the court.

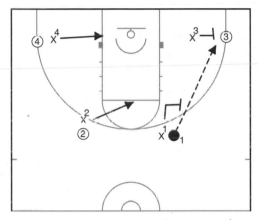

Figure 8.1 Defending passes around the horn: Make defensive adjustments on a pass from perimeter to baseline.

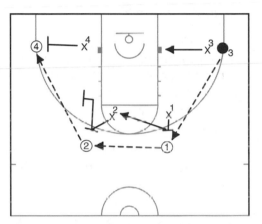

Figure 8.2 Defending passes around the horn: Make defensive adjustments on passes from corner to corner.

Defending Diagonal Passes

The diagonal passing entry into the shell drill adds three important new coverages to defend—longer passes, the skip pass, and live offensive sets. Begin the drill by explaining each defender's shifting position as the ball moves from player to player. To initiate the drill, the passing sequence begins with the perimeter player throwing a long diagonal pass to the corner. The corner passes to the opposite corner, and that receiver then passes out diagonally to the opposite perimeter player. After all four players have touched the ball, live action can begin. To teach proper player defensive coverage, the drill uses four-man play sets.

As the ball moves from player to player, coaches should stress the ball–you–man concept and emphasize coverage area, proper spacing, and close-out techniques. After the drill becomes live, the coach has an opportunity to evaluate the players' defensive abilities, speed, anticipation, and comprehension.

DEFENDING DIAGONAL PASSES

Focus

Diagonal pass drill passing and sliding techniques.

Procedure

Players begin in the half-court shell set. Players practice the same defensive slides that they used in around the horn. Players close out under control, and perimeter players sink and fill, according to the position of the ball and their positions on the floor. Follow these steps:

1. The offense makes three passes before the drill becomes live. The first pass goes from the perimeter to the far corner, the second pass goes baseline to baseline, and the third pass goes from the baseline diagonally to the perimeter. Before the defensive players begin their slides, the offensive players should practice the passing routine. After they have done that, add defensive slides and player movement as the ball rotates.

2. To start, the defender on the ball is up on the opponent in normal defensive position. The other guard defender is in help position, denying the middle drive. The defenders guarding the big men on the baseline start at the free-throw lane.

3. When the ball is passed to a big man in the corner, the defender rotates in a close-out stance to contain and influence baseline. The weak-side big man rotates to the free-throw lane, protecting against the drive (figure 8.3). These defenders work in tandem, as though tied together at the waist with a rope. In theory, when one goes out, he pulls the other to the free-throw lane.

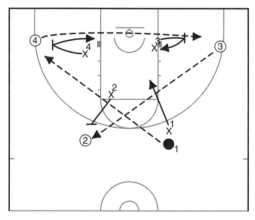

Figure 8.3 Defending diagonal passes.

Five-on-Five

After approximately 10 minutes of teaching defensive fundamentals on individual coverage, body positioning, floor balance, and close-out techniques in the shell drills above, the next 10 to 15 minutes should be follow-up work for five-on-five live half-court work.

FIVE-ON-FIVE

Focus

Scrimmage work emphasizing defensive execution, getting stops, rebounding, positioning, support and help off the ball, limited fouling, and the importance of each possession.

Procedure

Players begin on the half court five on five. Follow these steps:

1. Split the team into three teams of five, separated by different-colored jerseys. Assistant coaches are assigned specific teams, and the teams on offense rotate on each possession.

2. The team on defense has 10 possessions to make as many defensive stops as possible. At the end of 10 possessions, the teams rotate and another defensive unit steps in.

3. When all three teams complete their 10 defensive possessions, a winner is declared.

This drill is always spirited, and usually a second round of five possessions is played. Although this drill focuses on defense, it also touches on offensive execution. During early season practices, teams run their own team's offensive sets, but as you get into games, you may want to run upcoming opponents' offensive sets as part of your scouting report preparation.

Teams play good defense when players are alert, active, and aggressive and when they are constantly anticipating the next move from the offense. Players constantly move their heads, feet, arms, and bodies, depending on where the ball is. A defender guarding one pass away could be assigned to deny the ball, push the player out to receive the pass, or play soft and off. Players two passes away must recognize what their teammates are doing and either drop two steps toward the basket or adjust by moving to a closer support position. No one is ever static on defense.

Defensive Screening Sets

A single screen occurs when an offensive player rubs the defender off a stationary teammate (the screener) to get open for a shot. An inside big man on the low post usually sets the screen. In today's game, screens make it possible for players to get open for good shots and rotate passes as play develops. In almost every half-court offensive set, someone is getting screened, and defenders must anticipate the contact and avoid being ensnarled in a trap. To avoid being surprised by the kind of screen used, players and coaches must be alert to identify the screen and be prepared to counter it with good techniques. Following are the six most common screening methods: baseline screens, pin-downs, cross screens (including screen-the-screener sets), sideline and middle pick-and-rolls, and drag sets.

Defending Baseline Screens

Baseline screens are off-the-ball screens. Normally, good shooters use them to curl off a big man for a catch-and-shoot. The range of the shooters, as well as their individual skills, determines the route that they take. The defender must know the opponent's strengths and weaknesses to defend effectively. A whole range of individual player tendencies is available from scouting reports, game films, and scouting services. Does the offensive player prefer to come out off the screen left or right? Is the offensive player right-handed or left-handed? Does the offensive player like to dribble before taking a shot? Does he like to curl tight off the screen and attack the basket? Does the player like to fade? If crowded, will he put it on the floor or look to pass? Does he like to catch, measure the defender, and shoot, drive, or pass? Does the player favor going right or left? Coaches have access to this kind of information as it relates to all the drills explained in this chapter, but the information is effective only if used.

Baseline screens can be single or double, and the offensive player using the screen can curl, fade, or slide to the corner. The ideal way to defend this maneuver is to give the offensive player only one way to run. The defender must position himself to the opponents' right or left outside hip, whichever the case may be (not face to face), bend at the knees, and block the offensive player's path, forcing him to exit opposite. This positioning allows the defender to run step for step with the offensive player and avoid the screen or screens. The defender should always try to get small, avoid the screens, and never shortcut up the middle, thinking that he can catch up to the offensive player. A smart offensive player will win every time. For this stationary screen, the direction in which the defender intends to drive the offensive player should be predetermined.

DEFENDING BASELINE SCREENS

Focus

Execution, communication, and techniques versus baseline screen, single or double.

Procedure

Players begin on the half court five on five. Follow these steps:

1. O1 begins at the top of the key with the ball in the middle of the court, and O2 lines up directly under the net facing O1. O3 and O5 set a double screen on the left side of the free-throw lane, and O4 sets a single screen on the right side of the free-throw lane.

2. The play is designed specifically for O2, the team's best catch-and-shoot guard, to use the option of running off either the double screen or the single screen. O1 reads O2's cut and dribbles to the same side, looking to pass to O2 for a catch-and-shoot. This play is run directly at X2, who must do the work early. The defensive objective is to make sure that O2 has only one way to run. When O2 begins moving under the basket and to the net, X2 must position himself to prevent two issues: First, X2 should take a position on the left hip of O2 so that O2 only has one way to run, out the single side, and second, X2 needs to make sure that he has the right arm up and extended to prevent a direct pass from O1 to O2.

3. Single-side action: If O2 goes off the single side (figure 8.4), O4 will set the screen and post up on the low block. If O2 doesn't take a quick shot, O2 looks inside immediately for O4 on a post-up. If O4 is not open, he will turn and screen across for O5 or O3, whichever one is designated. As O2 makes a move and runs off O4 out the single side, X2 must get low and ride on O2's outside hip as O2 speed cuts off O4's screen. The offensive target is O2 for a catch-and-shoot, and X2 is responsible for disrupting O2's rhythm. If O2 does not get the shot, the offense will then go to different options based on their personnel.

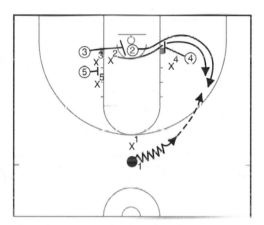

Figure 8.4 Defending baseline screens (single or double).

4. Double-side action: If O2 goes out the double side, O3 vacates his position as O2 makes his cut and O5 slides to the low post. O3 continues across the lane and runs off O4's screen on the weak side. X2 must again fight through the screen.

Defending Pin-Down Screens

This play occurs when an offensive player sets up deep on the block or wide to one side, free-throw line extended. The pin-down screen can occur on a ball reversal to the weak side, as illustrated in the drill that follows, or it can be a more complicated three-man technique that involves a screen and pass followed by a second screen and pass. The most common pin-down screen involves O5, positioned at the elbow or on the free throw line, and either O2 or O3, who sets up on the same-side low block. The pin-down screen takes place when O5 sets a down screen for the guard, who works off the screen and relocates to the top of the key.

COMPLEX PIN-DOWN SCREEN

A pin-down screen can be a moving screen like the one that Dallas runs for Dirk Nowitzki. Nowitzki usually sets the first screen to establish a low-post position, and then he works off the second screen to get open for his one-on-one fall-back jumper. In the 2011 NBA Finals, the complex version of this play occurred with the ball on the strong side as the offensive player with the ball dribbled to the free-throw line extended. The first pass occurred when Nowitzki, at the right elbow, turned and executed a screen for a teammate located on the right-side block. The teammate used Nowitzki's screen and relocated to the top of the key, where he received the first pass. After the ball handler passed to the top of the key, he immediately set the pin-down screen on Nowitzki's defender. The ball handler at the top of the key passed to Nowitzki, and he went one on one against his defender.

Defending this play is difficult. When the screen is set out high on the wing, the defender should crowd the offensive player. The defender must not go under the screen because doing so will permit a shot for the offense. This type of screen comes mostly out of secondary breaks with excellent shooters involved. The defender must maintain close pressure to contest the shot.

DEFENDING PIN-DOWN SCREENS

Focus

Execution, communication, and techniques versus the pin-down screen.

Procedure

Players begin on the half court five on five. Follow these steps:

1. Dallas executes the pin-down screen better than most teams, and they begin in a wide set with O1 taking the ball to the right-side free-throw line extended. O4 sets up at the elbow area just off the right-side free-throw lane in preparation for a pin-down screen for O2 on the low block, right side. O5 sets up on the elbow left side, and O3 is low toward the corner on the left side.

2. Play begins as O1 dribbles toward the right sideline, free-throw line extended. O4 sets a pin-down screen for O2 on the low block. O2 relocates to the top of the key. Defensively, this should be a two-player technique. Defender X4, guarding the player setting the screen on O2, opens up, gives space, and yells,

"Get through," or "Watch the screen." The offensive player setting the screen (O4) moves directly in line with defender X2, forcing the defensive player to alter his direction when chasing offensive player O2, who is relocating to the top of the key.

3. Defender X2, who is getting screened, must break down, get small, maintain contact, and be prepared to push his opponent away from the screen and follow as closely as possible. The screen occurs in a tight space, and the offensive player is looking to catch and shoot, so the closer the defender is, the better the defense is.

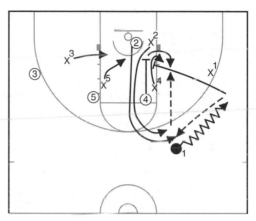

4. O1 passes to O2 and sets a second pin-down screen on O4's opponent at the low block. O4 uses the screen and rubs off O1 to establish a low-post position. X4 must break down, get small, maintain contact, and be prepared to push his opponent away from the screen and follow as closely as possible (figure 8.5).

Figure 8.5   Defending pin-down screens.

5. O2 passes to O4, who has the whole side cleared for him to operate.

Pin-down screens are effective in relocating players and creating mismatches on switches. In Dallas' case, the pin-down screen is a tremendous offensive tool.

Defending Cross Screens

The cross screen occurs when a small guard screens for a big center or power forward low on opposite blocks. Both NBA finalists used this offensive set: Miami had Bibby screening for James, and Dallas had Kidd and others screening for Nowitzki.

There are two effective ways of getting into the cross screen. First, the low-post feed can come from a direct pass when the guard begins on the low block, crosses the free-throw lane, and sets the screen for the center. The second technique can come off an indirect pass as the guard initiates the play from the perimeter position and runs into the cross screen. Both are defended the same way. For illustration purposes, the cross screen that follows begins with the guard on the perimeter.

DEFENDING CROSS SCREENS

Focus

Execution, communication, and techniques versus the cross screen.

Procedure

Players begin on the half court five on five. Follow these steps:

1. Player O5 sets up on the right-side low block. O1 begins the play with a pass to O3 at the free-throw line extended.

2. O1 runs a hard cut to the same-side low block while working into position to set a cross screen for O5. X1 must be alert to bump O1 as he moves across the free-throw lane in preparation for a screen on O5's defender.

3. The physical action begins as O1 moves across the lane, looking to set a screen on X5. In preparation for the cross screen, X5 must be in position to see both the ball and the opponent.

4. Both X1 and X5 must execute their defensive techniques to avoid getting caught in the screen. X1 forces O1 down and low so that O1 cannot get a good angle to screen X5. X5 steps toward O1's screen while maintaining vision, position, and hand contact with O5.

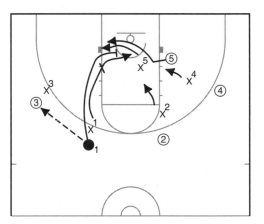

5. X5 pushes O5 down toward the end line under the block, and X1 steps directly in the passing lane in front of O5 and prevents O3's pass. X5 maintains contact with O5 and works to maneuver O5 off the low block (figure 8.6).

Figure 8.6 Defending cross screens.

6. The reason that O1 screens for O5 is to produce a switch. In this case, X5 needs to step back and make sure that O5 does not get across the lane on the inside. X5 must push with his arms and force O5 toward the baseline. Then X1, defending O1 setting the screen, bumps O5, slowing him down to give X5 time to regain position on O5.

DEFENDING CROSS-SCREEN, SCREEN-THE-SCREENER SETS

Focus

Execution, communication, and techniques versus cross-screen, screen-the-screener sets.

Procedure

When offensive teams see the defense forcing down crossing action and how the defense plays the cross screen, they will change and involve a third screener in the play, causing more defensive adjustments. Players begin on the half court five on five. Follow these steps:

1. Play begins with O1 in the middle of the court above the top of the key, O2 on the left block, O5 on the right block, O4 in the middle of the free-throw lane, and O3 on the left side, free-throw line extended.

2. O1 passes to O3 and moves directly to the right-side free-throw line extended. On O3's catch, O2 executes a cross screen for O5, who relocates to the left block. Both X2 and X5 must execute their defensive techniques to avoid getting caught in the screen. X2 forces O2 down and low so that O2 cannot get a good angle to screen X5. X5 steps toward O2's screen while maintaining vision, position, and hand contact with O5.

3. O4, on the free-throw line, sets a pin-down screen on O2's defender as O5 is moving across the lane. O2 uses O4's screen to flash to the middle of the free-throw circle, looking for a catch-and-shoot. O4 posts up on the right-side block. Defensively, the big issue comes into play with O4's screen on X2. X4 must bump O4 and slow up the pin-down screen (figure 8.7). It may also cause O2 to commit a three-second violation.

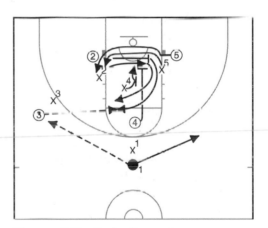

Figure 8.7 Defending cross screen, screen-the-screener sets.

4. O3 has three basic options. The first look is to O5 posting up, the second choice is to O2 at the free-throw line, and the third alternative is to reverse the ball to O1 by passing or dribbling.

Defending this set is difficult if the offensive team sets good screens. What is required is a coordinated defensive effort with a lot of talking, bumping, denying, and possibly switching on the last screen to prevent an easy basket.

Defending Pick-and-Roll Screens

The pick-and-roll screen on the ball is one of the most frequently used and effective offensive sets in basketball, often separating the good players from the great ones. The pick-and-roll is a direct attack on guards who cannot get over screens, post players who will not step out with the screener, and weak-side defenders who go to sleep on good jump shooters. Because offensive schemes offer many ways of getting into the pick-and-roll, coaches must have a well-developed defensive plan of attack.

Early on, the pick-and-roll was used between the guard with the ball and a big man setting the screen either on the sideline or, more often, at the top of the key. Today, the pick-and-roll has become an offense unto itself. The pick-and-roll is especially hard to defend when it is initiated by a skilled offensive guard who makes good decisions. Not all guards can run the pick-and-roll effectively, but the great ones make their living doing it; Steve Nash of the Phoenix Suns, Chris Paul of the Los Angeles Clippers, and John Wall of the Washington Wizards control their teams' offense by running the pick-and-roll almost exclusively. Good point guards have flexibility in knowing when and where to attack their opponent.

Choosing the time and floor location to run the pick-and-roll depends on the team's individual personnel: Some teams focus on the sideline, some like the middle, and others are exceptional in transition using drags (like the 2012 Miami Heat, with Dwyane Wade and LeBron James handling the ball). This requires the defense to define exactly how they are going to defend each procedure. Pick-and-roll screens on the sideline and in the middle are predetermined and less complicated to cover because the defense knows that they are coming. Currently, the problems that defenses must deal with are random pick-and-rolls and multiple cross screeners. More teams are using the run-in-to across the free-throw lane pick-and-roll technique.

Many techniques are used to defend the pick-and-roll: the trap, the hedge and get back (the defender guarding the player who is setting the screen takes a quick step out and shows himself as if preparing to trap the dribbler but is only buying time, or slowing down the ball handler, so that the teammate who is guarding the dribbler can catch up), the hard hedge (the big man steps out and does not let the dribbler split him and the other defender or turn the corner), the show or get through (the defender shows but backs off to help his teammate maintain a good defensive position on the ball handler), the soft play (the defender stays back and does not commit to attacking or faking at the ball handler), and the switch. The defensive method employed depends on talent, team speed and quickness, the ability to anticipate, and the opponent's effectiveness in running pick-and-rolls.

Regardless of where on the floor the offense runs the pick-and-roll or the defensive method used to defend it, the defender should follow three important rules:

1. The defender on the screen setter must communicate by talking and letting his teammate know that the pick is coming.
2. The defender on the ball must not let the offensive guard split him and the defender on the screener.
3. If the decision is to trap, the defenders trapping must stay in it until the guard passes the ball.

Sideline Pick-and-Rolls   The most important decision in defending the sideline pick-and-roll concerns how to play the guard with the ball. The defense must know the guard's tendencies. If the guard turns the corner and gets into the lane, will he pull up and take a jumper, drive for a layup, or draw and kick to an open teammate?

Determining the best defensive strategy depends on the skill of the ball handler. Going over the screen would make good sense against a good jump shooter, whereas going under is recommended against a player who likes to attack the basket. After the defense makes a decision about how to defend the ball handler, the focus is on what happens when a screen is set. What the defense does at the point of the screen dictates the action that follows. When O5 sets the screen for O1, X1 and X5 must know player tendencies and communicate their predetermined instructions. Any confusion here gives the offense the advantage.

DEFENDING SIDELINE PICK-AND-ROLLS

Focus

Execution, communication, and technique versus the sideline pick-and-roll.

Procedure

Players begin five on five on the half court. Follow these steps:

1. O1 dribbles to the free-throw line extended, pushing O3 to the corner. O5, at the high post, relocates to set a pick-and-roll screen for O1.

2. The first decision comes at the point of O5's screen on O1. The defense must predetermine its technique: stay with the opponent, go under, fight over, switch, or trap to create a team rotation process.

3. If O1 gets to the middle, the interior defense has to scramble. O1 has the following options:

   a. O1 can shoot the jump shot.

   b. O1 can pass to O5, who, after setting the screen, rolls to the basket.

   c. O1 can pass to O2 for the jump shot or drive and dish to O4.

4. Figure 8.8 reflects that a sideline trap has occurred and O1 has retreated toward midcourt. For this technique to be effective, X1 and X5 must stay in the double team, or trap, forcing O1 either to pick up the dribble or to pass the ball. In figure 8.8, O1 picks up the dribble and is forced to pass.

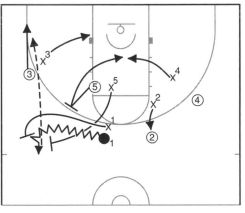

Figure 8.8   Defending sideline pick-and-rolls.

(continued)

Defending Sideline Pick-and-Rolls *(continued)*

5. The double team creates a rotation situation, and X3 and X4 must be alert to cover O5 as he rolls to the basket. O1 passes to O3, and X4 must rotate and cover O5, while X2 covers the middle area. (Had the pass been to O4, X3 would have been responsible for covering O5.) X5's responsibility on the pass is to rotate back toward the basket and pick up either O4 or O3, whichever one is open. And if the defensive trap works, O2 must sink and find O4 should X4 rotate to cover O5.

Middle Pick-and-Rolls   The middle pick-and-roll is difficult to defend because the screener is typically a big man who screens and then rolls to the basket. Alternatively, the big man may be a good perimeter shooter who pops out for the medium-range jumper. Defending these sets takes much practice and team coordination. The all-important defensive decision comes at the point of the screen, with O5 screening X1. How the defense handles this screen determines success or failure.

A defense that cannot control the point of the screen in a straight man-to-man will need to practice various methods and find an acceptable option. Many times on defense, a coach must choose the best of the worst options because of the talent disparity. Playing straight up on great players and great play sets may be the kiss of death. Dallas made an intelligent defensive adjustment in game 7 of the 2011 NBA Finals by playing zone against Miami. Dallas knew that guarding Wade, Bosh, and James man-to-man would be almost impossible, but the zone took Miami out of their patterns, their timing, and their comfort zone.

When trying to overcome a talent deficit, defending the pick-and-roll straight up is not an option. This process is complicated, and coaches may want to consider these options: a hard hedge and back (the big man steps out and does not let the dribbler split him and the other defender or turn the corner; the big man shows hard but does not let the dribbler penetrate); a trap, a soft open up and under (in which the defender stays back and does not commit to attacking or faking at the ball handler) in an attempt to eliminate O1's drive; or an automatic switch and play soft on O1.

Coverage options vary, but maintaining close defensive presence on both the ball handler and the screener is a major goal. The defense cannot give O1 an open drive, O5 a layup on a roll to the basket, or O4 an open 15-foot (4.5 m) pop-out shot rotating high off O5's dive to the basket. They must also contend with not allowing O2 or O3 open looks at three-point shots. This diagram shows the various shots that must be defended in the middle pick-and-roll.

DEFENDING MIDDLE PICK-AND-ROLLS

Focus

Execution, communication, and technique versus the middle pick-and-roll.

Procedure

Players begin five on five on the half court. Follow these steps:

1. O1 begins with the ball above the top of key. O2 is at the right-side free-throw line extended, and O3 is at the left-side free-throw line extended, both above the three-point line. O5 is located at the top of the key, ready to set a screen for O1, and O4 sits at the left low post, opposite the way that O1 will drive.

2. O1 runs the play to the right side. O5 sets up to screen above the top of the circle, the left shoulder toward midcourt. X1 and X5 must communicate and defend against O5's screen. Defending at the point of the screen means not letting O1 split X1 and X5 on the initial contact. Hearing a signal from X5, X1 can drop back even with O5, avoiding the screen and playing soft to keep O1 in front of him or X1 can attack O1, attempting to double up with X5. X1 may also use one of the other options mentioned previously.

3. Keeping O1 in front of X1 is the key. If X1 plays soft and stays in front of O1, then X2 and X3 can stay home and reduce the possibility of a three pointer. This also cuts down on O1's ability to draw and kick. In figure 8.9, X1 and X5 are able to contain O1.

Figure 8.9 Defending middle pick-and-rolls.

4. When X5 stays with the dribbler, O5 rolls immediately to the basket, forcing the defense to rotate. As O5 rolls to the basket, O4 pops up the lane, which puts the offense in an advantageous position for a high–low opportunity. To eliminate rotations, a defense can play zone, switch, or attack the ball handler to force him away from the screen.

Drag Sets The most difficult pick-and-roll to defend is the one set when the defense is retreating in transition. Any offensive player can establish a screening position or, as the dribbler is advancing, can set a screen on the defensive player, freeing up the dribbler to attack the basket. The drag pick-and-roll is a spontaneous, random act that occurs as the offense is progressing up the court, so teaching proper coverage is best illustrated by explaining, demonstrating, and practicing off hit or missed free throws.

Normally, the drag pick-and-roll is performed just after the dribbler enters the frontcourt to either sideline, permitting the dribbler to get to the middle. Exceptional ball handlers in the NBA like screens to be set at the top of the key, where they can explode down the middle for a layup or a draw-and-kick.

Drags, as well as random pick-and-rolls, are extremely difficult to defend, and ways to defend them must be constantly addressed.

DEFENDING DRAG SETS

Focus

Execution, communication, and technique versus drag sets.

Procedure

This drill emphasizes the importance of finding the opponent early and being prepared to help. Players begin following a made free throw. Follow these steps:

1. Begin by teaching backcourt sideline coverage. O5 inbounds the ball and gets it to O1, who begins a dribble attack up either sideline as the defensive team retreats.

2. As O1, who is attempting to elude constant pressure from X1, gets close to midcourt or to the high frontcourt sideline, O5, trailing down the middle, changes direction and sets a screen on X1 that enables O1 to get to the middle.

3. This defensive play is difficult because the defense is retreating and looking for their assigned opponents. In most cases, the best help is calling out the screen, and if X1 gets screened, X5 must switch, slow down, and string out O1 (figure 8.10). This action gives X1 a chance

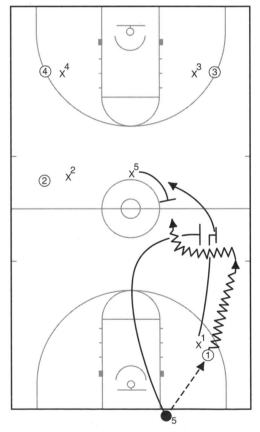

Figure 8.10 Defending drag sets.

to recover and get back to O1. What X5 must not do is let O1 penetrate middle off the dribble.

4. If O1 does beat X1, X5 must be prepared to help.

Defending the drag pick-and-roll is becoming more prevalent, and this drill simulates game conditions.

Disrupting Full-Court Transitions

Certain teams are hard to beat because of specific defensive attributes. Good examples include half-court defenses that challenge every shot, teams that take away dribble penetration, teams that limit offensive rebounds, teams that minimize the number of easy baskets, teams that stay out of foul trouble, and teams that limit or reduce the number of transition baskets that their opponents score. Limiting transition baskets is a matter of emphasizing a number of fundamentals. Following are some defensive principles that can be of assistance.

Rebounding   When designing offensive plays, a coach should always factor in offensive rebounders in case the shot is missed. To do this, designated players are required to go to the board on each half-court play. If the shot is missed and they cannot retrieve it, they are in good position to be the first line of defense and take away the opponents' quick outlet pass that initiates the fast break. Big men especially should extend their arms high and smother or clamp down on the rebounder, restricting an easy outlet. At best, a deflection or an interception results, and at worst an outlet pass is slowed down. Should the rebounder try to dribble out, one of the defenders should cover the player immediately. All of this is possible only when you teach designated rebounders to attack the boards and then add this defensive maneuver of containing the outlet and the dribble-out.

Stopping the Ball   The goal here is to stop an opponent's transition game. Stopping the ball in transition begins when offensive sets are designed. To slow down an opponent in transition, offensive plays should be designed to send three inside players to the offensive boards, one guard to the free-throw line looking for the long rebound, and one guard back to defend against the long pass. In this defensive formation, the inside players jam the rebounders, the guard covering the long rebound has the first pass out responsibility, and the guard back picks up and contains the first opponent crossing the midcourt line.

Lane Denial   The offense moves the ball up the court in transition in two basic ways: passing and dribbling. Passing is by far the quickest. For that reason, the big men should jam the rebounders to negate the quick outlet that is so important to the transition game. Scouting reports can provide valuable information about an opponent's transition game, such as whether they favor one guard over the other or whether the guards come back for the pass or leak out.

In a 3-1-1 tandem defensive alignment, the up guard has the responsibility to deny first and then stay in front of the offensive guard in case he receives the outlet pass. After the guard receives the outlet pass, is he looking to dribble up or pass long down the sideline? If the guard is looking to pass, that would mean that a teammate is leaking out. If the guard dribbles up, a defensive player must stay in front and contain him.

The first line of defense is to jam the rebounder, and the second is for the up guard to deny. Either way, the defense must contain and control the outlet guard receiver.

Helping In normal transition defense, big men must sprint back and provide middle containment support for the player defending the ball handler. Yet certain transition situations are difficult to defend against. If the offense turns the ball over out front, the defense is in a scramble and there is no help. A long rebound that the opponent catches on a dead run also puts the defense at a big disadvantage. These two situations eliminate the possibility of getting containment help from the big men. Quick offensive guards in today's game go coast to coast; therefore, all five defenders must sprint back, defend the paint, and protect the basket.

Switching Defenses

One of the most overlooked and underused techniques in coaching is the defensive procedure of switching defenses, as discussed earlier in the transition section. Most coaches begin learning man-to-man defense first and, for whatever reason, stay in that track without even considering zones and the ability to switch defenses as the game progresses.

The issue of defense is determining whom you must guard and recognizing those whom you do not need to guard. Regardless of the competition level, few teams have as many as three outstanding point producers, as did the NBA 2011 finalist Miami Heat, who had James, Wade, and Bosh, and even they did not win it all. When Dallas switched defenses and went zone, the game changed. Miami's shots came from different areas, offensive rebounds disappeared, and the flow and tempo of the game changed.

In close ball games, the momentum can change with one or two plays. Switching from a man-to-man to a box-and-one zone against a hot shooting guard can sometimes take that guard out of the game. Also, when a guard playing man defense against a high scorer might be relatively short, simply moving a taller defender on the scorer can affect and alter his shot. Similar adjustments would have to be made if the defense switches to a 1-3-1 half-court zone, trapping wings and corners, and making the offense use some nonshooters in the process.

Major advantages for switching defenses also emanate from the flexible manner in which this technique can be employed. Changing defenses can be done in many ways without making a big issue of the adjustment. For instance, players may be instructed to switch defenses during free throws, on dead balls out of bounds, after time-outs and substitutions, or on makes and misses. Some teams enjoy constantly changing defenses and relish in the challenge of changing from a full-court zone press to a 2-3 half-court zone and then switching back to a man-to-man on the first pass. Switching defenses is a creative way to coach and play, and it can produce great dividends.

PLAYING TO YOUR STRENGTHS

It's been said that, from a coach's perspective, offensive players are the gifted and skilled players whereas defensive players are categorized as physical and athletic—the heavily motivated, rugged players who are taught and understand their roles. Defensive players should take pride in the cliché that "defense travels," meaning that a good defense will keep a team in ball games. This notion is especially true for games in which a highly favored team fails to execute their offensive game plan. An excellent example of this circumstance occurred on January 30, 2011, when Duke, 19-2 and ranked third in the country, traveled to New York City for a game with unranked St. John's, which was 12-8 at the time.

The game was a home game for St. John's, but it was played at Madison Square Garden before 19,353 fans who were definitely pro St. John's. Duke scored 78 points, more than enough to win on most nights, but not this time. Individually and on paper, there was no way that St. John's could play straight up against the Blue Devils. The alternative was to gamble with a defensive strategy that would take Duke out of their comfortable half-court offense, and that's what St. John's did. From the opening whistle, St. John's showed a team defensive game plan that took Duke completely out of their offensive comfort zone, employing a full-court trapping man-to-man defense. Translated, they were man up but could double on the ball whenever they thought that they had an advantage. This strategy forced Duke to play at St. John's quicker tempo.

Few games better illustrate how defense can dictate offensive styles. Duke attempted to counter St. John's full-court pressure with an aggressive full-court defensive attack of their own. But the smaller and quicker St. John's team feasted on Duke's early confusion and shot layup after layup. The St. John's guards created turnovers and captured long rebounds as they attacked the basket with drives for fouls and easy baskets. Duke, on the other hand, attacked from the perimeter and hit only 1 of 21 three-pointers until late in the game, and ended up hitting just 5 for 26 overall.

Time and again, St. John's rebounded the long shots and attacked their basket with layups and put-backs. They led at half 46-25, and their continuous pressure never allowed Duke back in the game. St. John's used the entire 94 feet (28.7 m) with its smaller but quicker players, and their smothering defense forced Duke into a game that they did not anticipate.

St. John's pulled a major upset, beating Duke in a classic game by matching 40 minutes of aggressive defense with a dribble-drive offense. Defense, the common denominator for all basketball coaches, was instrumental in generating St. John's offensive attack. By changing their defensive strategy to a tenacious full-court press, St. John's upset one of the nation's premier teams. Although offense is the finesse part of basketball, defense becomes the equalizer.

DEFENSIVE UNIT COORDINATION

A number of specific team strategies, when managed properly, can work toward unity and harmony within the team concept. Player input, clock management and foul strategy, and end-of-game decisions are part of every game. As such, productive results are more likely to occur if coaches and players are involved and on the same page as it relates to these tactics.

Player Input

Coaches have varying opinions about how they incorporate, navigate, and validate the benefits of player input. The power of player input can be enormous, and I personally found it extremely significant and constructive. Our system encouraged player participation in all team policies and rules: our academic requirements and responsibilities, team dress code, team rules and policies that cover class and practice attendance, player conferences and meetings, and practice and game guidelines. We found that when players help make the policies, they are more prone to abide by them.

Players have many opportunities to approach the coach with input. For instance, players can approach the coach with questions and suggestions at practice the day before a game. On the day of the game, most high school, college, and NBA teams have shoot-arounds and hear scouting reports. In addition, a walk-through occurs before the game when all assignments are discussed. At each of these times, the coach should be willing to answer any questions. Another good time for player input is after pregame warm-ups when teams return to the locker room for last-minute instructions.

Player input may also be warranted is during time-outs. Observing the differences between high school, college, and professional coaches during time-outs can be interesting. At all levels, the entire coaching staff—the head coach and all assistants—often step out onto the court and move away from the players for a brief time. They discuss their strategy and give input, and then the head coach steps into the player huddle to discuss their assignments. More often than not, the coach draws the play; occasionally a player will ask a question or make a comment about execution, but never to change a play call. If a player wants to suggest strategy, he will do that just before the coach goes to the team huddle, although sometimes when a last-second shot is involved, a pro player might say, "Let me take him this time" or simply "I've got him," and the changeover works.

College and high school coaches go at this a little differently. When free throws are being shot, specific players—generally the captains—are in constant sideline discussions with the coach. More often than not, they are discussing either the defensive alignment or which play to run on the next possession. During time-outs, sometimes the staff does not meet away from the players, and the coach might go straight to the huddle while the assistant coaches, having been assigned specific players, make sure that those players know the play call as they leave the huddle.

When going for a last shot to win or tie a game, coaches may ask a player which side of the court he wants the ball on. Player input in situations like this is invaluable.

UNCC VS. SAN FRANCISCO

In 1976, one of my teams, UNCC, was playing in the first round of the NIT at Madison Square Garden. San Francisco was our opponent, and they had just pulled ahead by 2 points with 16 seconds to play. We had a time-out, with the ball frontcourt, side out of bounds. To continue playing that night and in the rest of the tournament, we had to make a field goal.

As the players came to the huddle I asked, "Who wants to take this shot?" Three players quickly raised their hands; two did not. So we set up a play. One of the two who didn't raise his hand inbounded the ball, and the other set a screen. The play was to go inside and look for a good shot and maybe a foul on San Francisco. We inbounded the ball, made a couple of quick passes, and inserted the ball inside on the low block to a freshman, Kevin King. After a nice ball fake, he pivoted left and shot a nice 10-foot (3 m) jumper that swished through the net. This basket put the game into overtime, and we won. Do I believe in player input? You bet; that player wanted the shot!

Clock Management

Clock management comes into play in every game. It involves time-outs, substitutions, foul situations, and when and who takes a last shot. Whether they are on offense or defense, teams need to practice situations where they are 1, 2, and 3 points ahead or 1, 2, and 3 points behind.

A classic example of clock management occurred when Indiana beat the number one ranked University of Kentucky Wildcats 73-72 in Bloomington on December 10, 2011. With 5.6 seconds to go, Kentucky was up 71-70. Doron Lamb was on the free-throw line for a chance to put UK up by 3 points. He missed the first and made the second, giving Kentucky a 2-point lead, and Indiana called time-out.

Here is where clock management came into play, because both teams had to execute perfectly to win. Indiana had to get an open shot and hit a two-pointer to tie and a three-pointer to win. Kentucky had to deny Indiana an open shot.

Kentucky's strategy was clear: With two fouls to give and with Indiana having to cover 94 feet (28.7 m) in only 5.6 seconds, Kentucky needed to foul in the backcourt and take a few seconds off the clock. Then they needed to duplicate the procedure for the second foul, keeping Indiana from getting an open look. Successful execution of this two-foul scenario would have been an outstanding job of clock management.

Indiana, on the other hand, was aware of the foul situation and knew that they had to be quick with the ball and avoid all contact. Kentucky's defense should have been in control of the game. They needed only to go man-to-man and foul the player catching the ball inbounds. But that did not happen.

Indiana inbounded the ball to Verdell Jones. He dribbled untouched into frontcourt and passed to Christian Watford, who hit a three-point shot with 7/10ths of a second on the clock. Indiana executed perfect clock management and won, whereas Kentucky failed to foul, and it cost them the game, 73-72.

Foul Strategy

Fouling is a fundamental component of basketball. Coaches and players must be on the same page and share the same viewpoint when it comes to when to foul and when not to foul. In chapter 5, "Offensive Priorities," we discussed the importance of free throws, citing how many games are determined by an open free shot (chapter 5). The free-throw figures included the entire game, not just end-of-game free throws. All free throws are important, so minimizing fouls and keeping teams out of the bonus is good strategy.

Another important fundamental to keep in mind is never to foul a jump shooter. Why? You might be giving up a 4- or 6-point play if the shooter misses the free throw and his team captures the rebound to hit another three-pointer.

Chapter 9, "Tactics for Special Situations," includes a thorough discussion of creating a foul policy that goes hand in hand with fouling strategies (chapter 9). Players must consciously limit their number of fouls, especially early in games. Players need to understand that the quickest way to reduce playing time is to pick up useless fouls.

But fouling is advantageous at times, and knowing who, how, and when to foul is crucial. Each foul should be a smart play that does not penalize the team. Players must learn and practice proper fouling techniques so that they conform to the rules. Coaches must instruct players how to give a foul to avoid intentional two-shot fouls. For instance, if your opponent is holding the ball and statistics tell you their ball handlers are poor at the free-throw line, then fouling them might just keep you in the game. Taking away a driving layup and making an opponent hit two 15-foot (4.5 m) shots is defined by some as fouling for profit. (On the other hand, the offensive team trying to control the game must keep the ball in the hands of their best free-throw shooters. To do this, they might have to substitute to get their best free-throw shooters into the game.)

Following 26 years of college coaching on through a 22-year tenure in the NBA, I encountered a number of differences between the various levels of coaching regarding defense in close games. Having worked with eight NBA head coaches, I found that they preferred to go man-to-man in game-ending situations where they had a 3-point lead with less than 10 seconds to play. In the college game, which doesn't have as many accomplished three-point shooters, coaches were prone to trap and zone. In either case, the rule of thumb was not to foul.

Following is a situation in which the defense failed to execute. The players may have been told to foul or to contain the ball handler, but neither occurred, and it almost cost Florida the game. Early in February 2011, the University of Florida had a 3-point lead with 6 seconds on the clock. Their opponent had the ball out of bounds with 94 feet (28.7 m) to navigate. Florida applied token pressure on the inbounds pass, but the opposing guard caught the pass in full stride and the defender on the ball was suddenly two steps behind. The guard dribbled straight to the top of the key and hit an open three-pointer to send the game into overtime (which Florida went on to win 65-61). Applying token pressure on the offensive guards to eliminate rolling the ball up the floor is a good strategy, but hard pressure that permits a quick ball handler to beat the defender and get an open look is certainly a bad mistake. But this is exactly what happened here. Did Florida intend to foul? Did they have a foul to give? Good questions. The only way to prepare for this kind of situation is through practice.

End-of-Game Decisions

Planning and practicing for late-game situations is important for both offense and defense. Here are two NBA illustrations in which input would have been extremely helpful. These two examples illustrate the complexities and difficulties that teams encounter. How a team defends a situation usually goes back to one of two theories. Theory 1 says do not let the opponent's star player beat you; make him give up the ball. Theory 2 says to play your opponent tight and make their star hit the shot. In the second situation, as you will see, a major miscalculation occurred.

Situation 1

In game 2 of the 2011 NBA Finals, Dallas beat Miami in Florida, coming back from a 15-point fourth-quarter deficit to tie the score. Here was the play: With 24.5 seconds remaining, the score was tied 93-93. Dallas had the ball out of bounds on the right side of the court, free-throw line extended. The inbounds pass went to Jason Kidd in the middle of the court. Kidd dribbled toward the sideline as Jason Terry set a pin-down screen for Nowitzki, Bosh defending. Nowitzki caught Kidd's pass slightly to the left of the free-throw lane line that runs from under the basket toward midcourt. Nowitzki was not quite straight on the basket upon receiving the ball. He made a great fake to the right, spun right to left, made a hesitation move that fooled Bosh, and drove left for an open layup to win the game with 3.6 seconds left. No defender rotated to help.

Five defensive ramifications to consider

1. Could Miami have doubled-teamed Nowitzki?

   Yes.

2. When was the best time for Miami to double-team Nowitzki?

   When he made his spin move.

3. Was there an opportunity to foul Nowitzki on his spin?

   Yes.

4. So why didn't Miami foul? Did they fear that he would hit two free throws?

   Dallas was not in the penalty.

5. Regardless of who drew the assignment to guard Nowitzki, did everyone know that Bosh needed help?

   They should have!

Situation 2

In an NBA playoff situation when I was an assistant coach, we were down 2 points with 26 seconds left to play. Our opponent had the ball in the front court, side out of bounds. All we had to do was get one stop, call a time-out, advance the ball, and get a good shot to tie the game.

We had many defensive options:

1. We could put pressure on the inbounds pass by putting a big man on the ball.
2. We could trap the player receiving the inbounds pass with our defender on the inbounds passer.
3. We could set up in a no-gamble defense, a 1-3-1 trap, double teaming on the first pass.
4. We could run and jump, forcing action.

But rather than take any of those options, our defensive assignment was to play straight-up man-to-man with no gambling and let the clock tick down. We were not supposed to foul, and after they took the last shot, we were to rebound, call time-out (there should be about three seconds left), advance the ball, run our play, and look to tie the game.

Discussing various options with your assistants is always a good policy, to make sure that all your bases are covered. This approach is especially relevant in the NBA, which has a 24-second shot clock and different rules that apply to advancing the ball. Unfortunately, this discussion did not take place in this game.

The plan backfired right from the get-go. The ball was inbounded to a crafty veteran point guard, Sam Cassell, who went to the middle of the court and began dribbling. With token pressure on him, we watched as the seconds ticked off. When the shot clock got to 0:03, Cassell made a quick move and shot the ball just as the shot clock expired, leaving 0:02 on the game clock. The ball hit the back of the rim and bounded high toward the sideline and went out of bounds as time expired.

Needless to say, after the game, our locker room was very quiet.

Coaches and players must practice situations and have specific plays for when they are down 1, 2, and 3 points, especially with 26, 10, 5, 3, and fewer seconds to get a good shot. In like manner, when a team is 1, 2, and 3 points up, they must have good plays for getting the ball inbounds. End-game strategy is vital, and only practice prepares a team properly.

Anyone who has ever coached knows that offense is a fickle companion. Some nights it simply disappears without warning. Shots will not fall, passes go astray, and the team gets in foul trouble, resulting in an unanticipated loss. Sometimes, it seems that poor offensive execution is contagious, affecting the entire team. On nights like this, defense is the only answer to give the team a chance to win. Players must be prepared to defend screens and to change from man-to-man to zone defense when strategies call for it. This is why practicing defensive fundamentals, including the shell drill, are so important. Defense is always a challenge, but it may just be the strategy that helps you escape defeat.

CHAPTER **9**

Tactics for Special Situations

Failure to prepare is preparing to fail. It's a cliché, but it's true. Coaches owe it to their players to have them ready for any tactical maneuver that the opposition might employ. They should cover all realistic strategic options with the team in practices leading up to the game. The more prepared that players are before competition, the more confident they'll be in executing both planned and spontaneous efforts to thwart the opponent's attack. Conversely, unprepared squads are susceptible to confusion, panic, and, ultimately, defeat. Two important areas get us right into the heart of preparation: an effective fouling policy and efficient use of time-outs. Let's examine these two primary strategic themes first as we discuss special tactical strategies. Later we cover pregame analysis to prepare your team for special situations.

CREATING YOUR OWN FOUL POLICY

As a college student, I officiated intramural basketball games as part of a class assignment. I learned firsthand that refereeing is difficult. Each game has its own rhythm, and trying to guess how the game will be officiated is strictly hit and miss. Coaches and players must get a feel for how the game is being officiated, and coaches need to help their players understand that they must adjust their game to the way that it is being officiated. For example, if officials are allowing rough play and lots of physical contact, players need to adjust and not complain. Good coaches understand that different officiating styles are part of the game, and they have their teams prepared to adjust accordingly.

Fouls are inevitable, so planning makes sense. Our foul policy came from my observations of how Coach Dean Smith substituted his players. I have no knowledge personally how deeply rooted this was in his philosophy, but for me, substituting on the first, second, and fourth fouls and involving back-up players in the process was a vital part of our game plan.

In this policy, the coach should have a designated substitute for each starter. When the first foul on a starter occurs, the predetermined substitute should report immediately to the scorers' table and replace the starter. This approach should be clearly understood, and the substitute has the responsibility of being prepared to enter the game. After the substitution policy is in place and each starter has a backup, the reserves know from the opening tip that they should put themselves into the game rather than wait for the coach to do it. Each sub should also be aware that the starter may return to the game on the next dead ball. Alternatively, the sub might play for a longer period. The basic reason for this early substitution policy is to prevent a player from picking up two quick fouls. Many times players commit an offensive foul, get frustrated, and immediately commit a foul on defense. Such a policy erases this potential problem. This policy also helps keep all backups mentally involved in the game from the opening tip, and it eliminates emotion from the decision of the coaching staff to pull the starter. For my teams, this first-foul substitution policy was an established part of the game plan. The entire team accepted this procedure.

This policy applies to the second foul in the same manner. But the second foul has greater consequences because it is important that a starter begin the second half with no more than two fouls. Thus, after the second foul in the first half, the starter should know that he will not play again until the second half. This part of my policy always took some persuading! Players believe that they can play without committing a third foul, but basketball is a game of reactions and emotions, and the role of the coach is to try to have the best players on the floor at the end of each game.

On a player's fourth foul, the back-up substitute should again insert himself into the game immediately (unless the player is told to wait). Never was this used more effectively than when my Purdue team played Duke in the championship of the Mid-East Regional tournament in 1980. Joe Barry Carroll, our 7-foot (213 cm) All-American center, picked up his fourth foul with about six minutes to go and with our team holding a 7-point lead in the game. His freshman backup, 6-foot-10 (208 cm) Ted Benson from Atlanta, reported to the scorers' table. With our lead, we wanted to work the clock down to where we could put Joe Barry back into the game with about three minutes to play. We had to control at least three possessions to eat up enough time for the plan to work.

The college game had no shot clock at the time, so our instruction to the team was to run our control offense (the LA offense guard to forward, reset), moving through the sequence at least twice on each possession before looking for a shot. Brian Walker, our savvy point guard, was in control and did an excellent job with this strategy. Brian started the play with the guard to forward pass. Then he cut through to the far corner, where the ball ended up back in his hands. After he received the ball in the corner, he dribbled out and restarted the offense. The only way that Duke was going to get the ball was to foul us. This decoy was not immediately apparent to them. Our plan worked, and we won the game, 68-60.

Zone defenses can be effective when trying to protect players and keep them in the game. Whenever one of our players had four fouls and we could not afford to have him leave the game, we usually went zone and placed him in the zone's least vulnerable spot, where he was less susceptible to picking up a foul on a drive or rebound. In Joe Barry's case, that meant that he became a wing player in our 2-3 zone rather than play in the middle. But if a guard picked up a fourth foul, we would usually go 1-3-1 and put him on the baseline.

USING TIME-OUTS EFFICIENTLY

Coaches need to examine, discuss, and clarify many details. One such detail involves when to call time-outs. In most cases, the ebb and flow of the game dictates when a time-out is needed, but there are exceptions, and I encountered a major one during a Final Four appearance with Purdue University in 1980. Purdue played UCLA in the first game of the Final Four in Indianapolis. UCLA had an excellent young team with Mike Sanders, Mike Holton, and Darren Day, highlighted by veteran Kiki Vandeweghe, a dynamic 6-foot-8 (203 cm) player who had excellent offensive skills. Purdue also had some outstanding athletes. Arnett Hallman was a superb athlete and a defensive specialist who was always assigned the opponent's top player—guard Isiah Thomas at Indiana, forward Kevin McHale at Minnesota, and all-everything Magic Johnson at Michigan State. The matchup between Hallman and Vandeweghe was a classic from the start of the game to the end.

One of those time-out exceptions that some coaches have to deal with occurs in nationally televised games. At that time there were three TV time-outs per half, and they were taken at specific intervals, such as at the 5-, 10-, and 15-minute marks, unless one of the teams took a time-out, which would nullify the TV time-out for that time slot. Another caveat of the TV time-out was that if a coach called a time-out to question a call or rule interpretation by the official and the ruling went in favor of that coach's team, no time-out was charged. If the ruling went against the coach, however, a charged time-out was applied.

The game was close as Hallman picked up a third foul early in the second half. At about the midpoint of the second half, Purdue had two time-outs remaining. During a scramble under the basket, a foul was assessed to Hallman with 10:49 to play. It was clear to me and my staff that the foul had been incorrectly given to Hallman when it should have been assessed to Purdue's Drake Morris. Although I felt with certainty that the foul was on Morris, I hesitated to question the call because I knew that if the appeal went against me, we would be left with only one time-out. Still, I appealed the decision but lost, leaving us with one time-out and four fouls on Hallman. As the game began to wind down, we had to use our final time-out. This circumstance put us at a significant disadvantage, because from a strategic standpoint we knew that we would need that other time-out at the end of such an important game. On a number of occasions we were 1 point down with the ball, and being able to call time-out would have been advantageous. We were not able to, and we lost.

Following that game, Louisville played Iowa, and as we sat watching the first half of that game, the officials who worked our game passed directly in front of where I was sitting. We nodded to each other, and after they were past us a couple of steps, one of them turned, came back, and said, "Coach, I am sorry, I missed the call." Always remember to value your time-outs; they are precious!

Another important lesson is understanding the value of time-outs, especially in a close game. Many times you'll see coaches let a 6- to 8-point lead dwindle down to one possession before they call time-out. To me, that policy has always appeared to result in the time-out being called just a little too late. In most cases like this, momentum has already swung to your opponent, and now you are in a panic situation. Rather than wait until your last possession, why not call time-out with three possessions left to give yourself greater flexibility? You may need to call another one immediately, but that's OK. You are trying to stop their run, and using a time-out for that purpose is warranted.

PREGAME ANALYSIS

One of the major differences between high school basketball, college basketball, and the NBA is game preparation. High school and college teams usually play 2 games per week, whereas NBA teams have stretches during the season when they may play 4 games in 5 nights or 8 games in 12 nights. High schools play approximately 25 games per season, colleges play 30 to 40, and the pros play around 100, counting preseason games and the playoffs. NBA teams often lose a day of practice because they play so many games back to back. Although the volume of games varies, some basic pregame preparation routines with video, scouting reports, personnel tendencies, and game-day walk-throughs are similar.

One of the crucial aspects of game preparation involves objective analysis of the two teams' comparative speed and quickness. The faster team should look to exploit that quickness advantage, both as a unit and in individual matchups. The slower team must try to control the pace of the game and emphasize fundamentals, ball fakes, and positioning. If the opponent has quicker guards, the coach should identify a player at another position who is capable of handling the ball in the backcourt.

During his tenure from 1996 through 2000 with the NBA Charlotte Hornets, power forward Anthony Mason was frequently used to help bring the ball up. And when I coached at UNC Charlotte in 1975 through 1978, we used our center, Cedric Maxwell, an outstanding ball handler with exceptional quickness, to break presses and get the ball across the 10-second timeline and into the frontcourt. Both of those big men had the skill and confidence to dribble the ball under pressure and initiate the offense. The daily full-court dribble drills (chapter 4) is thus an important source of information for the coach and team. This strategy helped UNC Charlotte offset Michigan's quicker guards to upset the number-one ranked team in the NCAA Mid-East Regional to go the 1977 Final Four.

Similarly, poor-shooting teams have to find other ways to score. Defense is often a great equalizer in such circumstances. Presses, traps, and a variety of zones—such as the box-and-one, matchup zones, and run-and-jump traps—can confuse opponents and make them tentative. Changing defenses can also create turnovers that result in run-out baskets. Those easy shots created by the defense certainly improve a team's field-goal percentage. Poor-shooting teams also have to hit the boards, both on the offensive end to convert missed shots into put-backs and on the defensive end to prevent second-shot scoring opportunities for the opponent.

The five key tactical situations that follow require significant pregame preparation:

1. Using the offensive clock
2. Attacking full-court pressure defense
3. Scoring plays from the backcourt
4. Scoring plays from the frontcourt
5. Executing against disruptive defense

PREPARATION IN THE NBA

Let's look at a specific play and point out the differences in preparation. To prepare for a pick-and-roll set, high school and college teams can practice against it for two days to perfect their technique. Seldom would they have to modify their strategy from practice to game. An NBA team, however, may face four different pick-and-roll attacks in a week, executed by a variety of talented players. By following an NBA squad through a four-game road trip, you can see how difficult it is to prepare.

Practice and preparation time for NBA teams diminishes as the season progresses. When playing four games in five nights, game preparation for the first game is the best. Preparation will involve practicing against the opponent's offense, a game-day morning walk-through showing an edited video of the opponent's play sets, a review of the opposing team's individual personnel, and defensive matchups against the opposition's play sets with specific player assignments. Just before the game, there is a scouting review and video session.

Following the game, the NBA team boards a charter flight to the next city, arriving at their hotel sometime between 1 and 3 a.m. Players meet the next morning for an 11 a.m. breakfast and watch the previous night's game video or a video on the opponent for that night. Players then rest until it's time to go to the arena. The early bus with rookies and seldom-used players leaves at 5:30 p.m. so that they can get in extra work. The veterans leave the hotel around 6 p.m. Following pregame shooting, a coach goes over the scouting report and show an edited highlight video. After the game, the team repeats the travel procedure of the night before. Practice the next day is generally light because the men who play major minutes need to let their bodies recuperate.

On the day of game 3, the players repeat the breakfast, video, rest, bus ride, pregame shooting, and locker-room procedures. After the game, they bus to the airport and travel to the next city. The fourth game on a road trip like this is difficult because fatigue, lack of adrenaline, and diminishing concentration begin to take their toll on the players; preparation is mostly scouting reports and videos. Quality of play suffers, and some teams get blown out when they are on the road for an extended time.

Allow sufficient practice time to cover each situation thoroughly, especially those in which quickness and pressure have significant effect. These five situations represent major areas of the game in which an offensive team lacking speed and quickness can be helpless if the coach has not adequately prepared them. One of the plays demonstrates how to use the clock to your advantage; six of the plays involve getting the ball inbounds against hard pressure in the backcourt; three plays entail scoring from the frontcourt, side out of bounds with a short clock; three plays include scoring from the frontcourt, baseline out of bounds against pressure; and the last three plays require that the coach be prepared for irregular zone defenses.

When the opponent is quicker or a team has to face a box-and-one, triangle-and-two, or diamond-and-one, the coach must be prepared to execute the offensive strategy with the correct play calls. All these situations are special because the defense forces the action with pressure and disruptive configurations. The offense must respond with an effective attack of its own.

The special situation game chart is a quick study of offensive plays that a coach can use when confronting pressure and disruptive defenses. This chart is shown in table 9.1. Teams must practice these tactical options with the player alignment that produces the best results. Coaches should be prepared to run more than one option to counter different looks and matchups.

Using the Offensive Clock

Since the shot clock came into existence in the mid-1980s, the game has become quicker and more fluid, eliminating ball control as we once knew it. After a few years of experimentation in various conferences, a 45-second shot clock was introduced in the NCAA men's game in the 1985–86 season.

After the shot clock became ingrained into the system, offensive control patterns such as the famous four-corners offense became obsolete. As previously mentioned, the four-corners offense had become the signature offensive set for Dean Smith, the great UNC coach. This set was a balanced spread offense with three out and two either on the blocks or in opposite deep corners. Because there was no shot clock, when some teams got the lead, they played keep away in this formation, spreading the floor and letting their best ball handler dribble the time off the clock. Scores were very low, and coaches who opposed this technique became irate when forced to chase an outstanding point guard who would dribble, pass to a teammate in one of the corners, sprint for a return pass, and then begin dribbling again. Defensive teams tried to double-team, but with the players spread in the corners, all they did was chase passes. Fouling the point guard, who was usually an excellent free-throw shooter, was the only way to stop the clock, and the game turned into a free-throw-shooting contest. The advent of the shot clock eliminated this offensive stalling tactic.

In the 1993–94 season, the men's shot clock was trimmed to 35 seconds. The current time limitation of 35 seconds in the men's game, 30 seconds in the women's game, and 24 seconds in the NBA controls the game and forces shots. No longer

Table 9.1 Special Situation Game Chart

Defensive attack	Offensive counter
Pressure full court (man or zone)	Alignment 1-4 • Option 1: guard pass • Option 2: big-man pass
Pressure full court (man)	Scoring plays from backcourt • Comeback option 5-3 • Step-out bomb • Transition lob • Fake-and-go • Line, baseline • Line, sideline
Pressure sideline frontcourt (SOB) • Vs. two-point shot • Vs. three-point shot	Frontcourt (SOB) scoring plays • Box double • X-out into pick-and-roll • Three-point X-out • X-out into single-double
Pressure baseline frontcourt (BOB)	Frontcourt (BOB) scoring plays • Inside pick-the-picker • Box, cross 2 • Line • Lob
Disruptive zones on the half court • Vs. 1-3-1 • Vs. box-and-one • Vs. triangle-and-two	Attacking disruptive defenses • LA offense • Triangle overload attack • Guards to block alignment • Three-man overload shot spots

SOB = sideline out of bounds
BOB = baseline out of bounds

do teams labor with strict control patterns because scoring and offensive execution now determine their fate.

Few teams run the flex, a control pattern, or the four-corners offense in today's game, but some offenses emphasize player and ball movement, good shot selection, and patience. With many big men declaring for the NBA draft and turning pro early, more teams have gone quicker with offensive sets that emphasize the dribble-drive options. Control still has a place, and a motion set with lots of screening and movement is one effective option. Another controlled variation is a box set with a three-man triangle rotation, as explained next.

The objective in the three-man triangle is to gain control of the game by using the clock to your advantage. This offensive set can be run for short or long periods depending on the game situation. This set is especially effective when you get in early foul trouble and have to keep key players in the game. You are looking for scoring opportunities, but not one-and-done quick shots.

THREE-MAN TRIANGLE

Focus

To gain control of the game by using the clock to advantage.

Procedure

Players begin on the half court. Follow these steps:

1. Begin in a 1-2-2 formation with O1 on the point, O5 and O4 at opposite elbows, and O2 and O3 on opposite blocks.

2. O1 dribbles to the right-side free-throw line extended, about 3 feet (1 m) from the sideline, keeping the dribble alive, as O2 fakes a corner cut and speed cuts, using O5 if necessary, to the top of the key, in line with O5.

3. O1 times the pass so that O2 is squared, not sideways, and ready to receive the pass. After making the pass, O1 proceeds to the low block right side.

4. On receiving the pass, O2 breaks down in a protective position using the right foot to pivot, dribbles left, and takes the ball to the left free-throw line extended. O3, on the left block, fakes a corner cut and speed cuts up the middle, using O4 if necessary, to the top of the key in line with O4.

5. O2 keeps the dribble alive and times the pass so that O3 is squared, not sideways, and ready to receive the ball. After making the pass, O2 proceeds to the low block left side (figure 9.1).

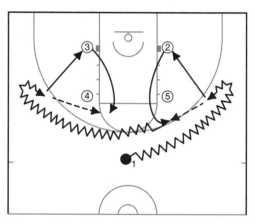

Figure 9.1 Three-man triangle.

6. On receiving the pass, O3 breaks down using the left foot to pivot, dribbles left, and takes the ball to the right free-throw line extended. O1, on the right block, fakes a corner cut and speed cuts up the middle, using O5 if necessary, to the top of the key in line with O5.

7. This triangle movement continues for a predetermined time or to a set number of rotations, at which time the team runs a specific set pattern. If the defense overplays on O1, O2, or O3, the opposite block player sprints diagonally to the top and the low players realign. If one of the ball handlers picks up the dribble, O5 and O4 immediately go to the ball handler's aid.

This set is effective for three guards and after you determine to attack the basket; it is also an excellent set to run either a sideline or middle pick-and-roll.

Attacking Full-Court Pressure Defense

The coach must consider four major areas when designing a full-court offensive attack versus man-to-man and zone pressure. Teams must carry out four specific steps to complete the possession and establish a defensive position:

1. A team has 5 seconds to get the ball inbounds.
2. After the ball is touched inbounds, high school and men's college teams have 10 seconds to get the ball across midcourt, while NBA and WNBA teams have 8 seconds; women's college teams have no time limit.
3. After the ball is in the frontcourt, the coach must decide whether to attack immediately or to set the offense and run a play.
4. After the attacking team scores or loses possession of the ball, it must get into a specific defensive alignment.

Each of these steps requires individual strategies dictated by the skills of the players. The 1-4 set described here is an effective attack against both man-to-man and zone pressure. Provided within this set are two options for getting the ball inbounds: the first to a guard and the second to a post.

1-4 SET VERSUS FULL-COURT DEFENSE, OPTION 1

Focus

Execution, passing, and reading versus full-court pressure.

Procedure

Play begins in the backcourt. For identification purposes, O1, O2, and O3 will be the ball handlers, and O4 and O5 will be the big men. The wide lanes designated right and left are described from the perspective of the offensive attack. Follow these steps:

1. The team lines up in a 1-4 alignment. The two ball handlers, O1 and O2, line up at the wing positions, and the big men, O4 and O5, line up on opposite elbows. The coach must put each team member in his strongest position on the court, the place where the player can be most effective.
2. Basic inbounding rules apply. Following scores, the player has five seconds to inbound the ball and can run the baseline. The player should never throw in from under the basket. He should use a two-handed pass and be aware that bouncing the ball on the end line will result in a turnover.

(continued)

1-4 Set Versus Full-Court Defense, Option 1 *(continued)*

3. The 1-4 alignment depends on all five offensive players to get the ball inbounds. No matter which way O3 goes, to O1 or O2, the play is the same. (The diagram has O3 throwing the ball in on the right-hand side, but teams must also practice going left.)

4. O3 passes to O1 and relocates to the middle of the free-throw lane. O1 catches, pivots, and faces the defender before dribbling.

5. O5 cuts diagonally across the midcourt line and looks for a pass.

O5 Is Open

6. O1 passes to O5 if O5 is open (figure 9.2).

7. On O1's pass to O5, O2 sprints across midcourt and looks for a pass from O5. O4 releases his position and goes opposite O5, filling the outside left lane.

8. O5 passes to O2 and fills the right lane.

9. From here, O2, O4, and O5 attack the defense, looking to score.

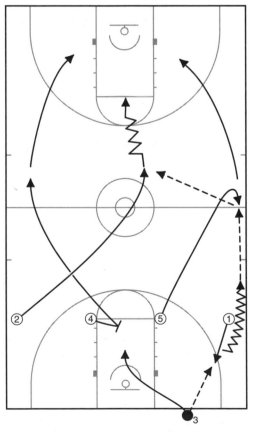

Figure 9.2 1-4 set versus full-court defense, option 1: O5 is open.

O5 Isn't Open

6. If O1 is unable to pass to O5 after receiving the inbounds pass, the next look is to O4 or O3. Dribbling in the backcourt is the last option.

7. As O5 vacates, O4 cuts to the ball, becoming visible to O1.

8. If O4 receives the pass, he turns and looks for O2. If O2 is covered, O4 passes to O3.

9. After receiving the ball from O1 or O4, O3 looks to rotate the ball to O2; O3 may need one dribble to establish a good passing angle.

10. After receiving the ball, O2 looks to pass to O1, cutting into the middle. O2 then fills the left lane as O5 fills the right lane.

11. When receiving the ball, O1 attacks the basket, and O2 and O5 fill the lanes (figure 9.3). O1 looks to pass, drive, or shoot the ball.

12. After the ball enters the frontcourt, the offense aggressively attacks the basket.

Aligning this attack with balance and spacing is crucial to good execution.

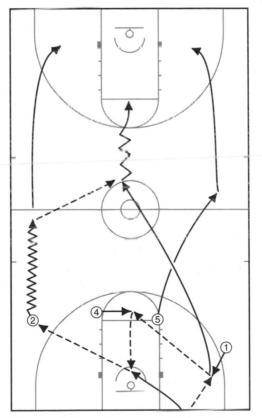

Figure 9.3 1-4 set versus full-court defense, option 1: O5 isn't open.

1-4 SET VERSUS FULL-COURT DEFENSE, OPTION 2

Focus

Executing, passing, and reading versus full-court pressure.

Procedure

Starting in the same setup shown in figure 9.2, play begins in the backcourt with an inbounds pass. Follow these steps:

1. The first inbounds option is always O1, but if a hard denial prevents O1 from receiving the ball, O1 still breaks to the corner looking for a pass.

2. O3's second option is the big man on the strong side (O5), who should come straight down the lane. Seldom do big men, especially 5s, defend deep in the backcourt, so O5 is usually taller than the defender.

3. The pass to O5 is a high pass over a smaller defender's head, especially when a defender is on the ball.

O1 Is Open

4. As O5 gathers the pass, his first look is for O1, who takes his defender to the baseline, plants the right foot, uses a quick reverse pivot, and sprints ahead of the defender, looking for O5's pass (figure 9.4).

5. On the weak side, O4 sees O5 break for the ball, so O4 sprints to midcourt, finds the open space, and buttonhooks, looking for a pass from O5.

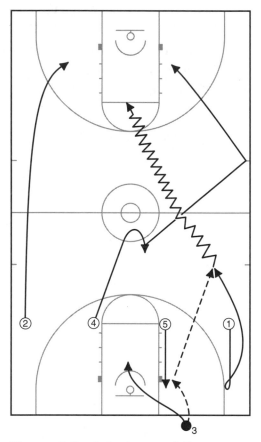

Figure 9.4 1-4 set versus full-court defense, option 2: O1 is open.

6. Now that the play is in front of O4, if he sees O5 pass to O1, O4 continues diagonally to the hash mark on the strong side and fills the right lane.

7. On the weak side, O2 sees the play develop and fills the left lane.

8. O1, O4, and O2 attack the basket.

O1 Isn't Open

4. The second passing option for O5 presents itself when O1 is unable to get open on the sideline cut. O5 has three options—O4 in the middle of the floor, O3 stepping inbounds, and O2 on the far sideline.

5. If the pass goes to O4, he has two options—O1 and O2. If the pass goes to O2, he has O4 in the middle and O1 cutting diagonally across the middle. O5's easiest pass is to O3, who is stepping inbounds.

6. Should the pass go to O3, his action is to move the ball to O2 and stay behind the ball in the middle of the floor as an outlet against pressure.

7. O2's action is to push the ball with a couple of dribbles, pass to O1, and then run the left lane (figure 9.5).

8. When O4 realizes that he will not be involved in the backcourt, O4 clears diagonally to the frontcourt hash line and runs the right lane, with O1 in the middle and O2 on the left lane.

9. As they attack, O1 decides whether to drive, shoot, or pass.

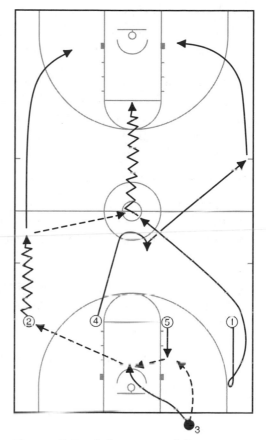

Figure 9.5 1-4 set versus full-court defense, option 2: O1 isn't open.

Scoring Plays From the Backcourt

Scoring off a play from the backcourt against pressure late in the fourth quarter is challenging. Specifically, getting the ball inbounds in this situation can be a problem for teams at all levels. To be successful, players who inbound the ball must be confident, must pass well, and must understand the rules, specifically when they can run the baseline and when they can only pivot but cannot take steps. They must also know that they cannot bounce the inbounds pass on the end line or sideline. Combine these necessary attributes with the fact that the inbounding player has only five seconds to get the ball inbounds, and this means that you need a player who is an accurate passer and has a cool head!

Selecting the right person to inbound the ball in late-game situations should be done carefully and with great thought. Sometimes it is a good strategy to insert a backup point guard to inbound the ball and use the starting point guard as the inbounds receiver. The intent here is to keep the ball in the hands of reliable ball handlers. While reviewing our NBA roster at San Antonio for a possible trade, the name Ed Nealy came up for discussion. Nealy was a burly 6-foot-6 (198 cm) substitute who was on the bubble. But before anyone could say a word, Bob Bass, the Spurs' general manager, said, "He's a keeper because he is great at inbounding the ball." Nealy made a 12-year NBA career out of doing the little things well.

Comeback Option 5-3

Here is a full-court inbounds play to use when the offensive team is ahead by 1 point with five seconds to go. The defensive team must steal the ball or foul immediately. The offensive players running the O3 and O5 positions must be excellent free-throw shooters.

COMEBACK OPTION 5-3

Focus

Look long but concentrate short to get the ball inbounds.

Procedure

The play is designed to get the ball inbounds against hard, full-court defensive pressure. Play begins in the backcourt. Follow these steps:

1. O1, on the end line, is the inbounds passer and lines up just outside the free-throw lane. O2 lines up about 10 to 12 feet (3 to 3.5 m) in front of O1, facing the opposite basket. O4 lines up 10 feet farther out on the court in a straight line with O1 and O2.

2. The major inbounds receivers, O5 and O3, line up on the middle of the free-throw line and on the weak-side low block, respectively.

3. As the referee hands the ball to O1, O4 sets a pin-down screen for O2. After a quick jab step inside to help O4 get a good screening angle on O2's defender, O2 breaks for the frontcourt. Only if O2 breaks open does O1 throw to him. After O4's down screen, he breaks to the strong-side corner, looking for the inbounds pass.

4. As soon as O5 sees O4 screen down for O2, O5 relocates to the corner of the free-throw line and O3 sets a back screen on O5's defender. O5 jab-steps and then breaks hard for the weak-side corner, looking for an inbounds pass from O1. After setting the screen, O3 cuts hard toward O1, looking for an inbounds pass.

5. O1 looks first for O2 and then for O4 in the right corner, O3 in the middle of the free-throw lane, and O5 sprinting to the weak-side corner (figure 9.6).

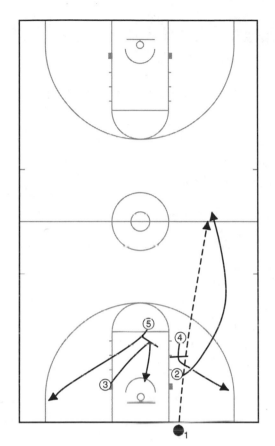

Figure 9.6   Comeback option 5-3.

Step-Out Bomb

The step-out bomb play can be run only following a score when a team is permitted to run the baseline. Teams use the step-out bomb play when the defensive team is desperate and gambling all out to get the ball. This play is effective only when all five defenders are in a full-court man-to-man press. This timing play takes practice and a touch of deception to be effective. Only through practicing the play can the coach assign positions. The player who shoots the ball should have good speed and the passer must be skilled at throwing the long baseball pass.

To illustrate in the following diagram, the players will be numbered, but when running this play in a game situation, specific skills determine player positions.

STEP-OUT BOMB

Focus

Scoring from the backcourt when the defense overplays.

Procedure

Play begins on the end line in the backcourt after a score. The play is specifically designed to score against a denial defense. O2 handles the ball out of bounds. O1 lines up at the strong-side elbow, and O4 is on the same side at the wing position, free-throw line extended. O5 lines up on the low block on the weak side, and O3 is at the elbow. O3 can also line up in the weak-side deep corner and just step out of bounds if his lack of speed is a factor. Follow these steps:

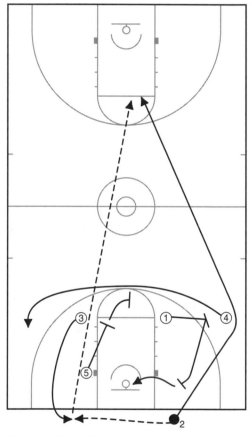

1. The play begins just before the official hands the ball to O2. O5 fakes a screen for O3, but O3 ignores the screen and sprints out of bounds on the baseline, where he receives a pass from O2.

2. During this action, O1 fakes a screen for O4 and screens O2's defender on the baseline. O2 passes to O3 and immediately sprints off O1's screen, running down the sideline looking for the long pass from O3 (figure 9.7).

3. For inbounds options, O1 looks for the ball in the middle. O5 sets up at the top of the key and lets O4 run off him toward the sideline. O2 is the primary option.

Figure 9.7 Step-out bomb.

Transition Lob

Teams that have good passers, jumpers, and players who make good decisions can run special lob plays off opponents' made free throws. The lob should be part of their transition offense, but they should not run it every time. They look to catch the defense unaware after time-outs or when new substitutes enter the game. The play can be extremely effective; defensive teams must be particularly alert to defend it properly.

TRANSITION LOB

Focus

Use the secondary break following opponents' made free throws.

Procedure

Play begins in the backcourt. Follow these steps:

1. Play begins on a made free throw. O4 inbounds the ball quickly to O1, who is cutting across the free-throw lane. O4 then trails the play up the middle of the court.

2. O2 and O3 run the lanes, and O5 runs down the middle of the court.

3. O1 passes the ball ahead up the sideline to O3 at approximately the free-throw line extended. Following the pass, O1 sprints even to O3 and then dives to the low block strong side.

4. O5 sprints to the top of the key and receives a pass from O3. O5 then rotates the ball to O2, who is at the weak-side wing position.

5. While the ball is being rotated, O1 moves up the middle of the free-throw lane and sets a back screen on X5. On O5's pass to O2, O5 steps to the left to set up the defender and then swiftly runs off O1's screen, looking for the lob from O2 (figure 9.8).

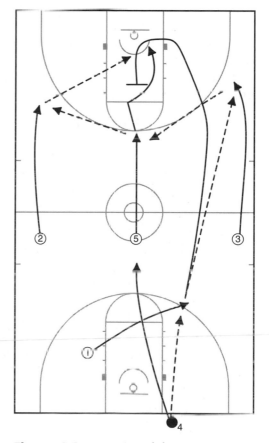

Figure 9.8 Transition lob.

Fake-and-Go

This play can be run effectively 10 to 15 times a season. Use the play at the end of the half or at the end of the game when little time remains on the clock and you are 94 feet (28.7 m) from the basket. Designing a set play with multiple options is better than just having someone go long and heaving the ball toward the basket. The fake-and-go is a good one in this situation.

FAKE-AND-GO

Focus

Backcourt scoring against pressure with a short clock.

Procedure

Play begins on the end line in the back-court. This skill-specific play requires a player, O4, who can throw the long pass, two good shooters, O2 and O3, on the wings, and a big man, O5, who sets a screen for a small man, O1, at midcourt. Follow these steps:

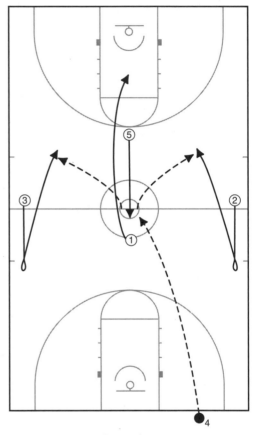

1. When the referee hands the ball to O4, O5 moves to the midcourt area and sets a screen for O1, who sprints to the basket. O5 then takes two or three quick steps into the backcourt with his hands even with his head, looking for O4's pass. The strategy is to get O5 open for a baseball pass from O4.

2. As O1 makes his move, O2 and O3 sprint into the backcourt, where O4 fakes passing to them. O2 and O3 sprint to the hash lines as though they are going to receive a pass. They then reverse pivot as O4 passes to O5.

3. O5 uses a touch pass to either O2 or O3 for the shot (figure 9.9).

Figure 9.9 Fake-and-go.

Line, Baseline

When no big men are available, the line is an excellent alternative against man-to-man pressure. Proper execution of this play depends on correct alignment of the players. The line can be run both when the inbounding player can't move the pivot foot on the throw-in and when the inbounder can run the baseline following a score. For the offense to score on this play, all five defenders must be guarding a player in the backcourt.

LINE, BASELINE

Focus

Backcourt scoring play with inbounds options.

Procedure

Play begins on the end line in the back-court. Follow these steps:

1. Player O3 has four passing options. All four players line up facing O3, approximately 12 to 18 inches (30 to 45 cm) apart. The players' routes are not scripted; instead, each reacts to the player directly in front of him and sprints to an open area. When O4, the first player in line, runs out, O5's defender must guard against the bomb, which allows O5 to get open going to the ball.

2. When the official hands the ball to O3, O4 goes away from defensive pressure and sprints to midcourt, looking for the bomb. O4 has the option to go either right or left.

3. O2 breaks in the opposite direction of O4, and O1, the third player, cuts opposite O2. O5 breaks toward O3, with both hands high, looking for the ball (figure 9.10).

4. After the ball is inbounded, the offensive players space themselves out and work the ball up the court. O3 is the safety.

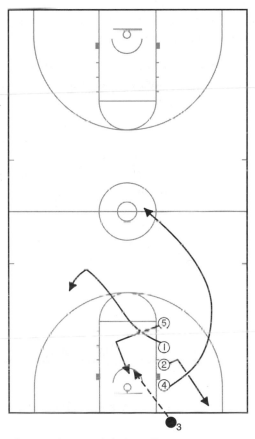

Figure 9.10 Line, baseline.

The line is an effective way either to score or to get the ball inbounds.

Line, Sideline

One reason that the line is such a good play is that it can be used effectively for all three inbounding areas—the backcourt baseline, the side court, and the front-court baseline. The play is not complicated, and with just a few modifications, it is adaptable and effective in most situations. On the side court, when the defense applies tight pressure, the players line up directly in front of O3, approximately 12 to 18 inches (30 to 45 cm) apart.

LINE, SIDELINE

Focus

Backcourt scoring play against defensive pressure, side out of bounds.

Procedure

Play begins in the backcourt, side out of bounds. Follow these steps:

1. O4 lines up 10 feet (3 m) off the sideline. O2, O1, and O5 are behind O4 in that order.

2. On O3's command of "Hike" or "Go," O4 peels off, circles the line, and sprints toward the basket. O2 breaks opposite O4. O1 breaks opposite O2, and O5 steps into the open area toward O3 (figure 9.11).

3. All four players are options. O3 must choose the right one and get the ball inbounds.

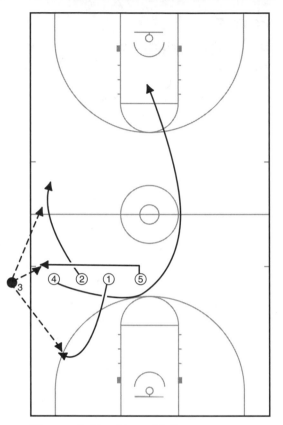

Figure 9.11   Line, sideline.

Scoring Plays From the Frontcourt

In a last possession situation when a team is behind by 3 or fewer points and has a time-out, specific issues arise. The biggest concern is getting the ball to the player who has the best chance of making the play. Coaches must keep in mind that whatever play the team runs, it must work against all types of defense. Therefore, if the defense denies the player designated to receive the pass, the other players must be alert and available for the inbounds pass.

Box Double

The amount of defensive pressure dictates whether the goal of the play is to get the ball inbounds and initiate a play or to attempt to score off the initial pass. This play, called the box double, is run from the free-throw line extended to midcourt and is designed to produce a score off the initial pass.

BOX DOUBLE

Focus

Looking to score from the frontcourt, side out of bounds.

Procedure

Play begins from the frontcourt, side out of bounds. Follow these steps:

1. Players line up in a box set. O5 and O2 are on the low blocks, and O4 and O1 are at the elbows. The player in the O4 position must be a good jumper because this play is a lob for him.

2. O4 sets a cross screen for O1. O1 fakes a screen on O2 and comes off O4.

3. O5 steps up to the free-throw lane and prepares to set a screen for O2. O2 sets a back screen for O4 and continues to the sideline off O5's screen as O5 opens to the ball.

4. O3 has four possible receivers— O4 on the lob; O1, who is coming to the strong-side elbow, O2 in the corner; or O5, who is stepping to the ball after O2 clears the screen (figure 9.12).

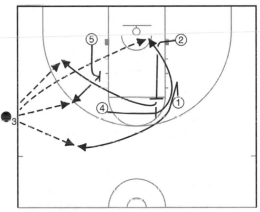

Figure 9.12   Box double.

X-Out

If the game clock shows 4 seconds or less, the player receiving the inbounds pass must make the play. Teammates should flatten out in the corners and not obstruct him. The player who receives the pass has plenty of time to catch, face up, and dribble a couple of times before shooting. The ball handler does not have time to run a play or gamble on a pass that may be deflected, bobbled, or mishandled. If the clock has between 5 and 10 seconds remaining, the player receiving the inbounds pass has time to run a pick-and-roll, looking to penetrate or draw and kick. The X-out play can be used in both situations, assuming that the player can create and get his own shot.

X-OUT INTO PICK-AND-ROLL

Focus

Execution and proper alignment, down 2 points with seven seconds on the clock, side out of bounds.

Procedure

Play begins in the frontcourt, side out of bounds. Follow these steps:

1. O1 lines up under the net. O2 and O3 line up at the free-throw lane extended, just above the three-point line. O5 sets up just above the free-throw line.

2. O3 cuts first and goes to the left-hand corner. O2 cuts off O3's back and goes to the right-hand corner.

3. After O2 and O3 make their cuts, O5 turns and sets a down screen for O1, whose job is to get open at the top of the key by going either way off O5.

4. O4 inbounds the ball and dives to the same-side block to rebound. The alignment is now set to run a specific play.

5. In most situations, the inbounds pass will go to the point guard (O1), who is generally the team's best ball handler and can penetrate.

6. When O1 clears O5 and O4 inbounds the ball, O5 relocates at the top of the key and sets a second screen for O1 (figure 9.13). O5 then pops out for a spot-up.

7. The team's best shooter (in this case, O2) spots up in the corner on the side to which O1 drives. The offensive team is down 2 points, so O1 looks to turn the corner and attack the basket.

8. O1 has three viable options—a drive, a pass to O5, or a pass to O2.

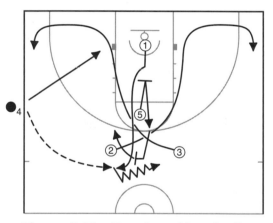

Figure 9.13 X-out into pick-and-roll.

This play is designed to get the best shooters in the corners, and the point guard penetrates to the basket for the layup or a draw-and-kick. If O2 is a good ball handler as well as the best shooter, it may be wise to have O1 and O2 switch positions. When diagramming these plays during time-outs, the coach should put the players in positions where they are comfortable. Coaches should know their players' strengths, such as which side of the floor they like to shoot from or whether they prefer to go right or left on drives. Practicing special situations, a crucial aspect of game management, allows coaches to gain this knowledge. The X-out into pick-and-roll play provides excellent opportunities for scoring by several players in a variety of ways.

THREE-POINT X-OUT

Focus

Execution and proper alignment, down 3 points, side out of bounds.

Procedure

Play begins in the frontcourt, side out of bounds. This play is designed to get a three-point attempt. Follow these steps:

1. The play begins with the X-out formation, which properly aligns the players. O4 prepares to inbound the ball.

2. Instead of going wide to the corner on their cuts, O2 and O3 dive to the low block on their respective sides of the court.

3. O5 sets a screen for O1, who receives the inbounds pass from O4.

4. On O4's pass inbounds to O1, O3 sets a cross screen for O2 as he sprints toward the corner. After making the pass inbounds, O4 immediately sets a second screen for O2, who runs a curl off O4, looking for a three-point catch-and-shoot.

5. After O1 clears O5's screen, O5 continues to the right-side low block and sets the last screen in the pick-the-picker screening technique for O3, who sprints to the three-point line looking for a catch-and-shoot.

6. After receiving the inbounds pass, O1 has three options: shoot if open, pass to O2 for a three-point shot, or pass to O3 for a catch-and-shoot three-point attempt (figure 9.14).

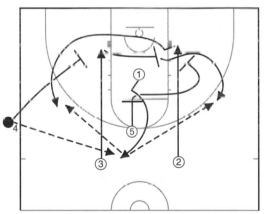

Figure 9.14 Three-point X-out.

This play is designed to get one of your best three-point shooters a shot. In today's game, the center, O5, may be an excellent perimeter shooter, so you may want to exchange O5 and O3's responsibilities for this special situation.

X-OUT INTO SINGLE-DOUBLE

Focus

Execution and proper alignment, down 3 points, side out of bounds, baseline set.

Procedure

Play begins in the frontcourt, side out of bounds. Follow these steps:

1. Players begin in the X-out formation. O1 receives the ball off the inbounds pass in the middle of the court, beyond the three-point line.

2. As the inbounds pass is being made, O3 relocates to the left-side free-throw line and O2 realigns directly under the net in the middle of the free-throw lane. O4, just off the left block, is in excellent position for the single-double action.

3. In order to establish a proper screening position, O3 sets up about 12 inches (30 cm) higher than O2 and steps into the free-throw lane for a cross screen for O2. O2 uses a jab step to the middle and goes off a staggered double screen, with O4 being the second screen.

4. After O2 clears O3, O3 uses O5's screen and cuts to the top of the key.

5. O1 can either pass to O2 or O3, who have the option of shooting or rotating the ball for a three-point shot (figure 9.15).

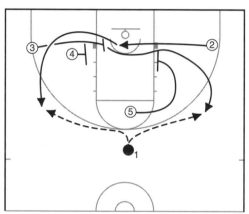

Figure 9.15   X-out into single-double.

In this play, the three best perimeter shooters should occupy the O1, O2, and O3 positions.

Inside Pick-the-Picker

People have two theories about baseline out-of-bounds plays. One promotes getting the ball inbounds and running a play, and the other advances the goal of scoring off the inbounds pass. The coach must take into consideration the normal variables of score, time of game, shot clock, floor position, and players in the game. This play, inside pick-the-picker, is designed to produce a score off the initial pass. The play works best when O2, or whoever is designated to run O2's route, is a great shooter. During the Michael Jordan era with the Chicago Bulls, this play was good for at least one basket a game, with Jordan being the shooter.

INSIDE PICK-THE-PICKER

Focus

Setting good screens with ball fakes and good passes.

Procedure

Play begins in the frontcourt, baseline. The basic play is normally run for O2, the shooter, to come off a double-stagger set by O5 and O4 for a catch-and-shoot jump shot from the corner. After running the basic set a couple of times, the play call changes and O2 becomes a decoy. Instead of going to O2, the play goes to O5 or whoever sets the first screen. Follow these steps:

1. O3 inbounds the ball on the baseline. O4 and O2 are set up on the strong-side and weak-side blocks, respectively. O5 is just below the free-throw line, and O1 is at the top of the key.

2. As the official hands the ball to O3, O5 sets a screen for O2 to work off him. But when the play is run for O5, O2 waits, then cuts when O5 gets lower on the block.

3. O5 is now on the low block opposite O3 who is inbounding the ball. O4 sets a solid back screen for O5, and O5 cuts to the vacated open space for a layup (figure 9.16).

Figure 9.16   Inside pick-the-picker.

Box, Cross 2

Sometimes the simplest plays are the most effective ones. The box set can be highly successful and easily disguised. Players need to learn three calls: cross, diagonal, and up. Each call indicates a screening angle. The players can then line up at any of the four spots and execute the play. For instance, in the cross action, the hot spot, or the shooting spot, is the elbow opposite the player inbounding the ball. The call "Cross 2" means that the play is designated for O2 coming off a cross screen. "Cross 3" indicates that O3 is on the hot spot, and so on. If the call is "Diagonal 4," O4 lines up diagonally to the player inbounding, and the player who lines up in front of the player passing the ball inbounds sets the screen. The offensive team should pick on a weak defender and get a layup or a foul by attacking the basket.

BOX, CROSS 2

Focus

Alignment, screens, cutting angles, and passes.

Procedure

Play begins in the frontcourt, baseline. Players are in a box set. Follow these steps:

1. O1 takes the ball out of bounds and calls, "Cross 2." O5 fakes inside as if he is going to get the pass and moves to the corner, pretending to be the primary target.

2. O3 calls out, "Back screen" and moves toward the defender guarding O2. O2 jab-steps to the sideline, setting up a cross screen by O4 on O2's defender.

3. O2 uses the screen and cuts down the middle, looking for a lob or layup (figure 9.17). O4 holds the screen on X2, opens to the ball, and goes to the basket as the second option. O1 fakes to O5 and looks for the O2 and O4 options. O3 relocates high as the safety.

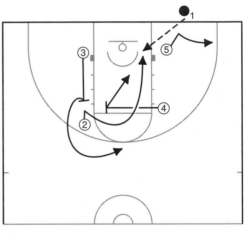

Figure 9.17 Box, cross 2.

Line

The line inbounds play is one of the most effective alignments. Besides being used in the backcourt, the line play can be used underneath the basket to score or to inbound and get the ball in play. The play permits the coach to assemble the line to be the most advantageous to the team and the talent at hand, changing the player alignment to inbound to a passer, a ball handler, or a shooter.

LINE

Focus

Inbounding the ball versus hard defensive pressure.

Procedure

Play begins in the frontcourt, baseline. Follow these steps:

1. O3 takes the ball out of bounds. The rest of the players line up approximately 12 inches (30 cm) apart. O2 is in the front of the line, lined up on the low block on the ball side. O1, O4, and O5 line up behind O2.

2. O1 cuts toward the baseline, goes around O2, and sprints up the middle, veering to the sideline and looking for the inbounds pass. As O1 makes the move, O5 jab-steps to the middle and goes to the corner, looking for the inbounds pass.

3. O4 steps inside the free-throw lane and screens down on O2's defender. O2 comes up the lane, veers to the elbow, and moves toward the sideline, looking for the inbounds pass.

4. Following his down screen, O4 steps to the ball as a possible receiver. O3 looks over the options and decides where to throw the ball (figure 9.18). Regardless of who receives the inbounds pass, O1 seeks the ball to set the offense.

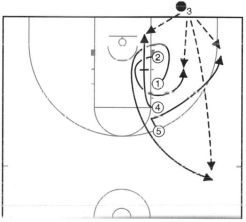

Figure 9.18 Line.

If a coach could choose only one out-of-bounds alignment, the line would be it. This play works against pressure, and with proper spacing, it is the most adaptable. When the defense applies hard pressure on the baseline, the line provides several effective options. The objective is to get the ball inbounds and into the hands of the point guard quickly. All four players in the line are possible options and must get open to receive a pass. The offensive players must be aware that defenders will try to hold them, so a determined mind-set to get open is required.

Lob

The frontcourt lob is another inbounds play used on the baseline. For the lob to be successful, players must execute a number of key components. The floor must be balanced so that those involved in the lob have room to operate. Deception is a major issue and must be executed properly, and the passer must read the defense and deliver the pass where the player dunking can make the play. In this situation, making the lob a priority is a matter of concentration and focus of both individual team members and the team as a whole.

LOB

Focus

Inbounding the ball on a lob versus hard defensive pressure.

Procedure

Play begins in the frontcourt, baseline. Follow these steps:

1. O1 takes the ball out of bounds on the right side underneath the basket.

2. O4 lines up on the left low block, O5 at the left elbow, O3 at the right elbow, and O2 in the right corner.

3. On the command "Go," O4 pretends to set an up screen for O5. O5 makes a jab fake to the outside as if he is going left.

4. O3 reacts immediately with a cross screen for O5.

5. O5 pivots off the left foot using O3's screen, cutting hard down the middle and looking for a lob from O1 (figure 9.19).

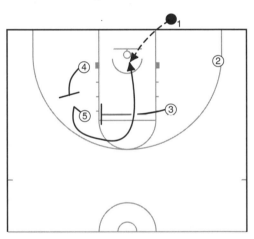

Figure 9.19   Lob.

Executing Against Disruptive Zones

The traditional theory for attacking a zone with a one-man front is to align the offense in a two-man front. And if the zone is a two-man front, the offense aligns in a one-man front. After the offense aligns itself properly, the players try to create a triangle, or an overload, pitting three offensive players against two defenders. The team's best shooters occupy at least two of these spots. This offensive strategy is sound until the defense throws up a box-and-one, triangle-and-two, or 1-3-1 half-court trap. Why? Because these defenses are designed to disrupt the normal zone attack.

The offensive team must be prepared, and preparation comes from practice. Zone defenses, especially those designed to disrupt, require special attention. Most coaches cover the basic 2-3 and 3-2 zones within their normal offensive sets, but defenses that disrupt the offense with traps, denial of the ball to the best player, and gimmicks demand special preparation. Coaches need a well-designed plan of attack to make sure that the right players are in the right spots to get their shots.

Let's look at three disruptive half-court defenses: the 1-3-1, the box-and-one, and the triangle-and-two. In all cases, the offense needs to be patient, align in an overload, maintain proper floor balance and spacing, and use player and ball movement to attack the offensive boards for rebounds.

Versus 1-3-1

A 1-3-1 defense is designed to keep the offense on the perimeter and eliminate layups. The LA guard-to-forward set (see chapter 6) is an excellent 1-3-1 example because it puts shooters in open areas and gives an opportunity to lob to a big man. In this misdirection play, the ball starts on one side and reverses to the other side for the attack.

VERSUS 1-3-1

Focus

Alignment and execution versus a disruptive 1-3-1 on the half court.

Procedure

Players begin on the half court. Follow these steps:

1. O2 starts the play with a pass to O4 and then cuts through to the opposite corner.

2. O5 screens away for O3 and relocates to the low block and out of the low defender's vision.

3. O3 cuts from the wing to the ball-side elbow, looking for a pass and a shot. O1 uses a V-cut to get open at the top of the key for the pass (figure 9.20).

4. As the offense begins to move and players realign, O4 looks at O3 coming in behind the middle man on defense. If O3 does not get the pass, he continues to the baseline on the ball side.

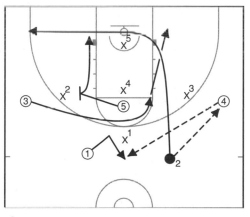

Figure 9.20   Versus 1-3-1: Pass to top of key.

(continued)

Versus 1-3-1 *(continued)*

5. O1 looks to lob to O5 as he steps into the lane behind the defense (figure 9.21). If that is not available, O1 takes a couple dribbles and passes to O2, who may have a shot or a pass inside to O5.

6. After making the pass to O1, O4 relocates to the elbow and forms a triangle with O2 and O5.

This set offers many opportunities for good shots, and someone is always on the boards.

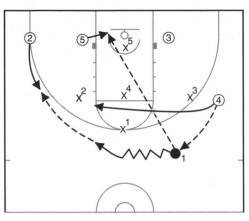

Figure 9.21   Versus 1-3-1: Pass inside.

Versus Box-and-One

The box-and-one is designed to guard one player man-to-man and to defend the rest of the team in a zone. The intent is to shut down a high scorer or at least limit the player's good view of the basket and reduce his points. Sometimes coaches assign the one man (in the box-and-one) to the opposing team's best ball handler, hoping to disrupt their playmaker. With some modification, the LA set (see chapter 6) accommodates our needs on offense.

VERSUS BOX-AND-ONE

Focus

Proper alignment and execution versus box-and-one.

Procedure

X2 is assigned to O2. Players begin on the half court in the LA offense. Follow these steps:

1. The offense begins by attacking the box. O1 initiates by passing to O3 and getting a return pass. O1 then passes to O2, who passes to O4. O2 dives to the strong-side block and screens X4.

2. O3 uses the screen on X4 and clears to the strong-side corner.

3. O4 passes to O3 and clears to the weak-side block (figure 9.22). O1 replaces O4 on the wing for the pass, and O5 remains at the high post in the middle and opens to the ball.

4. The realignment places O1 with the ball at the wing position, O3 in the ball-side corner, O5 at the high-post elbow ball side, O4 on the weak-side block, and O2 on the ball-side block, setting a screen on X4 and attempting to occupy two defenders.

5. O1, O3, and O5 establish a passing triangle, each looking for an open shot (figure 9.23). The objective of the offense is to find the open holes in the defense and get the best shooters to those spots.

6. If the point guard, O1, decides to reverse the ball on the dribble, O2 uses O4's screen for a turnout. In this scenario, O5 would stay at the high post and cross the free-throw lane to form a triangle with O4 on the block and O2 on the wing.

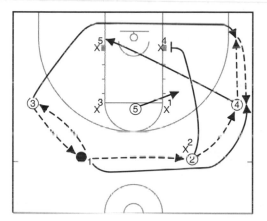

Figure 9.22 Versus box-and-one: Attack box.

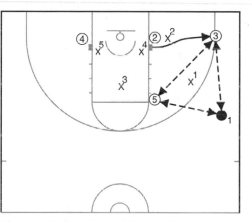

Figure 9.23 Versus box-and-one: Establish passing triangle.

Versus Triangle-and-Two

The intent of the triangle-and-two defense is to place enormous pressure on players who are not good perimeter shooters. These players may be effective close to the basket but are not skilled at face-up jump shots. The triangle-and-two is a mind game, inviting nonshooters to do things outside their comfort zone while applying constant pressure on the good shooters. But with patience and discipline, the offense will get good shots.

The triangle-and-two defense can be extremely effective. Auburn did a great job with it in playing eventual champion Syracuse to a 1-point loss in the 2003 NCAA tournament. The Auburn defense slowed the normally potent Syracuse offense by disrupting the tempo and flow of the game. When key players, scorers, and playmakers passed the ball, Auburn made it difficult for those players to get the ball back. Other Syracuse players then had to make big plays, such as getting rebounds, making assists, and scoring baskets, and they did. Syracuse won, but not before being tested.

VERSUS TRIANGLE-AND-TWO

Focus

Triangle overload for shooters and rebounders versus triangle-and-two.

Procedure

Players begin on the half court. Follow these steps:

1. Defenders X4 and X5 work in tandem to cover the baseline. When one slides out to cover a baseline jump shooter, the other slides across and covers the low block. X3 covers the middle and the top. X1 and X2 play man-to-man on the guards, inviting shots from O3, O4, and O5.

2. O1 passes to O5.

3. O1 and O2 dive to their same-side low-block positions (figure 9.24). O1 and O2 create congestion. They can screen the baseline defenders or cross screen to get open.

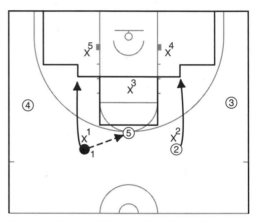

Figure 9.24 Versus triangle-and-two: Dive to blocks.

4. The blocked-off space indicates the open areas that the three undefended players can occupy (figure 9.25). The baseline corners, wings, and top of the key are the shooting areas.

5. For identification purposes, O3 has the ball, O4 is at the top, and O5 is in the corner. When working the right side of the court, O3, with the ball, creates a two-on-one situation with the corner, O5, and the baseline defender, X4, or with the top, O4, and the defender, X3. The left side is the same except that its baseline defender is X5.

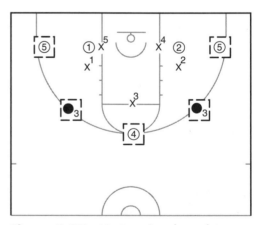

Figure 9.25 Versus triangle-and-two: Find open shots.

6. Ball movement with good passes between O3, O4, and O5, and taking up slack toward the basket will establish shooting range with open shots.

Make sure that the shooter is the right player and that rebounders attack the glass.

Disruptive defenses can cause problems for most teams. Going into a season-ending tournament, coaches must address the possibility that their opponent might try one of these unorthodox defenses. Teams that have nothing to lose will sometimes rally around a defensive gimmick such as the box-and-one, 1-3-1, or triangle-and-two to pull an upset, as Auburn almost did. Successful coaches prepare for all facets of the game, including full-court presses, inbounding the ball against pressure, and disruptive defenses, rather than waiting until game time to make adjustments.

Index

Note: The italicized *f* and *t* following page numbers refer to figures and tables, respectively.

A

academics 39
aggressiveness, in rebounding 100
agility training 5-13, 6*f*-11*f*
anaerobic training 2-5, 4*t*
angles, in passing 82-84, 83*f*-84*f*
anticipation, in rebounding 100
assistant coaches 39-41
athletic tools, for individual offensive skills 66-71
attitude 102
Auburn 255, 257

B

backcourt, scoring plays from 237-244, 239*f*-244*f*
Baker, Tay 36-37, 39
balance, UCLA for 131
ball 18, 21, 170, 215
    in defending ball side, one pass away
        181-182, 182*f*
    handler, defending 179-180, 180*f*
    kept out of middle 176-183, 176*f*-183*f*
    in middle, defending 182-183, 183*f*
    on-ball defense and 169-170
    in Screen on the Ball 97, 97*f*
    in Speed With the Ball 67, 67*f*
ball-side cuts, preventing 188-191, 189*f*-191*f*
ball–you–man position 170
base
    building 2-5, 4*t*
    for shooting 71-73, 72*f*
Baseline Pivot 91, 91*f*
baseline screens 99, 99*f*, 204-205, 205*f*
be in good physical condition, principle of 1-14,
    4*t*, 6*f*-13*f*
Benson, Ted 226
best players 26-27, 43-44
big players 113-114, 231
bounce pass 79-80
Box, Cross 2 249-250, 250*f*
Box Double 244-245
boxing out 100, 171-172, 192-194, 193*f*, 196
Box Out With a Step-Through 196
Bryant, Kobe 21, 23, 31, 33, 39, 77
burpees 7, 7*f*
Butler 20, 55-58, 55*t*-59*t*

C

Campbell, Elden 73
Carroll, Joe Barry 26-27, 152, 226

Cassell, Sam 222
center 31-32, 85, 111, 113-114
Change-of-Pace Dribble 88
character 42
Charleston Lowgators 17
Charlotte Bobcats 108
Charlotte Hornets 18, 31, 73, 77, 107, 228
chemistry, team 41-45
chest pass 79-80
Chicago Bulls 33, 37, 39, 69, 248
clock management 219
Close, Contain, and Contest 187-188, 188*f*
closing out 185-187, 186*f*-188*f*
coaches 14-15, 23, 30, 127, 172. *See also specific*
        coaches
    assistant 39-41
    player input to 44, 218-219
    as players 37-38
    roles and responsibilities of 34-35
    systems and 36-39
    team chemistry, leadership, and 41-45
Cohn, Jordan 169
Comeback Option 5-3 238, 239*f*
communication 168
confidence 71-73
consistency 43
cross screens 94-95, 95*f*, 207-209, 208*f*-209*f*
Cutting Off the Angle 184-185, 184*f*-185*f*

D

Dallas 172, 207, 212, 216, 221
decision making 102-103
defenders, characteristics of 167
Defending Ball Side, One Pass Away 181-182, 182*f*
Defending Baseline Screens 204-205, 205*f*
Defending Cross-Screen, Screen-the-Screener
    Sets 209, 209*f*
Defending Cross Screens 208, 208*f*
Defending Diagonal Passes 202, 202*f*
Defending Drag Sets 214-215, 214*f*
Defending Middle Pick-and-Rolls 213, 213*f*
Defending Passes Around the Horn 200-201, 201*f*
Defending Pin-Down Screens 205-207, 207*f*
Defending Sideline Pick-and-Rolls 211-212, 211*f*
Defending the Ball Handler 179-180, 180*f*
Defending the Ball in the Middle of the Court
    182-183, 183*f*
Defending the High Post 177, 177*f*
Defending the Low Post 178-179, 179*f*

Defending the Midpost 178, 178*f*
Defending Weak Side 180-181, 181*f*
defense. *See also* team defense
    choosing right defenses for team 172-174
    full-court pressure 233-237, 234*f*-237*f*
    overview of 165, 223
    switching 216
defensive screening sets 203-209, 205*f*, 207*f*-209*f*
defensive skills and tactics
    communication 168
    foundation of 17-18
    fundamentals 168-174
    hustle 22, 168-169
    for inbound plays 173
    man-to-man defense 30, 173
    objectives 175-197, 176*f*-191*f*, 192*f*-193*f*, 195*f*, 197*f*
    off-ball defense 170-172
    on-ball defense 169-170
    Wooden's 174-175
    zone defense 30, 173, 226-227, 252
Defensive Slide 8, 8*f*
defensive unit coordination 218-223
defensive value sheet 53-54, 54*t*
depth chart 54, 55*t*
Depth Jumping 12-13, 12*f*-13*f*
diagonal passes 201-202, 202*f*
Diagonal Pivot 90-91, 91*f*
Diagonal Screen 96-97, 96*f*
disruptive zones, executing against 252-257, 253*f*-256*f*
Double Pivot 90, 90*f*
Down Screen 93, 93*f*
drag sets 214-215, 214*f*
draw-and-kick 78-79, 78*f*-79*f*
dribble-drive offense 30, 147-151, 149*f*-150*f*
Dribble Pivots 87
dribbler, on-ball defense for 169
dribbling 74-76, 74*f*-76*f*, 84-88
drills
    Baseline Pivot 91, 91*f*
    Baseline Screens 99, 99*f*
    Box, Cross 2 249-250, 250*f*
    Box Double 244-245
    Box Out With a Reverse Pivot 194
    Box Out With a Step-Through 196
    Burpee 7, 7*f*
    Change-of-Pace Dribble 88
    Close, Contain, and Contest 187-188, 188*f*
    Closing Out 187, 187*f*
    Comeback Option 5-3 238, 239*f*
    Cross Screen 94-95, 95*f*
    Cutting Off the Angle 184-185, 184*f*-185*f*
    Defending Ball Side, One Pass Away 181-182, 182*f*
    Defending Baseline Screens 204-205, 205*f*
    Defending Cross-Screen, Screen-the-Screener Sets 209, 209*f*
    Defending Cross Screens 208, 208*f*

Defending Diagonal Passes 202, 202*f*
Defending Drag Sets 214-215, 214*f*
Defending Middle Pick-and-Rolls 213, 213*f*
Defending Passes Around the Horn 200-201, 201*f*
Defending Pin-Down Screens 205-207, 207*f*
Defending Sideline Pick-and-Rolls 211-212, 211*f*
Defending the Ball Handler 179-180, 180*f*
Defending the Ball in the Middle of the Court 182-183, 183*f*
Defending the High Post 177, 177*f*
Defending the Low Post 178-179, 179*f*
Defending the Midpost 178, 178*f*
Defending Weak Side 180-181, 181*f*
Defensive Slide 8, 8*f*
Depth Jumping 12-13, 12*f*-13*f*
Diagonal Pivot 90-91, 91*f*
Diagonal Screen 96-97, 96*f*
Double Pivot 90, 90*f*
Down Screen 93, 93*f*
Dribble Pivots 87
efficiency in 15
Fake-and-Go 241-242, 242*f*
Five-on-Five 203
Flex Offense 139-141, 139*f*-141*f*
Forward, No Ball-Side Cut 191, 191*f*
Forward-Oriented Attack 111-113, 112*f*-113*f*
Full-Court Shooting 75-76, 76*f*
Guard, No Ball-Side Cut 189-190, 190*f*
Guard-Oriented Attack 109-110, 109*f*
Guard-to-Center Pass Pattern 136-137, 136*f*-137*f*
Guard-to-Forward Pass Pattern 133-135, 133*f*-134*f*
Guard-to-Guard Pass Pattern 135-136, 135*f*-136*f*
Identifying Floor Areas 183-184, 184*f*
Inside Pass 81, 81*f*
Inside Pick-the-Picker 248-249, 249*f*
Jumping to Improve Timing 70, 70*f*
Line 251, 251*f*
Line, Baseline 242-243, 243*f*
Line, Sideline 243-244, 244*f*
Lob 252, 252*f*
Low Post, No Ball-Side Cut 191, 191*f*
Make 'Em to Move 125
Motion Offense 152-154, 153*f*-154*f*
Multiple Screens 95-96, 96*f*, 110, 110*f*
1-4 Front 149-150, 150*f*
1-4 Set Versus Full-Court Defense, Option 1 233-235, 234*f*-235*f*
1-4 Set Versus Full-Court Defense, Option 2 236-237, 236*f*-237*f*
One-Guard Front 148-149, 149*f*
Outside Pass 82, 82*f*
Passing Angles to the Low Post 83, 83*f*
Passing Angles to the Top of the Key 84, 84*f*
Power Cross Attack 116-118, 117*f*-118*f*

drills *(continued)*
    Power Down Attack 114-116, 115*f*-116*f*
    Pregame Warm-Up Shooting 163-164, 163*f*
    Rebound Jumping 10, 10*f*
    Rebound Put-Back 101
    Rope Jumping 11, 11*f*
    Screen on the Ball 97, 97*f*
    Shooting Off a Draw-and-Kick 78-79, 78*f*-79*f*
    Shooting Off a Step-Back Move 77, 77*f*
    Shooting Off the Dribble, Left Hand 75, 75*f*
    Shooting Off the Dribble, Right Hand 74, 74*f*
    Single and Double Screens 98, 98*f*
    Single Pivot 89, 89*f*
    Sit-Up 6, 6*f*
    Six-Basket Free Throws 121
    Soft Hands 68-69, 69*f*
    Speed Jumping 9, 9*f*
    Speed With the Ball 67, 67*f*
    Splits: Forward Makes Post Pass 157-158, 159*f*
    Splits: Guard Goes to Corner 157-158, 158*f*
    Splits: Guard Reverses 157, 157*f*
    Splits: Guard Sets Screen 156, 156*f*
    Step-Out Bomb 239-240, 240*f*
    Stop-and-Go Dribble 87-88
    Straight-Line Dribble 86
    Three-Man Triangle 232, 232*f*
    three-player screening 155-159, 156*f*-159*f*
    Three-Point Shooting 124-125
    Three-Point X-Out 247, 247*f*
    Thru 161-163, 162*f*
    Transition Lob 240-241, 241*f*
    Triangle Offense 143-146, 143*f*-146*f*
    Two-Basket Free Throws 121
    Two Touches 159-161, 160*f*
    UCLA Movement 132, 132*f*
    Versus Box-and-One 254-255, 255*f*
    Versus 1-3-1 253-254, 253*f*-254*f*
    Versus Triangle-and-Two 255-256, 256*f*
    Weak-Side Pin-Down 94, 94*f*
    X-Out Into Pick-and-Roll 246, 246*f*
    X-Out Into Single-Double 248, 248*f*
Duke University 27, 32, 55-58, 55*t*-59*t*, 217, 226

E
Ecroyd, Bob 20
efficiency 15
Ellis, Monte 108
end-of-game decisions 221-222
English, Alex 17
equipment 40
evaluation, player. *See* player evaluation
executing against disruptive zones 252-257, 253*f*-256*f*
experimentation, in games 19
extra work, seeking 16

F
fairness 43
Fake-and-Go 241-242, 242*f*

Felton, Raymond 108
five-on-five 202-203
flex offense 138-142, 139*f*-141*f*, 155
focus 15-16
Forward, No Ball-Side Cut 191, 191*f*
Forward-Oriented Attack 111-113, 112*f*-113*f*
forwards 31, 85
    in forward-oriented attack 111-113, 112*f*-113*f*
    in Guard-to-Forward Pass Pattern 133-135, 133*f*-134*f*
    in Splits: Forward Makes Post Pass 157-158, 159*f*
fouls 18, 170, 196-197, 197*f*, 219-221, 225-227
foundational skills, developing 17-18
free throw
    accuracy 106, 119, 120*t*
    as offensive priority 118-121, 120*t*
frontcourt, scoring plays from 244-252, 245*f*-252*f*
full-court pressure defense, attacking 233-237, 234*f*-237*f*
Full-Court Shooting 75-76, 76*f*
full-court transitions, disrupting 215-216
fundamental tips 106

G
game-day duties 41
games
    best players finishing 26-27
    experimentation in 19
    special situation game chart for 231*t*
    statistics for 40
Gasol, Pau 31, 113
genetic factors 66
Guard, No Ball-Side Cut 189-190, 190*f*
guard-oriented attack 108-111, 109*f*-110*f*
guards 30-31, 85, 108, 111, 151
    in guard-oriented attack 108-111, 109*f*-110*f*
    in Guard-to-Forward Pass Pattern 133-135, 133*f*-134*f*
    in Guard-to-Guard Pass Pattern 135-136, 135*f*-136*f*
    in One-Guard Front 148-149, 149*f*
    in Splits: Guard Goes to Corner 157-158, 158*f*
    in Splits: Guard Reverses 157, 157*f*
    in Splits: Guard Sets Screen 156, 156*f*
Guard-to-Center Pass Pattern 136-137, 136*f*-137*f*
Guard-to-Forward Pass Pattern 133-135, 133*f*-134*f*
Guard-to-Guard Pass Pattern 135-136, 135*f*-136*f*
guiding principles
    be in good physical condition 1-14, 4*t*, 6*f*-13*f*, 106
    be unselfish 20-23
    in early planning stage 27
    execute plan 18-20
    maximize strengths and minimize weaknesses 23-27, 24*t*-26*t*, 105-107, 217
    overview of 1
    play hard 14-16
    play smart 16-18

H
Hallman, Arnett 227
hands 30, 68-69, 69f
Harris, Del 131
Holland, Terry 122
horn, defending passes around 200-201, 201f
Hunziker, David 14-15
hustle 22, 61-63, 62t-63t, 168-169
hydration 2

I
Identifying Floor Areas 183-184, 184f
inbound plays, defending against 173
Indiana 219
individual offensive skills
    athletic tools 66-71
    decision making 102-103
    fundamentals 71-101, 106
    overview of 65-66
individual production 48
Inside Pass 81, 81f
Inside Pick-the-Picker 248-249, 249f
intelligence 16, 18
interval training 2-5
isolation, in triangle offense 145-146, 145f-146f

J
Jackson, Phil 37-39, 147
Jacksonville 19
Johnson, Magic 23, 33, 86, 105 106, 227
Jordan, Michael 21, 33, 39
jumping 69-70, 70f
Jumping to Improve Timing 70, 70f
jump shooters 170

K
Kidd, Jason 43, 221
King, Kevin 219
Kron, Tommy 172

L
lane denial 215-216
LA offense 127-138, 132f-137f, 155
layups, contesting 196-197, 197f
leadership 41-45, 108
learning, PRS promoting 48
Lincoln, Abraham 42
Line, Baseline 242-243, 243f
Line, Sideline 243-244, 244f
Line 251, 251f
line inbounds play 250-251, 251f
Lob 252, 252f
Low Post, No Ball-Side Cut 191, 191f
low-post-oriented attack 113-118, 115f-118f

M
Make 'Em to Move 125
man-to-man defense 30, 173
maximized strengths 23-27, 24t-26t, 105-107, 217

M (continued, right column)
Maxwell, Cedric "Cornbread" 34, 228
Mears, Ray 172
Meyer, Jeff 82
Miami Heat 172, 207, 210, 212, 216, 221
middle pick-and-rolls 212-213, 213f
middle-dribble penetration 183-188, 184f-188f
minimized weaknesses 23-27, 24t-26t
Morris, Drake 227
motion offense 151-154, 153f-154f
motivation 45, 49-50
Multiple Screens 95-96, 96f, 110, 110f
muscle action, stretch-shortening cycle of 12

N
Naismith, James 29, 119
National Basketball Association (NBA) 17, 23,
    30-32, 113, 206, 212, 216, 222
    player evaluation in 42
    preparation in 229
    rebounding in 100-101
NBA Development League (NBDL) 17, 37
NCAA tournament 20-21, 36, 53, 79, 129
    Duke in 27, 32, 55-58, 55t-59t
    free throws in 119, 120t
    three-point shots in 122, 123t-124t
Newton, C.M. 36-37, 129
New York Knicks 108
Nowitzki, Dirk 31, 43, 77, 106, 111, 172, 206-207, 221

O
objectivity, in PRS 48, 50-51
observation chart 24t
off-ball defense 170-172
offense, team. *See* team offense
offensive clock 230-232, 231t, 232f
offensive priorities
    designing offensive system 107-118
    fitting into offensive system 107
    forward-oriented attack 111-113, 112f-113f
    free throws 118-121, 120t
    fundamental tips for 106
    guard-oriented attack 108-111, 109f-110f
    identifying strengths and improving weak-
        nesses 105-107
    low-post-oriented attack 113-118, 115f-118f
    overview of 105, 125
    three-point shot 122-125, 123t-124t
offensive skills, foundation of 17-18. *See also*
    individual offensive skills
offensive value sheet 53-54, 53t
off-the-dribble shooting 74-76, 74f-76f
Okafor, Emeka 27
Olajuwon, Hakeem 76-77
on-ball defense 169-170
1-4 Front 149-150, 150f
1-4 Set Versus Full-Court Defense, Option 1
    233-235, 234f-235f
1-4 Set Versus Full-Court Defense, Option 2
    236-237, 236f-237f

One-Guard Front 148-149, 149*f*
Outside Pass 82, 82*f*
overhead pass 79-80
overload training 66
oxygen debt 3

P
participation survey 29
passer, activating 170
passing. *See also specific passes*
        basics 79-84, 81*f*-84*f*
        defending, around horn 200-201, 201*f*
        pass selection and 79-80
        vision and angles in 82-84, 83*f*-84*f*
Passing Angles to the Low Post 83, 83*f*
Passing Angles to the Top of the Key 84, 84*f*
Paul, Chris 17, 107, 210
performance, training for 14
performance rating system (PRS)
        application 55-58, 55*t*-59*t*
        components 50-54, 53*t*-55*t*
        hustle board and 61-63, 62*t*-63*t*
        implementation 51
        objectivity in 48, 50-51
        practical uses of 49-50
        reasons behind 47-48
        results 60-61, 60*t*
        scrimmage evaluation using 59
        statistics in 48, 55-60, 55*t*-59*t*
personal contacts 35
physical condition, good 1-14, 4*t*, 6*f*-13*f*, 106
pick-and-roll 210-215, 211*f*, 213*f*-214*f*, 246, 246*f*
pin-down screens, defending 205-207, 207*f*
PIT. *See* player improvement time
pivoting 88-91, 89*f*-91*f*, 192-194, 193*f*
plan, executing 18-20
player evaluation 42, 45, 47-49. *See also* performance rating system
player improvement time (PIT) 16
players. *See also specific players*
        best 26-27, 43-44
        big 113-114, 231
        as coaches 37-38
        efficiency of 15
        getting ball to 18
        goals of 24*t*-26*t*
        input from 44, 218-219
        multitalented 32-33
        roles of 29-35
        responsibilities of 34-35
        team chemistry, leadership, and 41-45
        as virus 22-23
play hard, guiding principle of 14-16
play smart, guiding principle of 16-18
Plumlee, Miles 32
plyometrics 5, 12
point guard 30, 85, 108, 111, 151
policies, trust and 44

position, in rebounding 100
post 83, 83*f*, 157-158, 159*f*
        defending 176-179, 176*f*-179*f*
        in low-post-oriented attack 113-118, 115*f*-118*f*
        no ball-side cut 190-191, 191*f*
power, training for 5-13, 6*f*-11*f*
Power Cross Attack 116-118, 117*f*-118*f*
Power Down Attack 114-116, 115*f*-116*f*
power forward 31
practice 17, 40-41
Predraft Combine, NBA 42
pregame analysis
        attacking full-court pressure defense in 233-237, 234*f*-237*f*
        offensive clock used in 230-232, 231*t*, 232*f*
        tactics for 228-257, 231*t*, 232*f*, 234*f*-237*f*, 239*f*-256*f*
Pregame Warm-Up Shooting 163-164, 163*f*
preseason program 2
PRS. *See* performance rating system
Purdue 226-227

Q
quickness 67

R
rebounding 100-101, 171-172, 215
Rebound Jumping 10, 10*f*
Rebound Put-Back 101
receiver, stepping toward 171
recruiting 39-40
releases 137, 137*f*
reverse pivot, boxing out with 192-194, 193*f*
Rice, Glen 18
Robertson, Oscar 32-33
roles 23, 29-35. *See also specific roles*
Rope Jumping 11, 11*f*
rules changes 29-30
Rupp, Adolph 36-37, 79, 128-130, 155, 172
Russell, Bill 22-23

S
St. John's 217
Sanders, Tom "Satch" 22-23
San Francisco 219
scheduling 40
scoring plays from backcourt 237-244, 239*f*-244*f*
scoring plays from frontcourt 244-252, 245*f*-252*f*
Scott, Phil 168-169
scouting 41
screening 92-99, 92*f*-99*f*
screening sets, defensive 203-209, 205*f*, 207*f*-209*f*
Screen on the Ball 97, 97*f*
scrimmage evaluation 59
secondary break 161
second shots, preventing 192-196, 193*f*, 195*f*
setting the table 148
shell 199-202, 201*f*-202*f*

shooting. *See also specific shots*
  base, visualization, and confidence for 71-73, 72*f*
  contesting 169, 196-197, 197*f*
  fundamentals 71-79, 72*f*, 74*f*-79*f*
  guard 31
  off the dribble 74-76, 74*f*-76*f*
  pregame warm-up 163-164, 163*f*
  step-back move 76-77, 77*f*
Shooting Off a Draw-and-Kick 78-79, 78*f*-79*f*
Shooting Off a Step-Back Move 77, 77*f*
Shooting Off the Dribble, Left Hand 75, 75*f*
Shooting Off the Dribble, Right Hand 74, 74*f*
shot clock 30, 222
shot selection 106
shuffle-cut 138. *See also* flex offense
sideline pick-and-rolls 211-212, 211*f*
Single and Double Screens 98, 98*f*
Single Pivot 89, 89*f*
sit-ups 6, 6*f*
Six-Basket Free Throws 121
Skinner, Al 138
small forward 31
Smith, Dean 29, 36, 128, 130, 155, 225, 230
Snell, John 172
Soft Hands 68-69, 69*f*
space, UCLA for 131
special situation game chart 231*t*
special situations, tactics for. *See* tactics, for special situations
speed 9, 9*f*, 66-67, 67*f*
Speed Jumping 9, 9*f*
Speed With the Ball 67, 67*f*
Splits: Forward Makes Post Pass 157-158, 159*f*
Splits: Guard Goes to Corner 157-158, 158*f*
Splits: Guard Reverses 157, 157*f*
Splits: Guard Sets Screen 156, 156*f*
statistics 26, 40, 48, 55-60, 55*t*-59*t*
step-back move 76-77, 77*f*
Step-Out Bomb 239-240, 240*f*
step-through, box out with 194-196, 195*f*
Stop-and-Go Dribble 87-88
Straight-Line Dribble 86
strengths, maximized 23-27, 24*t*-26*t*, 105-107, 217
stretch-shortening cycle, of muscle action 12
student participation survey 29
subjectivity, in player evaluation 45, 47-49
success, PRS and 49
support staff 39-41
Syracuse 255
systems, coaches and 36-39

T
tactics, for special situations. *See also* defensive skills and tactics
  executing against disruptive zones 252-257, 253*f*-256*f*
  foul policy 225-227

pregame analysis 228-257, 231*t*, 232*f*, 234*f*-237*f*, 239*f*-256*f*
  scoring plays from backcourt 237-244, 239*f*-244*f*
  scoring plays from frontcourt 244-252, 245*f*-252*f*
  time-outs used efficiently 227-228
team chemistry 41-45
team defense
  alignments 199-217, 201*f*-202*f*, 205*f*, 207*f*-209*f*, 211*f*, 213*f*-214*f*
  defensive unit coordination 218-223
  playing to strengths 217
team offense
  analysis of 154-155
  dribble-drive offense 30, 147-151, 149*f*-150*f*
  flex offense 138-142, 139*f*-141*f*, 155
  LA offense 127-138, 132*f*-137*f*, 155
  motion offense 151-154, 153*f*-154*f*
  overview of 127-128, 165
  triangle offense 142-147, 143*f*-146*f*
Terry, Jason 172, 221
three-man triangle 231-232, 232*f*
three-player screening drills 155-159, 156*f*-159*f*
three-point shot 30, 122-125, 123*t*-124*t*, 131
Three-Point X-Out 247, 247*f*
Thru 161-163, 162*f*
time-outs 218, 227-228
timing, in rebounding 100
training
  for agility and power 5-13, 6*f*-11*f*
  anaerobic 2-5, 4*t*
  overload 66
  for performance 14
Transition Lob 240-241, 241*f*
transition to opposite side, in triangle offense 145-146, 145*f*-146*f*
Transylvania University 14-16, 20, 154, 172
trash talking 17
travel 40
triangle offense 142-147, 143*f*-146*f*
trust 44
Two-Basket Free Throws 121
Two Touches 159-161, 160*f*
2-2-1 full-court zone press 127

U
UCLA 128-132, 132*f*, 174, 227
Union College 20
University of Cincinnati 33, 36, 39, 154
University of Connecticut 27
University of Florida 220-221
University of Kentucky 1, 14, 36, 53, 79, 128-129, 172, 219
University of North Carolina 29, 34, 36, 168-169, 219
University of South Florida 19, 49
unselfishness 20-23

V
Versus Box-and-One 254-255, 255*f*
Versus 1-3-1 253-254, 253*f*-254*f*
Versus Triangle-and-Two 255-256, 256*f*
video 40, 44
Virginia Commonwealth University 21
virus, eliminating 22-23
vision, in passing 82-84, 83*f*-84*f*
visualization, for shooting 71-73
volunteers 51

W
Walker, Brian 226
Watford, Christian 219
weaknesses, minimized 23-27, 24*t*-26*t*, 105-107
weak side, defending 171, 180-181, 181*f*
Weak-Side Pin-Down 94, 94*f*

weighted performance criteria 52
Williams, Gary 138
wing pass 171
Winter, Tex 37-39
Wooden, John 36-37, 59, 128-131, 155, 174-175
workout 4*t*, 23, 24*t*-26*t*
World University Games 49

X
x-out 245-248, 246*f*-248*f*
X-Out Into Pick-and-Roll 246, 246*f*
X-Out Into Single-Double 248, 248*f*

Z
zone defense 30, 173, 226-227, 252
Zoubek, Brian 32, 58

About the Author

Lee Rose began his coaching career starting at the high school level and then moving on to assistant coaching jobs at the college level before landing the head coaching and athletic director position at Transylvania University in Lexington, Kentucky.

In 1975, the University of North Carolina at Charlotte hired Rose as head coach and athletic director, and UNCC was soon rewarded for the move. Rose compiled a 72-18 (.800) record in three seasons at the school, and he was named the *Sporting News* National Coach of the Year in 1977 after leading UNC Charlotte to the NIT finals in 1976 and the NCAA Final Four in 1977.

Rose left UNCC in 1978 for Purdue University, where he took his first team to the NIT finals and the next year's squad to the 1980 Final Four, compiling a 50-18 record as the Boilermakers' coach. He then accepted the position of head coach at the University of South Florida, a school with a basketball program only 10 years old at the time.

As a college head coach, Rose compiled a .705 winning percentage (388-162). Equally impressive, he was named Coach of the Year in every conference in which he coached: Kentucky Intercollegiate Athletic Conference, Sun Belt, and Big Ten. He was inducted into the Kentucky Athletic Hall of Fame in 2001.

After his collegiate career, Rose went on to serve as an assistant coach for five NBA teams: San Antonio Spurs, New Jersey Nets, Milwaukee Bucks, Charlotte Hornets, and Charlotte Bobcats. In addition, Lee was vice president of player personnel for the Milwaukee Bucks. Rose has also served as an NBA consultant and coaching supervisor for NBA Developmental League coaches. The NBA also recruited him to coordinate and conduct the on-court instruction and drills at the NBA pre-draft camp for over 15 years.

One of Rose's proudest accomplishments is the work that he and his wife, Eleanor, do to reverse low educational attainment in Kentucky's Fifth Congressional District in conjunction with Forward in the Fifth (a nonprofit organization and an affiliate of the Center for Rural Development). Since 2005, Rose has been to 42 counties in this Appalachian region. He has spoken to more than 11,000 middle school students, encouraging them to stay in school and to use their education as a stepping stone for future success.

Lee is still actively involved with Forward in the Fifth in Kentucky and works with the Men's Homeless Shelter of Charlotte. He and his wife live in Charlotte, North Carolina.